Praise for Susan Doherty and

# The Ghost Garden

"This is a book I wish I could have written. Susan Doherty's eyes, ears and heart show us professionals who our patients really are and what their lives are really like. We should all see the person before the diagnosis."

Dr. David Bloom, medical chief,
Psychiatric Disorders Programme, Douglas Institute

"As a neuroscientist who understands the brain and its disorders, I know I still share the unconscious negative bias towards patients with schizophrenia. Yet in the startling detail of these stories about lives lost, Susan Doherty reveals the enduring humanity that resides within the souls of all persons suffering from this dreadful disease. She has given a voice to those unfortunate human beings who have long been unheard."

Dr. G. Rees Cosgrove, neurosurgeon, Harvard Medical School

"I'm thirty years old and have been in and out of the system for twelve years. It's about time a book came out that showed the mentally ill the way we actually are—as sentient and as competent as everyone else, though we might appear to be different. I loved reading these stories of unfairly marginalized people, some of whom I know personally. This book is the start of greater acceptance."

Katharine Cunningham, resident of Nazareth Community

"Being able to reach out to people with a severe mental disorder without the self-protective measures that come with being a mental health 'professional' is an uncommon gift. Susan Doherty has it, obviously.

Her account of her relationships with people with severe mental illness will bring you very close to them, and safely so. Reading her book might even make you a better person."

Dr. Pierre Etienne, associate professor of clinical psychiatry, McGill University

"This compassionate, perceptive and absorbing book chronicles the lives of people who have not let themselves be entirely crushed by the random cruelty of what used to be called insanity. Since more than one in four people is touched by mental illness personally or in their families, I recommend this readable, valuable book to everyone."

Dr. James Farquhar, psychiatrist, Douglas Institute

"With her brave and generous reporting from the front lines of intense human suffering, Susan Doherty delivers a fundamental challenge to everyone inside and outside the mental health system: what do we owe people who have lost their minds? Her poignant and harrowing profiles of men and women diagnosed with schizophrenia make a compelling case for the transformative power of personal compassion and tenacity."

James FitzGerald, author of
*What Disturbs Our Blood: A Son's Quest to Redeem the Past*

"A luminous, fierce and loving portrait of our brothers and sisters who suffer in ways that can appear bewildering and frightening; that can deplete the compassion even of those who love them most— ways in which the abiding human need for connection is obscured by personal chaos. *The Ghost Garden* in itself is a signal and compelling act of connection, leavened with humour, clear-eyed yet packed with hope."

Ann-Marie MacDonald, novelist and playwright

# The Ghost Garden

INSIDE THE LIVES OF SCHIZOPHRENIA'S
FEARED AND FORGOTTEN

Susan Doherty

Random House Canada

PUBLISHED BY RANDOM HOUSE CANADA

www.penguinrandomhouse.ca

Random House Canada and colophon are registered trademarks.

Library and Archives Canada Cataloguing in Publication

Doherty, Susan, 1957–, author
    The ghost garden : inside the lives of schizophrenia's feared and forgotten /
Susan Doherty Hannaford.

Issued in print and electronic formats.
ISBN 978-0-7352-7650-5
eBook ISBN 978-0-7352-7651-2

    1. Schizophrenics.  2. Schizophrenia.  I. Title.

RC514.H36 2019          362.2'6          C2018-905694-0
                                         C2018-905695-9

Book design by Rachel Cooper
Cover image © leisa hoppe / FOAP / Getty Images

Printed and bound in Canada

10 9 8 7 6 5 4 3 2 1

Penguin
Random House
RANDOM HOUSE CANADA

*To Brenda Pichette*

*If I can stop one heart from breaking,*
*I shall not live in vain;*
*If I can ease one life the aching,*
*Or cool one pain,*
*Or help one fainting robin*
*Unto his nest again,*
*I shall not live in vain.*

—EMILY DICKINSON

# Contents

# An Invitation to the Ghost Garden

I DID NOT INTEND TO WRITE A BOOK ABOUT PEOPLE who live with schizophrenia. But in October 2009, a door opened in front of me and I unexpectedly found myself face to face with a group of highly misunderstood souls. The door was to an elevator that required a special key to gain access. It carried me up to a locked ward. I'd never gone anywhere in the hospital where the doors shut tight behind me. My legs were a little shaky and my heart was thumping as I stepped off the elevator into a hallway where listless men and women in various states of undress regarded me with suspicious eyes. Grooming was non-existent. Their slippers whispered to the linoleum as they shuffled along, many in flapping hospital gowns, murmuring to themselves.

I was there as a new volunteer to meet a woman I'll call Camilla. Her doctor had described her background to me only as "troubled." I wore a zebra-print cotton dress, and as it turned out, on that day Camilla was wearing a zebra-print cotton top. She gave me the once-over as she came towards me, a penetrating gaze that seemed to burn a hole right through to my core. But we became friends that afternoon and we remained friends until the hour of her death—a relationship that altered us both.

Months before that first trip to a locked ward for the extremely mentally ill, I had come to this hospital—the Douglas Institute—to do research for a novel set in 1930s Montreal that touched on the era's heartbreaking psychiatric practices. I spent many hours in the library and archive department, where I watched a vintage black-and-white movie of a patient undergoing shock therapy. I saw photos of a terrified woman with strips of cloth jammed into her ears to block unwanted voices. I read the case histories of people who'd been dropped off at the hospital by their families and never reclaimed. The hospital was so candid and transparent about historical treatment options that after I was done with my research I wanted to reciprocate their generosity in some way. So I offered my time as a volunteer. If I'm honest, what I'd seen in the archive and on the hospital grounds also weighed on my conscience. It was clear that people were still being cast off, shunted aside, even shunned, and I wanted to help.

John Matheson, a priest who headed the volunteer department, interviewed me for more than three hours. He asked me a hundred questions, none of which seemed to have any relevance to mental illness. We talked about whales, of all things. Then I had to pass a police check. After all that, I assumed I would be tasked with filing documents or some such clerical chore, maybe working at the foundation or a reception desk. Instead, Matheson asked me to befriend Camilla. I said okay, though I admit I was not only frightened but also unsure whether I was up to the job. She lived on a ward for the chronically mentally ill.

But, somehow, Camilla and I came together as two people. She taught me that having even a single friend is not a given when your mind has been claimed by a psychotic disorder. She taught me about shame, addiction, sexual abuse, homelessness, and the true meaning of condescension. She didn't use words to articulate those themes; rather, I saw her plight with my own eyes. People with schizophrenia often live far outside the boundary of acceptance.

I was not given a laundry list of what was wrong with Camilla, nor a description of a past that would define her today or limit her tomorrows. The days and weeks and years after I met her honed my understanding of schizophrenia, and led me to advocate on behalf of those who were unable to do so for themselves. That first friendship led to another and another, and soon I was transfixed by the lives of the marginalized and forsaken. My ability—if you can call it that— to connect with people who have been pushed to society's margins made me long to gather and communicate their stories.

And then, in the middle of all these extraordinary encounters, a dear friend from elementary school asked me if I would write the life story of her sister, a woman who has struggled with severe mental illness for decades. Caroline Evans (not her real name) is now in her sixties, and has cycled in and out of hospitals and group homes looking to be cured for thirty years. She has never been able to elude schizophrenia. It's an edgeless, unknowable, looping odyssey, which no one drug or treatment regimen will fix. To the burden of the person already suffering from voices in their head and other horrors, add stigma, isolation, and marginalization. The easy path was to view Caroline as an incurable, obese, crazy lady, but I couldn't stop thinking that at one time she had been just like me. In all the most important ways, she still is. Her experiences have become the spine of this book.

I first met Caroline in 1967 when she was in grade four, over fifty years ago. She was a bubbly, white-blond nine-year-old with an infectious laugh, who showed no hint of what was in store. At the age of twenty-one, something changed within her brain and she began to experience violent sexual hallucinations, delusions, and paranoia. Caroline herself also wanted me to tell her story in order to tease out, if I could, the reasons why she has had grave difficulty maintaining recovery and to present a set of circumstances that might be familiar to and have meaning for others. The mistakes that were made in Caroline's life and treatment are lessons for family members who find themselves drawn, unwitting and unwilling, into the chaos of mental illness.

Since 2011, I have had hundreds of phone conversations with Caroline as she has crawled back into the darkest corners of her memory, places she thought were either inaccessible or best left undisturbed. I probed. She answered. We have laughed and we have cried over the telling of her life, but it's her honesty that has driven the writing. And the text, as a result, is scattered with her thoughts: frank reflections on a tattered life and the hard lessons she has learned.

Intermingled with Caroline's story are eighteen vignettes of the men and women who have also spoken to me of their deepest desires, unmet longings, and unimaginable hurts. For some, I am their only friend. The loneliness I have witnessed is beyond the beyond. What began for me as a weekly volunteer commitment has transformed into a need to shed light on the truth of debilitating mental illness. To prove that hope exists. Without this first-hand experience, I would not have been able to understand the hurdles of a misunderstood condition that still deeply frightens us as a society, even as we seem to grow more comfortable talking about depression and anxiety. Without my friendships, I would not have been able to do justice to Caroline's story or articulate the tangled nuances of psychosis that plague the people I write about.

I've changed all the names and some identifying details, but the stories in this book have been sanctioned by those who have suffered, be it patient or family member. (I have not changed the names of the doctors and health professionals I quote for their insights into both Caroline's long history, and the treatment of schizophrenia in general.) I didn't set out to do this, but I have inadvertently created a forum that allowed the psychologically afflicted, medicated or self-medicated, the walking wounded, to voice their truths. Those who are ignored and stepped around on the streets, the homeless who cycle in and out of wards and through rooming houses, are hardly seen as human, and are left to wander in a ghost garden—an interior haven where emotional pain can be suppressed.

Along with Caroline and my other friends, the heroes of this book are Caroline's sisters, who shared details that were shameful and painful, always with an eye for who would benefit from the reading. It has taken years to piece the story together, since everyone involved remembers each traumatic situation through his or her own lens, though each has suffered the emotional toll. Schizophrenia is a devastating disease. It's chronic, frightening, and isolating.

My hope is that this book will help family members and others pinpoint warning signs and thereby, perhaps, be in a position to identify incipient mental illness—thus preventing the harrowing lives experienced by the people I have written about. The thread of Caroline's story, and the dozen-and-a-half other snapshots, show how the condition, if left untreated, can play havoc with all that represents a life well lived. I believe it doesn't have to. It mustn't.

And if that lofty goal proves hard to reach, at least I can tear down some of the fences that prevent us from seeing those with schizophrenia as intelligent, productive, engaged, hilarious, beautiful, poetic, insightful, maternal, responsible human beings—and, above all, worthy of love.

# 1

# Kill the Devil

CAROLINE EVANS LEFT HER APARTMENT ON MCCARTHY Avenue with a one-way bus ticket shoved into the pocket of pink drawstring pyjamas that doubled as pants. It was the morning of Friday, July 31, 2002, the beginning of a sweltering long weekend in Ontario. She boarded the number 106 bus bound for the Ottawa General Hospital, and something about her startled eyes guaranteed the seat beside her stayed empty, despite the early morning rush. At the check-in window of the emergency department, she asked, perhaps too politely, to be admitted. Caroline's hair was a nest of knots, her blouse a crust of tomato soup stains, but the distracted nurse turned her away, missing vital signs of an unwashed woman distracted by a hailstorm of voices in her head.

Instead of taking the bus back to her three-bedroom townhouse, Caroline trudged home on foot. It took over ninety minutes in steamy thirty-degree weather. Hilary and Simon, Caroline's roommates, were not home. All three of them had messy histories of mental illness and they had come together because they couldn't afford to live alone. At the front door, Caroline took a deep breath to try to calm the tidal wave of messages now sounding in her head.

She walked up the steps to her bedroom, which smelled of sweat, cigarettes, and used Kotex pads, and peeled off filthy white socks that hadn't been washed in weeks. She lit a cigarette, drawing hard, ran her hand through her stiff hair, then sat down in her usual chair and closed her eyes.

On the table, next to her overflowing ashtray, was a pile of birthday cards, Hallmark messages of love and support from her siblings, and an unwashed plate where dry cake crumbs mingled with more cigarette butts. Her birthday in mid-July had been the single best day of her summer, especially when the phone rang and she could talk to her sisters and brothers. Her youngest sister, Peggy, had dropped off a chocolate cake. Hilary and Simon had laughed when Caroline needed help blowing out the candles, blaming her lack of wind on her smoking and the fact that she was getting up there in age. What was left of Peggy's cake was still on the kitchen counter, attracting ants.

What happened between that Friday and Sunday morning is lost to the voices in Caroline's head. What she does know is that near noon on Sunday, she filled a large kettle with water and placed it on the stove to boil. The instructions from the gang of voices were clear and specific: *Kill the devil.* As the kettle hissed like a tomcat, she knew what had to be done.

Caroline carried the kettle from the kitchen to the blue velour living room couch where Hilary lay asleep. She leaned down and poured boiling water into Hilary's ear, where the voices said the devil was breathing.

Hilary's screams filled Caroline with horror. Something had gone terribly wrong. Not only was the devil not dead, her friend was hurt, her skin bubbled and blistered. Covering her ears to block out Hilary's shrieks, Caroline watched her friend stagger across the room in a screaming panic to call 911. Caroline, though she had lived agonies herself, had never witnessed such pain in another person.

When Simon saw what had happened, he fled the townhouse, leaving the front door wide open. He roamed the nearby streets, knowing he should call someone but uncertain as to whether he should tell Caroline's family. How could he snitch when Caroline had helped him time and again when he was down and out? No one had been his friend like she had; she had taken him in when he couldn't find a rooming house, let alone buy a Pepsi or a pack of cigarettes. At a nearby phone booth, he sank to the ground and rocked from side to side, his arms cradling his knees. Should he tell one of her sisters what Caroline had done, or shouldn't he?

Back at the townhouse, six police officers and an ambulance arrived at the scene. Hilary had such severe burns on her ear, face, arm, back and chest that she had difficulty moving anything but her lips, which quivered with the mournful sound of her crying. The emergency team gently placed her on a stretcher then carried her out to the flashing ambulance. Hilary had stopped crying, and the ensuing silence was eerie—only broken when the siren was turned on as the ambulance peeled away.

Caroline was huddled near the window, still holding the kettle, as two of the constables took a careful look at the room—inexpensive, lumpy furniture, mismatched lamps, a scratched coffee table, but no signs of a skirmish. In the kitchen, there was bread on the counter, milk in the fridge that wasn't past due, blackish bananas in a fruit bowl. The crusty, tired birthday cake. They turned back to the woman with the kettle—the obvious culprit—and soon Caroline was handcuffed and being led outside, where a few neighbours stood watching in groups of two and three. The officers pushed Caroline into the back seat of a police vehicle and drove her to the Elgin Street police headquarters, where she was charged with assault with a weapon. White-faced and obedient, Caroline had not said a word.

——

Caroline's sister Rosalind was at home in Osgoode, a small nearby town, listening to Majic FM 100, a contemporary Ottawa radio station, as she and her husband Connor lazed on the back deck with their dogs. An announcer was describing a dire situation in the Hunt Club area of the city, where a woman had allegedly poured boiling water on a housemate. Rosalind had no idea that the woman involved was her sister until Simon managed to get himself off the phone booth floor and call her. He sounded stricken and confused. "It was terrible. It was terrible. It was terrible," he repeated. Then, "They've taken Caroline. She's gone to jail."

A panicked Rosalind and her husband got in the car and headed for Ottawa, as Majic 100 continued to broadcast details of the incident every hour. How could this be Caroline? Though she'd had her struggles, she was gentle, a pacifist, someone who chronicled her life in Hilroy notebooks and often spoke of nature's beauty. She copied inspirational quotes on scraps of paper that she jammed into the back pockets of her jeans. *"Treat your mother with love and care for you'll only know her value when you see her empty chair."* She could be insightful and humane. She lavished affection on animals, especially dogs. She gave money and cigarettes to strangers, and Rosalind had seen her cry when she spotted a dirty, homeless man propped against the wall at the train station. This seemed so out of character.

Rosalind couldn't help but remember Caroline as a bubbly little girl—part of their outsized clan of ten boisterous youngsters jammed into one medium-sized suburban home in Pointe-Claire, Quebec, a neighbourhood of Montreal's affluent West Island. Peanut butter sandwiches, school bags, dental appointments, Halloween costumes, winter boots, birthday parties, restaurant outings, ski lessons, Christmas presents, and everyone packed in the wood-panelled station wagon. And adding to the friendly pandemonium were dogs, big jumping-up-on-the-couch Irish setters shedding tumbleweeds of feathery red hair. How had it come to this?

It was hours before Rosalind and her husband managed to track Caroline down to lock-up, where a booking officer told them they didn't have the right to see her until the following morning at the courthouse, where she would be arraigned. They went home feeling like hostages to shadowy events beyond their control.

The next morning, Rosalind and her younger sister Peggy made their way to court. The car was hot and airless, the radio a welcome distraction as long as it wasn't Majic 100. They spoke of Hilary, in the burn unit of the Ottawa Civic Hospital; they'd heard from a social worker that she was alive and not fighting for her life, as they had feared. The sisters had been up all night.

"Had Caroline and Hilary been arguing? Did they have a fight?" Peggy asked.

"I don't know. Simon was a mess on the phone. He couldn't tell me anything."

Neither of them could come up with a reasonable explanation. More than anything, Rosalind and Peggy were scared—clammy hands and looping butterflies. Had their sister tried to kill Hilary? Maim her? Had she been planning to hurt her, or was it an impulsive act? No matter Caroline's intention, she could go to jail for a long time.

To get to the courtroom where Caroline was to be arraigned, they had to take a very long ride down a shiny escalator.

"I've taken that steep ride many times in my mind over the years that followed," Rosalind says. "The entire place was spotless. Such juxtaposition. The whole incident felt dirty. The courtroom was windowless and dark—air-conditioned and cold in contrast to the sweltering summer day outside."

Rosalind and Peggy sat on a bench with dozens of spectators, mostly the friends and family of other defendants. They worried about Caroline—the sister they knew would be in agonies over having hurt Hilary. Caroline had done some crazy things over the years, but physically attacking a friend still seemed out of the question. Caroline and Hilary had met on a psychiatric ward and their shared journey of emotional pain had cemented their loyalties. They'd seemed inseparable. Hilary was someone Caroline had laughed with and cooked with—a confidante.

As well, Caroline's night in jail would have surely compounded her stress levels; mounting stress had been the biggest contributor to her earlier psychotic breakdowns. What shape would she be in? Rosalind knew Caroline could be provocative and aggressive while in a psychotic state. What if the jail guards had little experience with mental illness? She had visions of them beating her sister.

Then the sisters saw her: it took two policemen to escort a handcuffed Caroline to the glassed-in defendant box. The fierceness of her blue eyes, the way her splotched face was contorted with rage, and her defiant resistance frightened her sisters. When Caroline spotted them, she erupted. "I don't fucking know them!" she screamed. "They abused my son. Up the ass. They tried to kill Matthew. I need to find my real family." Caroline shouted her accusations over and over, pointing at her sisters with her chin since her hands were shackled behind her back.

"She looks like she hasn't slept for days," Peggy whispered, head slumped, as she and Rosalind cowered in their seats.

The judge banged her gavel and the bailiff forced Caroline to sit down. The officers who held her wore black leather gloves to guard against bites, as though Caroline were a rabid animal. It was a soul-crushing moment for Rosalind and Peggy, and tears stung their eyes to see the stranger their sister had become.

The other accused were in the room to face charges of drunken and disorderly conduct. Most would be paying fines and family members would be taking them home. The sisters wouldn't be able to do that. Caroline was not even capable of making a plea of guilty or not guilty, a court-appointed psychiatrist testified, and so she was taken back to her cell, still cursing her sisters.


The people who loved Caroline began to formulate a plan. Her sisters knew they needed to hire a lawyer to fight her case. Neither Rosalind nor Peggy knew where to begin, nor where it would lead, but the sight of their sister overtaken by mental anguish bound them together as never before. Her violent act, her arrest, the officers in leather gloves, signalled an end to all the illusions they had clung to when it came to Caroline's hurdles, namely, that she would eventually have the life they had—career, marriage, untroubled motherhood. But it was only the beginning of their true reckoning with her mental illness. It was as though some invisible force had hauled Caroline down an irreversible crash course. How would they deal with the wreckage?

In the car, after court, before she turned on the ignition, Rosalind said to Peggy, "This is schizophrenia." Over the years, Caroline's doctors had checked the boxes of half a dozen other conditions, including depression, mania, bipolar illness, postpartum depression, social anxiety, and even something called "attention-seeking tied to lowered self-esteem." They drove home in silence, contemplating where this new road might take them.

———

Rosalind and Peggy waited seven days before going to see Caroline, because they couldn't stomach being screamed at again. They felt vulnerable, shamed by Caroline's outrageous verbal assault in the courtroom. Even though they could rationalize that she was not in her right mind, her words had been deeply humiliating. A court official had told them that she would be medicated while in her cell. The sisters hoped that, if nothing else, the drugs would eliminate her delusion that Rosalind and Peggy were the enemy. They wanted the sedative aspect of the drugs to kick in before they saw her a second time.

While they waited, they spent endless hours reconstructing the facts, privately and then with each other, and finally with their two older sisters. (The Evans brothers had bailed out of the business of dealing with Caroline a long time ago.) Someone needed to check on Hilary's progress, compile a list of criminal lawyers, and figure out what Caroline's rights were in this new situation. Hardest of all would be telling their mother.

They were also still struggling to reconcile this new Caroline with the person they'd known, who could be erratic, and had had earlier hospitalizations, but was on her good days a pacifist, a caring person, a passionately thoughtful mother to her two sons. Caroline used to have fits when Matthew, her first-born, tripped, as toddlers do, and scraped his knee. She had breastfed him for twenty-four months. She'd tried to be the best mother she could be for Kyle, her second child, too, though her sisters had to admit it had been a contentious decade since she lost a custody battle over her sons, who now lived with their father. Caroline had once written a ten-page letter of complaint to a grocery store because there was water on the floor in the produce section. It was excessive by any measure, but she was worried someone might slip. She offered to help her sisters move apartments without being asked. And no matter the hour, she was there if a friend needed to talk.

Rosalind struggled with waiting so long before visiting Caroline, but her sister's deed had been deeply frightening. She spent tortured nights tossing and turning, imagining her own daughter lying on the couch where Hilary had been sleeping. Caroline had come to Rosalind's house for weekend visits; she slept over on a regular basis, and stayed longer at Thanksgiving and Christmas. The fear of being attacked by her own flesh and blood froze Rosalind. But she also knew that Caroline was desperate for support. And forgiveness.

As the sisters made calls to legal professionals, looking for help, they wondered whether Caroline could even be held responsible for a crime, given the shape she was in. But one thing was now crystal clear: it was no longer possible to think their sister would recover without massive interventions. For fifteen years they'd pitched in to help Caroline get back on track when she couldn't stay in school, and had put up with her emotional tirades and a host of other inexplicable behaviours. But this time they could not see how Caroline would be able to walk away from what she had done, and perhaps she'd even have to serve a jail term. And then there was the victim. Rosalind had called the burn unit again to ask after Hilary, and received the sickening information that she would likely have permanent hearing loss. The third-degree burns on her neck and face would take years to heal, not to mention the emotional wounds caused by the attack.

How would anyone trust Caroline after this, even the members of her family? Who had the time and/or the desire to manage Caroline's situation? Out of guilt as much as anything, they asked themselves why it had taken a crime to expose the shakiness of Caroline's condition.

———

"The first time we spoke to Caroline after she was arrested, it was a typical jailhouse meeting, just like you would see in the movies," Rosalind recalls. They sat in a divided room reeking of industrial cleaner that didn't cancel out the smell of trapped sweat and pungent body odours. A glass window with ancient peeling bars separated them from their sister.

When she closes her eyes, Rosalind can still put herself back in that room, with its drab yellow walls where the paint had chipped away, and the dirty rainwater stains beneath the window ledges. There was a grey linoleum floor, worn thin in spots, that should have been replaced years ago, and the counter in front of where they sat on metal chairs was sticky, as if a sugary soft drink had been spilled on it, leaving a gummy residue.

Caroline was no longer shrieking at them, but was deflated, weepy, and unbearably sad. With pleading eyes, she asked for understanding and forgiveness. Her hair was a filthy, tangled nest, and her teeth hadn't been brushed in days. Despite whatever pills she had been given, it was obvious she hadn't been sleeping. Her raw nose and crimson eyes betrayed endless hours of crying—a distillate of panic and hurt.

Rosalind says, "It's unimaginable to see your sister or brother like that. Unreachable. Deep in psychosis. Nothing you say penetrates their thinking." Rosalind, who worked for the Canadian Red Cross as a national first aid specialist, knew she herself was experiencing shock at the sight of her sister—her mouth went dry and she felt faint from the emotional stress. As Rosalind took in Caroline's total defeat, she thought she might vomit, and felt desperate for a glass of water. But at least Caroline was recognizably Caroline again. There was a little relief to be found in that.

Peggy picked up the phone to talk to Caroline, replacing the receiver each time she was done talking, until the couple next to them told them they didn't have to hang up after each exchange. Rosalind laughed at the absurdity, and then so did Caroline. Soon the three sisters were in fits of giggles, releasing much pent-up tension. They drew stares, but the laughter gave them a flicker of hope that all was not lost.

Their helpful neighbours, well-dressed and articulate, were there to visit their daughter, and looked as though they didn't belong. Rosalind and Peggy felt they didn't either. How did girls from the West Island of Montreal end up in jail? Their father was a doctor. They were well off growing up. The two sisters kept bumping into the same wall: why had Caroline done such an incomprehensible thing? They were nauseated by the stench of the place, and terrified for Caroline. If they were honest, they were terrified *of* her too.

As their visit stretched on, Rosalind whispered to Peggy, "I need a shower so badly. I've never felt more unclean."

Except for the brief moment when she laughed with them, Caroline remained numb, limp, cheerless, and devoid of all anger. When Rosalind told her that Hilary was still in hospital, and badly hurt, Caroline put her hands over her ears to block out the words. She began to cry softly, then stammered, "I needed help, but no one would help me. I went to the hospital, but they wouldn't take me."

"We'll hire a lawyer. We'll do everything we can. Try your best to sleep," Rosalind said.

When Caroline was led away, the two sisters couldn't wait to find the shiny escalator and get outside. They drove straight away to their mother's house to impart the news that Caroline was in jail. Their mother, Isabel, lashed out in anger, "Well, that's a good place for her." Rosalind and Peggy were stunned into horrified silence until she collapsed into a nearby chair and sobbed with bitterness and regret. It was as though the seams of her body were opening up to let out years of contained distress.

After leaving Isabel, they called the Ottawa Civic Hospital to see if they could visit Hilary. They were told by a member of the nursing staff that Hilary wanted nothing to do with anybody connected to Caroline. And then a social worker came on the line to relay Hilary's exact words: "Stay away from me. Don't ever come near me again." Words that shred closure, invite humiliation. With no other way to console Hilary, they sent a bouquet of flowers, and a heartfelt apology on behalf of their sister, who had not yet been able to say a single word about the incident. The day Caroline poured boiling water in Hilary's ear, both women lost something irretrievable.

# 2

# Tank

IN THE 1960S, A BABY BOOM DECADE WHEN FAITHFUL Catholic families could be large, ten children still raised eyebrows. Dr. Arthur Evans and his wife, Isabel, not only had ten children, they had them all within a period of twelve years.

Their children remember that Arthur gave his wife a sloppy French kiss at the front door on his way to work every morning, and at the end of every single day he scooted up the five stairs from the foyer to the kitchen to wrap himself around her backside. He cherished his wife from the day of their vows until he drew his last breath. For her part, Isabel seemed to have an infinite supply of love, happily going from one pregnancy to the next and welcoming each addition to the family—the more the merrier. On the living room mantel, in a sterling silver frame, was a testament to her union with Arthur: a black-and-white photo of the ten children lined up like the shiny von Trapp family, each child as beautiful as the next.

Yes, the money had to stretch a long way with such a large brood, Isabel's time with each child was at a premium, and the ten siblings tended to bicker as children do. But Isabel hoped that their closeness in age would translate into unshakable relationships as adults. A raucous house full of children meant happy, controlled chaos on some days and bitter rivalry on others. All of it was normal large-family stuff—the orange Popsicle-stained lips, somersault contests on the grass, ball toss, and double dutch on the driveway, alongside fights in which her children pummelled one another hard enough to split the drywall.

The family was the envy of many. Arthur was a respected doctor, Isabel an involved mother who rarely said no to her children's desire for new footballs, roller skates, and bathing suits. The entire clan seemed healthy and wholesome, the children aimed towards bright futures.

During one summer in the late 1960s, Caroline remembers spending each waking moment in or near the backyard pool of their new house in Pointe-Claire, wearing a fuchsia bathing suit that stretched over her chubby tummy and disappeared into the crack of her fanny. She was happy, and laughed easily, even though her brother Ian, two years older, could be merciless about her less than perfect body. He began to call her Tank when she was in grade four, a taunting label that stung.

To counteract Ian's teasing, Isabel told Caroline her blue eyes matched the paint along the bottom and sides of the concrete pool, and reminded her that she was an outstanding swimmer for her age. When Ian continued to ride her about being fat, Caroline did her best to brush him off. She was a radiant nine-year-old, too busy playing and cuddling her scruffy cocker spaniel to have a care in the world.

That summer, Arthur took her to dog shows; he adored animals as much as she did. The following Christmas he chose Caroline to be an elf on the helicopter that would carry Santa to the grounds of the hospital where he was the medical director. No other sibling had ever ridden in a helicopter, or helped distribute Christmas presents to sick children. Such outings meant the world to Caroline at a time when being singled out by Arthur was rare for any of them, and when being constantly targeted by Ian had begun to feel disheartening. Rosalind recalls that her parents, especially her mother, realized that Caroline needed a bit more attention from them than their other children. As a toddler, Caroline had been nicknamed Britches for the way she hung on to Isabel's leg.

As a mother, Isabel was in a league of her own. She could entertain vast numbers of kids in her home and in the backyard pool, with or without her own children nearby. (I was one of them.) She taught them how to swim and do water ballet, how to knit and draw. She baked endlessly, and had a lenient attitude towards the everyday chaos of wet towels and shrieks from the pool. She did have rules about the kids helping with dishwashing, laundry, and bed-making, but not oppressive ones. "She didn't ride us," says Peggy. Her dining room table always had space for a neighbourhood kid, since she was cooking for an army anyway.

Like all five of Isabel's daughters, Caroline had lots of friends, rode her bicycle everywhere, loved doing cannonballs into the pool from the diving board in summer and skiing, skating, and tobogganing in winter—an unremarkable and frictionless suburban upbringing.

Her five handsome brothers were football players and wrestlers, trophy winners and quarterbacks, notorious for their size and toughness among the schools of Greater Montreal. During Sunday dinners, when they still lived at home, her brothers regaled the family with highlights from their sweaty contests on the mat or in mud-spattered fields, reliving goals scored, miraculous passes, heroic tackles. Two of Caroline's older brothers were all-star athletes, and were tapped for university teams. There was also a constant parade of girlfriends drawn to these handsome boys, and Isabel welcomed them all.

Of all ten children, though, Caroline may have had the lightest touch, the best sense of humour, the most sympathetic outlook. She was completely lacking in guile or artifice. She shared her ice cream cones with the dogs, stooped to speak with stray cats, forgot to remove her nose plugs after she stopped swimming, then laughed when the marks stayed on her skin for hours. She baked cookies for the mailman and created homemade Mother's Day cards, agonizing over the sincerity of the wording. Her gaze—from pale-blue eyes that in a certain light seemed otherworldly—was always direct.

She loved books and writing, wanted to act, yet also wanted to enter the health care field, following in the footsteps of her father. Always, there was her irresistible belly laugh, the infectious kind that drew friends to her side. She was uncomplicated, kind, and quick to forgive. For a long time she even managed to forgive Ian for being a bully.

But eventually, the way he picked on her became an escalating source of angst for Caroline. Ian, handsome and blond, a muscular running back and championship wrestler, was relentless about Caroline's size. She was chubbier than her siblings and, in a litter of ten, perhaps the easiest prey. Ian left her alone at school, where he struggled academically, but at home he used Caroline as a punching bag. When Rosalind looks back, she is certain Ian's academic issues, especially his difficulty with reading, were at the root of his bullying behaviour; he responded to his own stress by tormenting his younger sister. Peggy was also subjected to Ian's cruelty, but Caroline was his prime target.

Still, no one took Ian's behaviour too seriously, and Isabel, in particular, chalked it up to ordinary sibling rivalry. How could she possibly referee all the fights for the phone, the shower, the diving board, drives to the mall, the use of the iron, new running shoes, the washing machine, hair accessories, or sports equipment when she had a never-ending list of other things to take care of? She viewed sibling discord as a fact of life in any family, not just large ones like her own. She did intervene now and then, smacking Ian in the hope that a slap would smarten him up. She had a sharp tongue, too, which she used mostly on her sons. "Stop being an ass," she said to them on many occasions. Isabel was one woman looking after ten people, eleven if you counted Arthur, and her basic view was that one day they would all grow up and these childhood bumps and lumps would be forgotten.

And when her children became adolescents, she mostly took the path of least resistance. She viewed their experiments with sex, drugs, and underage drinking as part of what kids get up to, a normal testing of limits. Naturally, her children admired her leniency on these fronts. In effect, she closed her eyes, crossed her fingers, and hoped her teenagers would use good judgment. Perhaps she actually decided to forsake the heavy lifting of rigorous discipline to make room for more important values like acceptance and tolerance, and for more mundane work like shopping and cooking and getting everybody from place to place.

As they grew older, the ten children drifted into two groups, the five eldest in one and the five youngest in another, a mixture of boys and girls in each pack. Rosalind was one grade above Caroline, and Peggy was three below, all three in the younger group. By the time Caroline began grade seven at the junior high school in 1971, the oldest five were either studying in downtown Montreal or New Brunswick or living their lives in Alberta and British Columbia. Arthur and Isabel were starting to imagine a life after kids, even though five still lived at home. It was no secret that Arthur, in particular, was longing for some breathing space from parenting and the demands of his medical career. Isabel and Arthur couldn't wait to pack their bags and be Canadian snowbirds in Florida, a doting couple—and only a couple—once more. It was also no secret among his children that he wanted and needed all of Isabel's attention.

"My dad was beyond intelligent," recalls Rosalind. "We never needed an encyclopedia because every time we asked him something, he knew the answer. Schooled by the Jesuits, he had a real sense of authority and elitism about him, but he chose to spend his spare time fishing and hunting with the maintenance men at the hospital. He always preferred the company of blue-collar men to the highly educated doctors."

But the demands of his job meant he had limited time for recreation, and limited emotional resources to spend on his children. He often decompressed from the strains of the day with a couple of stiff drinks, sitting in the living room with Isabel. Peggy thinks now that he was slowly killing himself with alcohol, but so were other fathers of the era who drank martinis at noon followed by pre-dinner cocktails. Every evening, Isabel happily applied her lipstick and joined him for a drink, encouraging him to let the worries of the day melt along with the ice cubes in his crystal tumbler.

In September 1974, when Caroline was fifteen and going into grade ten, she began school tanned, toned, and synchro-swim fit from the rigours of daily acrobatic routines in their backyard pool. Ian had left the province for a university on the east coast of Canada, and the house was calmer without him. Caroline boarded the school bus every morning brimming with anticipation about her day. That year she was chosen as a member of the student council, played guard on the basketball team, and had a dozen girlfriends.

That was the year Caroline was obsessed with two boys she knew at St. Vincent high school: Darren Fulton and Joey Cartwright, both older. Crushes were normal, of course. What was abnormal, according to Rosalind, was that Caroline insisted her feelings were reciprocated. She even claimed that Darren had been asking her out on dates. Darren and Joey were popular and handsome, adored by all the similarly popular girls, and Caroline didn't stand a chance with either boy. Peggy and Rosalind accused her of being a liar: how could she make those outrageous claims! But that was the only small shadow on a standout year, and one that Rosalind, Caroline's closest sister in age and the person Caroline admired the most, pretty much ignored in the flurry of her own graduation from grade eleven.

In 1975, when it was Caroline's turn to enter her senior year at St. Vincent, she had high hopes of continuing the success of the year before. But she didn't make the senior basketball team, even though she had been on the squad since grade seven. Lots of people get cut from teams, her mother reassured her. "That's just life."

The next blow came when she was not chosen for hall monitor, a nod of recognition for outstanding students in the graduating class. Caroline, the vice-president of the student union the year before, had been counting on it, and rode the bus home trying hard to hide tears of rejection.

Without daily practice with the basketball team, her weight began to inch up. When Ian came home for Christmas, he picked up where he had left off, reminding his sister that she was an unsightly embarrassment. She also had skin problems. "Who doesn't?" Isabel said, which was little comfort to her daughter.

As the year progressed, Caroline's grades plunged. Her attention span was not what it had been, and completing homework assignments became near impossible, a fact she kept to herself until her report card arrived, revealing that she'd dropped to 50 percent in two subjects and lagged behind in all the others, even English, which was her passion. Although never at the top academically, neither had she been anywhere near failing. Isabel had seen her children go through ups and downs, so once again she didn't make a big deal of it. At parent–teacher interviews, when Caroline's teachers expressed their concerns regarding her falling grades and inattention, Isabel shrugged it off. "She'll be fine," she'd say. "She's trying to find her way." Hadn't those same teachers worried about Ian, she liked to point out, and he'd made it to university?

Then, in March, Caroline contracted mononucleosis. She spent several weeks isolated at home, too tired to study. The upside: she was delighted to have her mother all to herself, even if her marks hit new lows.

As the St. Vincent school year came to a close, bingeing on bowls of ice cream and chocolate chip cookies were among her only pleasures. But that led directly to more unhappiness—excessive weight gain. By her final month of high school, five-foot-three Caroline weighed nearly 160 pounds. High-waisted, wide-legged bell-bottoms were popular and hers were hand-embroidered with yellow and pink daisies at the hem, a look that suited nobody, least of all Caroline. Pairing the bell-bottoms with fringed peasant blouses with giant bell sleeves and wooden clogs that squeaked when wet, she tried her best to belong, but she felt diminished next to her beautiful sisters, and invisible beside the popular girls at school—the ones her crushes actually wanted to date.

Eating cartons of ice cream became a regular Friday night replacement for friendship. It was a vicious circle: the more she isolated herself, the more her friends stopped calling, and the more she needed a gallon of Ice Castle maple walnut.

One of her high school friends remembers that Caroline declined all social invitations, from the Christmas sleigh ride to evening sledding on the hill at the local golf course to rec room parties. Her mono was a legitimate excuse, but after she had recovered, she would say she was coming, then not show up. Eventually her friends stopped asking her to join them.

In her own mind, she had become the weakest link in a family of trophy winners. There didn't seem to be a hook in the real world on which to hang her particular dreams: dog shows and poetry, one-woman synchronized swim routines in the backyard pool, knitting, creating homemade macramé plant hangers, hanging out with her mom. Perhaps hardest of all, she didn't have a best friend; she felt alone in a crowded house and invisible in a high school of two thousand students. Until she could stand out in some small way, she was adrift. Where was the girl who had played guard on the basketball team, had her legs painted with spaghetti sauce during Spirit Week, told hilarious jokes in Mr. Hakim's French class? She was lying around doing nothing on the top bunk in her bedroom or grooming the dogs, while worrying that she was too much of a nothing to have a social life.

To cap off a disastrous year, in May she was not asked to the graduation dance—the bookend to a year of social, physical, and emotional disappointments. A week before the dance, Isabel persuaded one of her sons' friends to take Caroline, and Arthur even paid for the boy's tuxedo rental. In lieu of a limo, another brother acted as chauffeur. Rosalind stayed up all night to sew her a beautiful bubble-gum-pink gown with puffed sleeves and an eyelet ribbon across the bodice. Pulling the evening together was a genuine rescue executed by several family members, and for at least a moment or two that week Caroline knew she wasn't invisible to them.

At the dance, Caroline resurrected an exuberant version of her old self, a side of her personality that had gone silent since the early days of September. Sandra, a close friend from the basketball years, remembers she was the "firecracker of the party," gyrating on the dance floor as though she were Tina Turner. (Caroline's erratic behaviour that night is still talked about more than forty years later, as old acquaintances try to pinpoint the moment at which their sweet friend moved from stable to anything but.)

Over the years of her childhood and early adolescence, Caroline was one of ten siblings vying for attention, but it was only as high school came to an end that she truly began to feel insignificant, sand-wiched between two beautiful blond sisters with lively social lives who maintained good grades. When it really mattered to Caroline, the phone had rung for Rosalind and her younger sister Peggy but not for her; armour-clad by looks and athleticism, neither Rosalind nor Peggy seemed to face the difficulties Caroline encountered. Peggy was the dream girl in her grade, idolized by most of the boys her age and older. And beautiful Rosalind excelled in the sciences, which raised their father's hopes that she was the one who would follow him into a medical career. Caroline's sister Sharon was already studying to be a nurse, and Lorraine had a natural instinct as an entrepreneur. Two of her older brothers were engaged, which to Caroline was the surest sign of happiness and success. She felt as if she was the only marble not in a groove.

No single item on Caroline's list of high school setbacks was cause for alarm, but the accumulation of events was a warning sign nobody noticed. When Arthur worried about what was going on with their daughter, Isabel insisted that Caroline was just a kid and had her whole life to figure things out. Arthur wanted all his children to pursue lofty professions such as medicine and law, but she was more pragmatic. Isabel herself was self-assured, happy, and generous. She had been a doctor's assistant when she was in the military overseas, return-ing home to a job as a keypunch operator. She had forsaken the idea of a nursing career to nurture a family—and her husband. Traditional to the core, she believed that, for a woman, love trumped work, and she wanted that same kind of trajectory for her five daughters: healthy, lov-ing relationships, laughter, companionships that would endure. She had an intrinsic faith in every one of her ten children, although she reserved her most fanatical devotion for Arthur, who had been an academically gifted boy who'd weathered a solitary childhood in a divorced family.

———

Maybe Isabel was also thinking that her beloved Arthur had endured far worse challenges in his childhood than anything Caroline had encountered. His father's first wife died after giving birth to two children, and although his father remarried, and Arthur was born of that second marriage, he did not find happiness in his new union. His parents divorced when Arthur's mother developed a severe kidney illness and could no longer raise her own son, let alone her two stepchildren. When she chose to return to her birthplace in Holyoke, Massachusetts, Arthur was sent to a French-language Montreal boarding school, Saint-Jean-de-Brébeuf, where his separation from his distraught mother, his father in Toronto, and his two half-siblings caused him great anguish.

His parents' divorce, rare for a Catholic couple in the 1930s, stigmatized their son at his Jesuit-run school. And, unlike the other boarders, he had nowhere to go on the weekends. Pierre Trudeau, a fellow student, invited him home on occasion, igniting a friendship that lasted a lifetime. But Arthur, by then fully bilingual, mostly filled the empty spaces in his life with long hours of studying, a passionate pursuit of learning that led him to graduate with high honours.

Arthur went on to medical school and became a renowned doctor. His tenacity was further rewarded with a plum job as executive director of a regional Montreal hospital, an acknowledgement of his work ethic, intelligence, and specialized medical skills. But Arthur believed his biggest gift was finding and marrying Isabel. She was immensely proud of her spouse and the way he had triumphed over his fractured upbringing. She knew Arthur wanted to erase his unhappy, solitary childhood with a large family, and she had obliged. With that many offspring, at least Arthur would never be alone again. And he was deeply appreciative of the way she mothered all ten children, which seemed mysterious and wonderful to a man who had been raised and educated by priests and scholars, his own mother lost to a chronic illness.

Years later, Rosalind learned a detail of her father's past that would prove telling, given what later unfolded for Caroline. A few weeks before Isabel and Arthur were to be married, Arthur called off the wedding. He had second thoughts because it turned out his older half-sister, Marilyn, suffered from manic depression, perhaps even schizophrenia, and had had a breakdown in the late 1940s, a year before Arthur was to marry Isabel. She would go on to spend long periods incarcerated for "insanity" in a Toronto institution. She too had been scarred by death and divorce. Her condition was a closely guarded and shaming family secret. Although the science had not yet proven any genetic links, and heritability was a new idea, Arthur worried that whatever had upended his half-sister's life might be passed on to the next generation, and he told his fiancée that it might be a mistake to bring children into the world. Isabel scoffed. "For better or for worse," she said.

Caroline graduated from St. Vincent high school on a warm June evening in 1975 amid a throng of capped and gowned classmates. For the eighth time, her father's brown station wagon glided onto the football field, a once-a-year makeshift parking lot, and he and Isabel went inside to sit beneath basketball nets, ceiling fans, and looping crepe paper streamers—proud parents celebrating the launch of their eighth child. Maybe they were thinking "only two to go"—just Kevin and their youngest, Peggy. Caroline had curled her long blond hair, and when her name was called from the podium, she teetered across the stage on a sister's white high heels. For a moment, she glowed with the promise that all things were still possible.

3

# At Seventeen

CAROLINE BEGAN CLASSES AT JOHN ABBOTT COLLEGE, A
CEGEP in Sainte-Anne-de-Bellevue, in September 1975. She had
chosen a health science stream that would lead her to a nursing degree.
Even though she had little aptitude for the science courses—the
thrust of the curriculum—she had a strong desire to be a nurse, perhaps partly to please her dad and also to follow in the footsteps of
Rosalind and Sharon, who had both chosen careers in health care. But
after a month, she dropped out. She couldn't complete the homework
assignments, overwhelmed by her inability to focus. Her mother,
unperturbed, thought a temporary break from school would be a positive opportunity to regroup.

With no classes to attend, Caroline took a short trip with her parents to the Niagara region, where Sharon was living and working as a
nurse. Isabel hoped Sharon might have some good advice to share
with her little sister. It didn't work out: Caroline had several bouts
where she locked herself in the bathroom to cry, and Sharon was
unable either to console her sister or to coax her out. Sharon hadn't
been home much during Caroline's calamitous final year of high

school, and she was mystified by the change in her normally good-natured and even-tempered sister.

Back home and at loose ends, Caroline became fixated on music—in particular the hit single "At Seventeen" by Janis Ian. She played the track over and over, mesmerized by the soulful lyrics, identifying with Ian's depiction of a mournful sad-sack life. The words seemed to speak directly to her—from the basketball and hand-me-downs references to the line about desperately remaining home: *A . . . girl in hand-me-downs . . . they only get what they deserve . . . To those of us who knew the pain of valentines that never came, and those whose names were never called when choosing sides for basketball . . . inventing lovers on the phone . . . when dreams were all they gave for free to ugly duckling girls like me . . .*

Rosalind said, "It all resonated, especially the line about inventing lovers on the telephone. She listened ad nauseam for months, driving us all insane. She was so excessive that she wore us all down until we were really hard on her."

Caroline had turned seventeen the previous July. Janis Ian was the sister she needed, a woman who understood the heartbreak of inferiority.

In January 1976, Caroline signed up at a community college theatre school. She dropped out after six weeks. Though Arthur had boasted about her only performance, most of the other students had long years of singing and dancing under their belts. In March, she registered at a hairdressing school, and dropped out after two months. Nobody knew quite what happened that time, but to become a hairdresser it was not enough to have been born with beautiful hair. More importantly, Caroline had not connected with the other girls, who seemed glamorous and sophisticated whereas Caroline was homey and laid-back, anything but a style maven. She felt woefully inadequate. She didn't belong anywhere.

But nobody else was worried, least of all the most important person to Caroline—her mother. Isabel just assumed that her daughter wasn't ready to be a student or learn a trade, and that eventually she would know what to do with her life.

Caroline spent the summer living at home and babysitting neighbourhood children, and did not register for any classes that fall. She was reluctant to try anything new for fear of more failure.

By November, she was in meltdown. Many days she couldn't stop crying, sobbing into her folded arms, collapsed in an armchair, until it got dark enough to crawl under the covers in bed. She seemed utterly defeated and inconsolable, but bit by bit she managed to pull herself together, with liberal amounts of her mother's attention. Then, in January, through a family connection, she got a job in the classroom of an elementary school as a teaching assistant for students with special needs. It was a good fit. It didn't matter to the kids that she wasn't lithe or trendy, because she was patient, tolerant, and relaxed.

It was a lazy, ordinary Saturday morning the following summer. Someone was jumping into the pool, dogs were barking, and one of the cats was shredding the pleated corner of the chesterfield. Elton John was on the record player. "Goodbye Yellow Brick Road." It was pyjamas and cornflakes as usual at the oblong kitchen table surrounded by a dozen well-worn Windsor chairs. Rosalind and Ian were home from university, but that morning it was only the girls gathered with their mother at the table; Ian was nowhere in sight.

"Mum, I need to tell you something," Caroline said. She added more sugar to her mug of tea, stirred, then gazed from Rosalind to Peggy and finally to her mother. She had celebrated her nineteenth birthday one day earlier. The baby doll pyjamas she wore, frilly pink-and-white bloomers under a Swiss dot sleeveless top, still bore the store tags. Her tanned legs were stretched across the seat of a second kitchen chair. Finally, she said, "I've been sexually assaulted."

Her mother and sisters were speechless. Isabel lit a cigarette, inhaling deeply to collect her thoughts, and looked at all three of her daughters, then back to Caroline.

"I've been sexually assaulted," Caroline repeated. "By Dad. And Ian." There were ten seconds of silence. "Ian locked me in the bathroom and did things to me. And Dad . . ." Her voice trailed off.

Rosalind erupted. "Don't be ridiculous, Caroline. What a bunch of horseshit."

"Remember when we were living in Saint-Laurent, Ian sold me for twenty cents so that one of his friends could put his hand up my shirt." Caroline looked from face to face for sympathy and support. The family had lived in Saint-Laurent until Caroline was eight years old. At the time they moved, Ian would have been only ten.

"You're so full of crap," said Peggy, who was sixteen but seemed older. As the youngest of ten in Isabel's permissive household, she'd seen her siblings get up to a lot of questionable stuff. But this? And her dad too? Not possible.

Isabel needed to light another cigarette to get past the moment. No one thought to call Arthur into the conversation, despite the fact that he was in the living room reading the paper.

Both of Caroline's sisters got up from the table to scramble eggs and pour glasses of orange juice. When Rosalind sat down again, she looked Caroline in the eye and accused her of making up provocative lies to get their attention. As far as she was concerned, Caroline had been burning bridges in the credibility department since grade ten, when she told those stories about the popular boys chasing her. Yes, she'd been bullied by Ian, so this might be her idea of revenge, but how could she smear their father in such a shocking way?

Isabel at last found her voice. "He may not have enough time with you kids, but he is always moral and fair." She knew Caroline had been struggling, but this time she had gone too far, and in a calm voice she proceeded to set her daughter straight. In a crowded house, she pointed out, it would have been impossible for Arthur to do anything to Caroline that would have escaped her attention, or someone else's. "Such nonsense." Isabel said nothing about Ian.

But Caroline did not back down. When Isabel got up to clear the dishes, lighting another cigarette from the one she was smoking, Rosalind and Peggy rolled their eyes at their sister, who wavered when she saw nothing but revulsion and scorn etched across the faces of her two closest siblings.

"What is the matter with you?" Rosalind could not hide her contempt. Caroline lifted one of the dogs onto her lap and buried her face in the red, silky fur, crying in frustration and confusion. In that moment of divided loyalties, one of the strings that had held them all together was cut. No one thought to raise her accusations with Ian, and no one dared mention them to Arthur.


Several days after the scene in the kitchen, Caroline invited her friend Fern to come over. He was three years older than she was, big and burly, with a kind face and a fondness for films. They'd met a few years earlier at a student-run high school talent show at St. Vincent. Fern, already a part-time DJ, had earned a standing ovation by impersonating Elvis.

The entire house was empty—a rare occurrence, especially in August, when so many family members were home from school. It was a muggy summer night, and she'd invited him for a swim in the pool. Caroline had been attempting to turn their relationship into something more, though she knew Fern was going out with another woman. Caroline wanted one more chance to change his mind.

Fern had agreed to come over only so he could let her down gently, and in person.

The front door was open, and Fern found Caroline in the kitchen, already in her bikini. She had poured two beers, but when she looked at him, he felt as though she didn't recognize him. "Her eyes were glassy and bugged out of their sockets like she was possessed," he remembers. "It wasn't Caroline who was staring at me. I thought maybe she was on something, maybe a doobie, or something stronger. I walked closer and she pulled a carving knife out of the kitchen drawer. The kind of knife you cut meat with."

"You get away from me and you stay away from me," she told him.

Fern could see how hard she was gripping the wooden handle of the knife. "I tried to be light. I said, 'Caroline, it's me—Fern. You know, Elvis from the talent show. Caroline? Caroline! What are you doing?' I asked her to put the knife away, and she did, but I knew there was something wrong with her. I said goodbye, and left. I saw her a week later, and she was her old self again. She never mentioned the knife, and it was as if it hadn't happened."

Fern had mentioned this strange incident to Rosalind's boyfriend, Connor, who happened to be a friend of his, but neither of them knew what to make of it. They didn't tell anyone else. Fern now wishes he hadn't let it drop. "It's one of my deepest regrets."

The following summer, Caroline took the train west to Alberta and worked as a chambermaid at the Banff Springs Hotel, a grand railway hotel that opened in 1888. Rosalind was also in Alberta for the summer, working as a waitress at the Jasper Park Lodge. As far as she or any of the rest of the family knew, Caroline hadn't said or done anything untoward since she'd made her accusations, which they'd all nervously buried. It was as if Caroline had never uttered the words "I've been sexually assaulted."

In the summer, both hotels augmented their staff with students from Ontario, Quebec, and the Maritimes, who were offered train tickets, to and fro, in exchange for minimum-wage jobs. There was great competition for the chance to spend a summer in the Canadian Rockies, and Caroline was proud when her application was accepted.

One weekend she hitchhiked the 289 kilometres of winding mountain roads from Banff to Jasper to visit Rosalind. They ate pancakes at Smitty's, hiked near the Maligne Canyon, and had a lakeside bonfire with a dozen of Rosalind's friends—an evening of singing, drinking, and camaraderie. Rosalind felt a rare ease that weekend in her connection to Caroline, which had been strained by the accusations of sexual assault. And Caroline had exceptional gossip to share: She told Rosalind that she was the chambermaid for the famous stars of a popular TV show *Starsky & Hutch*. Paul Michael Glaser (Starsky) had been in a near-death motorcycle accident, she said, and was lucky to have lost only an arm and a leg. He was recuperating in her section of rooms. He planned to spend the entire summer in Banff before returning to Hollywood. Caroline was looking out for him, she claimed. They had become close friends. Rosalind was thrilled for Caroline. The story didn't seem all that outrageous: the famous Alberta hotels, close to pristine glaciers, the Columbia Icefield, and hiking and cycling trails, did attract politicians, high-profile actors, and rock stars. She did wonder, much later, why it hadn't occurred to her to ask her sister how the actor could still have a television career with two missing limbs. What she did think about was how much Caroline needed to be needed. If anyone could resurrect someone's flagging spirits after an accident that catastrophic, it was her sister.

And Rosalind hadn't seen Caroline this radiant in a very long time. She had shed the high school weight, and seemed to have shed all of her troubles as well. The sisters had a wonderful weekend together, re-establishing a sibling bond that had been sorely tested.

Rosalind now looks back in wonder. "For twenty-nine years I believed that the actor who played Starsky lost his limbs in an accident. Then I searched on the Internet and realized that she had invented it all, maybe sparked by another tragic accident. A male actor named James Stacy had been in a terrible motorcycle accident in 1973, was struck by a drunk driver and lost two limbs. The woman on the bike with him died in the crash. What would I have done if I had known? Probably accused my sister of more lies. I wish I could say that I would have seen it as a sign of her deepening difficulties. But back then, none of us knew anything."

Caroline returned to Montreal in late August, hoping to go back to school. Though she had missed the deadline to re-register for fall classes at John Abbott, she decided she'd take some science courses in January to prepare to enrol full-time in nursing the following fall.

She had four months on her hands, and no responsibility beyond babysitting, so when an acquaintance named Stella Simpson invited her to go island-hopping in the Caribbean, she leapt at the chance. They lived around the corner from each other, and had been witness to each other's singular lives. Stella had also attended St. Vincent, where nuns in long, flowing habits taught geometry, as well as guilt for anything sexual outside the confines of heterosexual marriage. Stella was alternative. Jet-black hair cut short. She wore dark jeans and a shirt with the sleeves cut off. No shimmery eyeshadow, ponytail, or acquiescent behaviour. She studied home economics because it was required, not because she wanted to sew a pink velvet pillowcase or make popovers. Caroline was her antithesis: blond, blue-eyed, curvy, and mostly a hippie. It was their outlier status that joined them like Velcro, though Caroline was crushed to be an outsider whereas Stella gloried in her alternative niche. Stella was also unusual because of her sexual orientation: even in high school she was an "out" lesbian, multi-pierced and tattooed at a time when body tampering was scandalous. She set herself far apart from the teenaged Barbies and Kens who lived to blend in.

In 1978, being openly gay was a bit scandalous in a suburban neighbourhood like Pointe-Claire, a place that enshrined traditional families. If a gay teenager had the courage to come out, his or her family rarely shared the news with the neighbours. If homosexuality was misunderstood in Quebec, it was openly discriminated against in the Caribbean. But Stella didn't give a damn what people thought of her, and Caroline found that attitude a thrilling liberation. She couldn't wait to spend her nights sleeping on the hot sand at the edge of the sea, or in a hammock slung between coconut palms.

They drove to Florida in Stella's dented second-hand gas guzzler, then flew to the Caribbean island of Bequia. From there, they planned to visit the Grenadine Islands, St. Vincent, Dominica, and Barbados. Flights between islands could be had for peanuts. The first night, they found a hotel for ten dollars next to a bar serving island drinks in vases. Each subsequent night they consumed vast amounts of inexpensive pina coladas and daiquiris, listened to calypso music, and found their way to the beaches to dance with the locals under a star-hooded sky.

It sounded like the trip of a lifetime, but a month later, when they returned to Montreal, Caroline seemed tentative and nervous. She confided in her sisters that one night she had been raped by a black man on a beach in Barbados. Her sisters were openly skeptical of this story. (Rosalind looks back now with regret, realizing it was another cry for help that went unheeded.) Caroline had thrived in the structure of a regular job at the Banff Springs Hotel; roaming the islands with no set agenda or place to stay had unhinged her.

# 4

# This Girl Is Not Right

AT ABOUT THE SAME TIME CAROLINE RETURNED FROM the Caribbean, Arthur quit drinking. Isabel had made it plain that she was tired of his sullen behaviour and gruff resentments. She was also frankly worried about the amount of alcohol he was consuming every day. She persuaded him that he was setting a bad example for the children, especially their two oldest sons, who were both struggling with alcohol. But at the heart of Isabel's urging was a deep-seated fear that her husband would get sick. She could not conceive of a life without Arthur.

Arthur had kept himself at arm's length from child rearing, partly because of the demands of his job and partly because he was a man of his generation. He tried his best to be an attentive father on weekends, taking his brood skiing and tobogganing, and he liked nothing better than being asked by his children for his opinion with regard to careers and how best to become independent. Still, he carried a large amount of guilt over his abilities as a parent, and that was an easy lever for his wife to pull. But as with everything to do with Caroline's parents, the real motivating force was Arthur's love of Isabel, especially after a car accident—in the early morning, with no alcohol involved—where

Isabel had broken her leg. Then he had a close call when his car went over the median while he was driving on the highway, and that clinched it. Isabel was the one person who loved him unreservedly. If nothing else, she deserved all of him. He never drank again.

To his dismay, according to his youngest, Peggy, his problems didn't vanish, and neither did his anger and resentments. "Memories don't go away," Peggy says, "just because the screen you hid behind is gone. He had more clear-headed time to examine his conscience about all of us." His new clarity of mind brought home the responsibility he bore for deciding to raise ten children. He had two sons who were alcoholics; his eldest was so deep into addiction he had difficulty holding down a job. Caroline's unaccountable conduct caused him a different kind of alarm. When she claimed to be adopted one night at the dinner table, he couldn't resort to booze to dull his perception that something was wrong with his daughter. For the first time, he contemplated the idea that his daughter had begun to exhibit some of the same behaviours that led his sister to spend years in an institution. Arthur was devastated.

Isabel tried to comfort him out of his worry, as she always did, offering optimism and abiding love. Their children would thrive and survive, she said. It helped him close his eyes to Caroline's aberrant thinking. When Isabel had broken her leg, it was an unassailable fact; he could verify the crack with an X-ray. With a plaster cast to support her leg, the bone healed. Caroline's symptoms didn't show up on any X-ray, just rumbled their warnings like the sound of distant thunder.


Caroline made it through the long winter after her distressing Caribbean holiday, getting by with babysitting, retreating to her room to play music, and, in the credit column, getting marks in two science courses that were good enough for her to enrol in nursing school, which would start in September 1979.

But then, at the family cottage that summer, Caroline met Andy and fell hard into her first true romance. Andy was slim, blue-eyed, and boyishly handsome. He was spending the summer with an uncle in Lachute, a tiny Laurentian town about an hour north of Montreal. He had few responsibilities, a wide-open agenda; the two were soon inseparable.

It turned out that Andy liked to get high. And soon Caroline did too. They experimented with magic mushrooms, and though Caroline was nervous, Andy assured her that mushrooms had been consumed for a thousand years in Mexico for their medicinal, therapeutic properties. Getting high on shrooms made them laugh, made them interpret the glowing neon landscape with awe, turned the lyrics of their favourite songs into epiphanies. And when they ran out of mushrooms, they smoked weed, then carried the canoe to the edge of Sir John Lake and slipped into the water at dusk to paddle out so they could be inside the sunset. In the dark, they danced on the sand under the soft edges of the moon, Andy's arms wrapped around her shoulders.

When, as the summer wound down, Caroline decided to put her nursing plans on hold, no one could hold it against her. She was the picture of rosy-cheeked happiness. Even though Andy had never been west of Ontario, Caroline had the bright idea to move them both out to Alberta, a place where she'd spent such a glorious summer. They rented an apartment in Edmonton, confident they would find a way to pay for it. Caroline got a job in a garden shop. Andy worked in construction here and there, though he was a little vague about how he was actually earning the money he brought home. Still, an entire year passed relatively peacefully.

But then Andy started to call Rosalind every now and then to report that Caroline was saying things that didn't add up, along with telling him obvious whoppers. He confided that he was worried her changed behaviour was a result of their drug use, and that he wanted to end things but didn't have the heart to do so. Instead, he began to see another woman, and when Caroline caught on, he didn't deny it, and he also didn't end the second relationship. Distraught, Caroline showed up at a job site where he was framing new houses and pleaded with him to come home, willing to say or do anything to keep him close. In response, he began to disappear overnight. When he was at home, he was stoned all the time. He hardly slept. Neither did she. Caroline worried he was spending too much money on drugs, and was anxious that he had become a dealer. When someone pounded on the door of their apartment in the middle of the night, her fears were confirmed.

After that incident, he was gone for good. He never even packed his belongings. When he didn't pay his share of the rent for three months running, Caroline had to admit it was over. Unable to stop crying, she packed up her things and booked a flight home to Montreal, seeking refuge again with her parents.

Arthur, who'd been so happy that he and Isabel were finally on their own, did not greet her warmly.

Three days after she got back, on a long weekend when a few siblings were also home, Caroline was at the kitchen table, drinking coffee with her mother, the very same table where she'd once accused her father and brother of sexual assault. She picked that moment to tell her mother that she had had a miscarriage that morning. Caroline became distraught, clearly experiencing the loss of something. Peggy, Rosalind, and Kevin came running from the family room as Caroline moaned and cried, holding her belly, inconsolable.

43

"Oh, for God's sake, Caroline. I have had enough of you," her mother yelled.

Isabel's outburst silenced them all. Except for Caroline, who cried harder. Rosalind, visiting from Toronto, felt a deep compassion for her younger sister at that moment. There was hardness in their mother's voice that felt personal.

Rosalind says, "That moment was the death of many things for Caroline: perhaps the loss of a pregnancy, of her love affair with Andy, of her self-esteem, independence, her pride too, given she'd been dumped without explanation." But the most damaging blow of all was the loss of her mother's support—the woman who had been saying for years, "This is just a phase." Isabel was as distressed and overwhelmed as her daughter, which meant neither was much use to the other.

That night, when Caroline was more or less composed, she picked up the old thread about Darren Fulton, confiding that she'd been calling him again and that he was once more infatuated with her. Rosalind thought but did not say, *Here you go again with the lies.* She knows now that the glittery delusion was Caroline's attempt to ride above the crushing wave of Andy's disappearance. It didn't make the idea seem any less true to Caroline when her sisters pointed out that Darren had long departed Montreal to embark on a singing career and that he was in a committed relationship with somebody else.

For some reason, it was on that night, while she listened to her daughter fabricate stories while in a state of distress, that some kind of door at last unlocked in Isabel's mind, allowing her to see what she had long denied. The following morning, she called Arthur at work and had him paged. "This girl is not right," she said when he finally called home. She beseeched Arthur to find a psychiatrist through his web of contacts at the hospital. Discreetly, of course. It was deeply embarrassing to Isabel that the family was at the point of seeking out mental health workers to help ease Caroline's psychic pain, but something had to be done.

The siblings didn't know what to make of their sister's lying. They rolled their eyes at her, tired of hearing about Caroline's make-believe dates, assaults, rapes, sexual abuse, and miscarriages. They were sick of all the ways she tampered with the truth to create a story where she was either the heroine or the besieged—a ridiculous, sometimes sordid fantasyland. Any empathy they had had for a struggling sister was draining away. Kevin said, "She made her bed. Now she has to lie in it."

5

# The Blue Box
# Under the Bunk Bed

CAROLINE HAD HER FIRST PSYCHIATRIC APPOINTMENT
in October 1981 at the Lakeshore General Hospital, a hastily organized
visit with a man Arthur had known for years. The doctor interviewed
her on her own, standard practice with an adult patient, leaving her
sister Sharon, who had accompanied her, in the waiting room as they
talked for two hours. He was a kindly father figure with tufts of white
hair growing from inside his ears and great listening skills. When he
greeted her, shaking her hand, Caroline pulled herself together, showing not a hint of her worrisome behaviour.

   She'd agreed to the appointment to placate her mother, but Caroline
did not want anyone to know she was seeing a psychiatrist. People
consigned to the infamous "4-East" ward at the Lakeshore General had
been the target of the worst kinds of teenage derision in high school,
stigmatized as loonies, as people who babbled senselessly and couldn't
care for themselves. Lock them up, medicate them, and throw away the
key. She had read *Jane Eyre* in English class, and knew what happened
to mad women: they were barricaded in the attic, shunned, and feared.

Caroline felt shame that she'd been sent to see a psychiatrist, on her own behalf and also on her father's, who was in charge of the entire hospital. The night before the assessment, Caroline had overheard her parents quietly talking about quirky Aunt Marilyn. They rarely spoke about her, and Caroline knew they were worried sick she might be on the same path.

She and her siblings didn't find out the whole of Marilyn's story till much later. Their father's half-sister had been an accomplished, brilliant academic who had earned a master's degree in library science in 1944. Her troubles had started when she met a man in her Sunday prayer group. They began to date, and then Marilyn got pregnant. For a single woman of any faith in the 1940s, unwed motherhood was a stigma; for a devout Catholic like Marilyn, it was an unimaginable shame. She could not contemplate an abortion; not only was it illegal and dangerous, it was a mortal sin. So she carried on with the pregnancy, making a concerted effort to keep it secret by hiding under voluminous drapery, all of which added to her mental distress. As she grew closer to term, she wrestled with whether she should keep the baby: she had the financial means to raise a child, and a deep desire to be a proper mother, maybe to make up for the losses of her own birth mother and the stepmother who had walked away. In the end, she gave the baby up for adoption because it was the proper thing for an unwed Catholic to do. But it was a shattering decision.

After she gave the baby away, she covered her head whenever she left the house, preferring to be unseen by the outside world, especially men. And soon she was over the edge of depression and into full-blown psychosis, a breakdown that culminated with her running naked down Bay Street in downtown Toronto. That episode led to her committal.

During much of the 1950s and 1960s she lived in the asylum at 999 Queen Street West in Toronto, whose grey walls imposed not only physical but social barriers. Arthur visited her during her incarceration. The wards were crowded and dark, and the smell was unimaginable. The "screamers"—people in extreme distress—were restrained in straitjackets or tied to their beds. There were very few treatment options, apart from sedatives, shock therapies, and ice baths; the doctors had far too many patients to attempt any sort of talk therapy. Patient-to-patient violence inside the institution was unavoidable, and this led to further aggression as the staff wrestled the combatants into harnesses attached to bed frames. If their symptoms were severe enough, patients simply stayed on indefinitely, usually forsaken by their family and friends. It left a demeaning, unresolvable imprint on Arthur's fragile psyche.

In the late 1950s, Marilyn was treated with a new drug, chlorpromazine, the first antipsychotic medication. It suppressed her symptoms, but there was nothing curative about the miracle drug that had been heralded as a saving grace for the mentally afflicted. Sedated, she was able to leave the institution for longer stretches, but the drug blunted her capacities and emotions, and she was never again able to work or lead a normal life.

Occasionally, she did come to visit her brother and his family in Pointe-Claire. While Arthur never told his children she'd been locked up, they knew that their idiosyncratic aunt had suffered a "nervous breakdown" of some kind. On one visit, during Expo 67, she had arrived at the Dorval train station wearing a thick cloth over her head, clearly once more on the brink of psychosis. Arthur, who had brought some of his children along to greet her, was mortified. The irony was that in her attempt to be invisible, she drew more attention to herself—and ridicule from her nieces and nephews, who laughed behind her back about her cloaked head.

Caroline was determined not to be a source of shame for her father, and also determined not to follow in her troubled aunt's footsteps. For two hours, she spoke to the psychiatrist about her desire for a nursing career, her failed romance with Andy, her love of poetry and theatre. She was gentle, candid, and forthright about her disappointments. Her distress made sense to the psychiatrist. He wrote in his report that she was a "leftover flower child of the 60s," that her head was in the clouds, that she was uncertain of her future, but that she appeared to have normal yearnings. His theory was that she was "acting out" as an experiment in self-discovery. His diagnosis was like a winning lottery ticket for Isabel, who wanted nothing but confirmation that her daughter was typical, average, and "normal" even if she was behaving inappropriately at the moment. Isabel went back to believing that Caroline's errant behaviour was an attention grab that would pass.

The psychiatrist's kindness, rather than his insight, had also done wonders for Caroline. She was reassured by her conversation with a person in authority who accepted her artistic and sensitive leanings, and also by his non-judgmental compassion. They didn't think to book a second appointment. After all, there was no need.

The respite was brief. When Rosalind came home from university for Thanksgiving weekend, she thought it would be fun to follow the usual turkey and stuffing in the festooned dining room with a family session of Monopoly or Scrabble. As she was searching for the board games in the girls' bedrooms, she found a blue cardboard box hidden under a bunk bed. Inside was a sheaf of 8½ -by-11 loose-leaf sheets covered in Caroline's handwriting. She had filled dozens of pages with graphic detail about violence—rape, fondling, and penetration perpetrated by her father, by her antagonistic brother Ian, and by another older brother, Stuart. The penmanship was tidy, each page numbered. "My father put out his cigarettes on my thighs," she had written.

A shocked Rosalind took several minutes to calm down, then pulled Ian into a bedroom, where she questioned him behind a locked door, holding the box. Ian refuted the allegations, insisting he had never laid a hand on his sister in that way. Rosalind remembers how scared he was, but in his own defence he attacked his accuser with anger, disgust, and contempt. "She's contaminated water," he said.

Together, Ian and Rosalind decided to trash the papers without confronting Caroline or telling their parents. Ian was white-faced and stricken, and Rosalind, who had forced herself to read every horrible detail, was mortified that Caroline even had those kinds of perverted thoughts. They tore the paper into shreds, then tossed them into two separate garbage cans in the garage so there was no chance anyone could put them back together.

Rosalind did share this latest outrage with Peggy and Sharon. For a moment or two, Sharon remembers, she couldn't help but wonder, "Did this really happen? The details were so specific about family members, and I asked myself, could this be true on some level? The sheets of paper in the box had the potential to create so much family stress and division. We all started looking over our shoulders, and wondering who was telling the truth."

It was too late to do Caroline much good, but one outcome of the discovery of the blue box was that Ian stopped bullying her. In fact, he cut off all contact with her.

On that same weekend, Caroline was campaigning on behalf of her father. She'd decided he needed to be properly honoured by the entire West Island community. She claimed she would organize a large-scale event at the rock quarry in Vaudreuil, as unlikely a place as anyone could imagine to celebrate a renowned member of the medical community. Of course, it never got off the ground. The siblings who knew about the contents of the blue box couldn't believe the contradiction, but by then most of Caroline's siblings met most of her utterances with derision. Yes, she'd had some disappointments in life, but not enough to justify her becoming a fantasist and liar. At one time everyone except Ian had been sympathetic to Caroline's struggles, but now they felt offended by her ideas and accusations, and confused by her emotional swings. One day Caroline was quiet and withdrawn, and the next she was buoyant and self-absorbed. She still had her generosity of spirit, an infectious belly laugh, and she loved her sisters without reservation. She especially idolized Rosalind, who had scaled social, athletic, and academic heights that Caroline could never manage. Rosalind now wishes she had had more insight back then, more compassion, when a sympathetic shoulder from the person Caroline admired most might have made a difference. But at the time, Rosalind was just deeply confused, exasperated, and sometimes scandalized by her younger sister.

With the all-clear from the psychiatrist—and no knowledge of the blue box—Isabel decided it was time for Caroline to move out of the parental home. Arthur was enthusiastically in favour; both of them thought their daughter would benefit from the responsibility of having her own place. Isabel found a tiny apartment on Elm Street in Beaconsfield, near the train station and the Gary Taylor Centre, a school for children with special needs. Isabel hoped Caroline might secure a part-time job at the centre. Since her daughter had so many special needs herself, she quipped, she would fit right in. She wasn't just making a slightly mocking joke: she really did think that her patient and generous daughter had a built-in capacity to improve the lives of children with intellectual deficits.

It turned out she needed credentials she didn't have to work at Gary Taylor, but thanks to a few calls made by her father, Caroline did secure a job as a nursing assistant at the Lakeshore General. From the first day, she excelled, showing a natural empathy for the patients. Galvanized by her success at the hospital, she applied to the nursing programme at John Abbott for the third time. And for a moment or two, Caroline's mother and sisters were able to shake off a few cobwebs of worry.

Caroline was still hurting from her collapsed relationship with Andy when she met Gilles Varga. "I remember that he had a lot of plants in his apartment," she told me with a laugh. "It made me think that he could keep things alive."

At the time, Gilles was driving a cab for a living, and spent his evenings either playing pool with friends or in the bar, called the Caboose, at the "Mapes"—the Maple Inn on Lakeshore Road in Pointe-Claire. The Caboose had been a raucous place in the seventies, when stubby bottles of Labatt 50 sold for $1.05 and drug dealers were a fixture— visible to some but invisible to others. Once a respectable lakeside summer resort, the Mapes had become a place where police raids were routine, as were closures for permit violations.

By the eighties, when Gilles met Caroline in the side bar of the inn, known dope dealers were barred from the premises, and there was a doorman to keep out the riff-raff. Still, Caroline didn't much like the undertone. She preferred Shawn's Pub on St. Charles Road, a local hotspot with snaky lineups every Friday and Saturday night. Soon she and Gilles were drinking and dancing most weekends at the pub, where several of Caroline's old high school friends also liked to hang out. Fern was the DJ—another draw as far as Caroline was concerned. He'd known Gilles for years, and worried that Gilles was too old and too experimental for his fragile friend. He kept an eye on Caroline from his perch at the turntables spinning tracks from the Pretenders and Michael Jackson. Though he'd put the unsettling knife incident behind him, he was still uneasy about what went on beneath Caroline's bubbly exterior.

Gilles was confident and chatty, and bore an uncanny resemblance to Andy—blond and handsome. The couple's early days were filled with dancing and drinking, and visits to Memorial Beach and the local arboretum, all of it accompanied by a healthy dose of recreational drugs and tequila shots. In other words, nothing out of the ordinary. Isabel thought Gilles was as much of a featherweight in the reliability department as her own daughter, and worried about the drugs. But, as usual, Caroline was her best self in a relationship, and that was enough to counteract her mother's uncertainty. Soon the couple was living together on Cartier Avenue.

Caroline's friend Dannah remembers visiting them after Caroline had called a dozen times imploring her to come over. "I drove down from the Laurentians. When I got there, the place was a mess, which was so unusual as she was a neat freak. Caroline wasn't herself. She was my sweet friend from elementary school. Of all my girlfriends, she had the biggest heart. She looked like shit. 'What have you done to yourself?' I asked her. 'This isn't you.'" After the visit, Dannah stopped taking Caroline's calls, figuring that her friend was simply a druggie. "I cut her off. I knew I couldn't save her."

Rosalind, who moved to Vancouver around the time Caroline moved in with Gilles, can't recall that her sister had any interest in drugs beyond occasional use. But she knew that something was going on inside her sister, a kind of shifting and shattering that was impossible to decipher. Sometimes Rosalind would get five calls from Caroline in one day, and then nothing for a week. A chameleon, she was either flat on the phone or crazily exuberant, and there seemed to be no reason for either state. It was a relief, that September, when she heard Caroline had actually started nursing school.

Two months later, Arthur organized a sixtieth birthday party for his beloved Isabel. They would soon be putting their home on the market and spending six months a year in a warm climate, and he wanted everyone in the family to come home for a big celebration of their mother. None of the sons were able to come, but Rosalind and Lorraine flew in as a surprise for Isabel, and Sharon and Peggy came from Ottawa. Rosalind remembers that Caroline sat alone at the dining room table, her head buried in her homework, through each joyful reunion at the front door.

Friday night was a casual dinner at home, everyone chatting easily, catching up, excited to be part of Arthur's surprise. Caroline was withdrawn and silent, easy to overlook in all the excitement. But eventually she whispered in Rosalind's ear that she needed to talk privately.

Behind a closed bedroom door, away from their parents, Caroline told first Rosalind and then her other sisters that she was four months pregnant. For a moment Rosalind wondered if once again she was seeking attention, but there was no denying Caroline's thicker waist and voluminous breasts, her wobbly chin and overflowing eyes. She desperately needed their support before she told Isabel, but Rosalind, for one, was on the verge of angry tears that Caroline had derailed the family reunion with her stupidity and carelessness. Why had she chosen that weekend to break the news? Why not after the birthday party? This was supposed to be Isabel's special moment, Arthur's toast to their long marriage, despite the inevitable ups and downs. Rosalind ached for her father, who had wanted the weekend to be a confirmation of Isabel's declaration "For better or for worse."

But it was impossible to keep it a secret. The news was like the crack of a baseball bat to the side of Isabel's head. The look on her face said it all. It was more than disappointment or anger—it was dread. They were a prominent Catholic family and Isabel cared deeply about the opinions of her friends and neighbours. They would judge her a careless mother for having a daughter who was pregnant outside the confines of marriage. And underneath the shock and humiliation was a deeper worry. Did Caroline have enough stability to be a fit parent? Did Gilles? He had to marry her, if she was going to keep the baby, but was that a good thing? Caroline's blue eyes overflowed with tears of remorse and the sting of their judgment. She was panicked by her situation, but nobody reached out with a kind gesture.

In fact they were unkind, immediately disinviting her to the birthday dinner, which went ahead without her the following evening at the Willow restaurant in Hudson, a nearby waterfront inn. It was a moody, rain-drenched night that matched Caroline's gloomy quarantine. She remained huddled in a chair, alone in the house on Lakeshore Road, while the family was out toasting Isabel. She had nine siblings, a live-in boyfriend, a baby on the way, two parents, and there she sat under a mammoth mountain of failure, of distance, of separation. Isabel had been her sounding board, her connection to the family, the person who had almost always risen to her defence. When the car drove off to the birthday dinner without her, her world got very small.

Rosalind now cries when she thinks back on that weekend, a pivotal moment of Catholic guilt and shame, and pictures her sister, treated like a pariah. Even at the time, when she realized that Caroline's textbooks were, in fact, baby-raising books she had borrowed from the library, her regret was profound. Years later, she asked Caroline for forgiveness, which Caroline was only too eager to give.

Caroline knew one thing for certain: no matter how her family treated her, she would keep this baby. The decision at first was a curse, and then a blessing, and finally both.

# Camilla

Camilla and I have become regulars at a Tim Hortons in LaSalle where the staff is not unfriendly to customers who talk to themselves. Though she's a slim 120 pounds, Camilla is wheezing and breathless from the short shuffle from the car to the coffee shop—the result of ever-decreasing lung capacity and a lifetime of zero physical exercise. She's a spectacle with her wild bleached hair that resists all efforts at taming. She has dropped eleven dress sizes since she was at her heaviest, weighing in at 285 pounds, the result of decades of antipsychotic medication.

We order, and she slips her false teeth into place from a box in a pocket in order to eat her chocolate glazed doughnut. The icing clings to her dentures. When Camilla sips her double-double, her hands shake from tardive dyskinesia, a permanent neurological disorder caused by her constant high-dose usage of antipsychotics.

In the middle of our coffee she excuses herself to go outside for a smoke, pulling a cigarette from a box she carries tucked inside her saggy bra, next to a plastic lighter. Purses get stolen, she tells me. Camilla smokes as many cigarettes as she can get her hands on. It would be eighty a day if she had her way. She once traded a suede fringed jacket she'd been given from the Montreal Women's Shelter for five cigarettes.

When she had a one-room bedsit in Verdun, she fell asleep holding a lit cigarette. Her dyed hair caught fire and melted the top half of her face. The months of painful recovery did not stop her from smoking, a habit that is highly correlated to mental illness. Although a plastic surgeon grafted new skin over her scars, the bluish translucence of her forehead is a shiny giveaway of the damage. She went straight from surgery to the extreme psychosis ward at the Douglas Institute, a place she has been in and out of for decades. Five years after the fire, she lives in a group home. The contents of her charred apartment are long gone, including the only photograph of a baby boy born to her forty years ago, the pregnancy a result of rape.

It took months of coffee dates, but Camilla eventually parsed her life to me in one-line fragments. Her experiences are not uncommon among people whose mental illnesses have robbed them of jobs, relationships, and purpose.

Camilla was four years old when her father ran away from the family, leaving her mother, a barbiturate addict prone to depression, to raise four children alone. Camilla and her three siblings were soon placed in foster care. Her siblings were eventually all adopted. Camilla was not, but she shows not a hint of self-pity or bitterness.

In 1970, when she was twenty-one, Camilla was raped, ended up pregnant, and then carried the baby, Jason, to full term under the glare of small-town condemnation for being an unwed mother. She had no vocabulary to defend herself and zero support from social services. Although she'd been academically gifted in high school, she was soon penniless and alone.

Desperate, she asked her mother if she could come stay with her for the final two weeks of her pregnancy. When her mother refused, Camilla had her first psychotic episode and tried to kill her mother with a breadknife. As a result, her newborn son was taken away from her. The wounded give birth to the wounded.

After losing Jason, Camilla boarded a Greyhound bus for Montreal in an effort to start a new life. She has been on welfare since the day she arrived; crippling anxiety and depression have eclipsed all her efforts to find meaningful work.

Not being chosen for adoption was the beginning of a long string of rejections. Somewhere in the middle of the scroll of sorrows that she unfurled for me, she stood at the altar in a wedding gown purchased at Goodwill for sixteen dollars, waiting for a fiancé who didn't show up. After that, she turned off the tap of her emotions. For a long time she didn't laugh or cry, her numbness as strong as anaesthetic.

Together, Camilla and I decided to search for the baby she'd given up. Huddled over my computer at the library, we called every single person in the province of Ontario with a name close to his. We finally found her son in Thunder Bay, living in semi-sufficiency at a psychiatric facility, a ward of the province of Ontario. His life, like hers, was waylaid by anxiety, and speaks to the genetic heritability of mental illness.

Camilla was stoic about where he'd ended up. She began to make weekly calls to her long-lost son from my cellphone. Those five-minute conversations gave her purpose. She sent cards to him on every occasion, underlining the message with a black felt-tip pen: *I love you Jason.* At the time of today's coffee date, she has seen him just once.

His birth, their separation, their shared illness is a hurt buried so deep that the only outward sign of her feelings is her rocking back and forth and humming when she tells me about him. As soon as she is composed again, we hold hands and eat doughnuts. She loves to hold hands. Her fingers are stained deep rust from nicotine, but her skin is soft. I can't help but wonder if her path would have been different if she had been allowed to keep her son. Camilla's reconnection to Jason has allowed her that singular place to give and receive love.

One Thursday, after our coffee at Tim Hortons, we bought clothes for Camilla's ever-shrinking body. Her weight loss happened so quickly, I was sure she had cancer. She refused to be tested; she told me she was finally happy, so why would she want any more bad news? And why would she voluntarily go anywhere near a hospital—her associations with hospitals have mostly been traumatic. During her first hospital stay, her baby had been taken away. All her other confinements were attached to her mental illness. What she *did* want was *new* jeans and penny loafers. She had the pennies.

At a brightly lit Winners store, she grew anxious and hummed to comfort herself. In the change room, she stripped off her old clothes, found in the charity bin, her deep, hacking smoker's cough alarming the sales clerk waiting with me.

Camilla emerged from the change room to show us her new pink-ish jeans and frilled blouse. She decided to wear them out of the store, and I asked the clerk whether she had a garbage bin for the old ones, which reeked of urine and stale tobacco.

"Of course," she said, and we dumped them. Then the sales clerk snipped off the price tags with a sunbeam smile and took a step backwards to scrutinize the effect. Stepping close again, she pulled Camilla's new jeans a little higher to hide several inches of Depends that rose above the waistband.

"Coral is your best colour," she said.

Empathy shows up when you least expect it.

## 6

# Lego Bricks at the Daycare

BY THE TIME CAROLINE TOLD GILLES SHE WAS PREGNANT, it was too late for a termination. He must have felt blindsided, but he stepped up, marrying Caroline in December 1983. There was no white dress with a train, no bridesmaids, no tiered cake with marzipan icing, no champagne toasts, no something borrowed, something blue, and no thrown bouquet. So much for Caroline's dreams of her perfect wedding day.

Still, Isabel had organized a small dinner to mark the occasion. She had come around to the inevitability of the baby, and thought it best that the child had two legitimate parents. Neither she nor Arthur wanted the darker scenario, where Caroline and the baby lived at home with them. Both were too worn out to raise an eleventh child.

Caroline, now five months pregnant, wore a navy-blue dress with a snowflake pattern on the bodice and sleeves. She curled her blond hair with fat rollers, wore pink drugstore lipstick, and gave Gilles a card, inscribed with her wish for an everlasting marriage. Though he had needed to be convinced to marry her, with his parents likely giving him a big push to do the responsible thing, he looked every bit the willing groom on his wedding day, in a slim-cut grey suit with a navy tie and a red rose in his lapel—a nod to Pierre Trudeau, his father-in-law's friend. There were eight at the dinner, including the bridal couple and Arthur and Isabel. Gilles's parents came to celebrate, but no one else from his side of the family. Only Donald, of Caroline's nine siblings, was there, along with his wife, Pauline. They lived nearby in Dorval. Her sisters, having come home for Isabel's sabotaged birthday party, said they couldn't afford to come again.

To her enormous credit, Caroline embraced the way her face and breasts and hips were overtaken by the pregnancy. She loved shopping for cribs, diaper pails, and receiving blankets. She had a husband, and a baby coming, which meant she had found a way forward. With her mother once more in her corner, her joy bubbled up like sparkling wine, a further testament to her love for Isabel. It was her older brother Donald who had unexpectedly helped bridge the gap, by reminding Isabel that a Beaconsfield girl had had a baby in grade nine at St. Vincent, and the family had survived the scandal.

In February 1984, Caroline and Gilles rented a small house in Île Perrot. Matthew was born in April. By July, they'd set up a red swing set and a plastic slide in the back garden, along with patio chairs beside the flowering dogwood, under the canopy of oak trees. Gilles was handy. He hung curtains, bought spider plants for Caroline's homemade macramé slings, and could just as easily fix the roof as the toaster. The couple swore off all drugs and alcohol in an effort to be good parents.

Gilles got a part-time job as a cashier on a rotating shift at a cafeteria that opened at 6 a.m. and closed at 11 p.m. To make ends meet, Caroline, who had once more dropped out of nursing school, took on three jobs. From 7:30 to 3:30 she worked at a daycare, where she was able to bring the baby. At 3:45 p.m. she brought Matty to his paternal grandmother's house and worked the four-to-midnight shift as a custodian and case room aide at the Lakeshore General. She delivered meals to patients, collected bins of laundry, restocked the nursing station with sterile gloves and gowns. On weekends, she cleaned houses. Caroline pumped and stored milk using a machine she rented, with a motor that sounded like a washing machine. She could churn out four to five bottles at a time. She once went eighteen days without seeing her husband because his shifts and her brief stints at home never aligned.

It was a time of high stress and even higher fatigue, but it was mitigated by the joys of motherhood. She delighted in being able to slather love and affection on Matthew. She kept up the pace for sixteen months, functioning on adrenalin, umpteen cups of coffee, and the intoxicating baby smell of her little boy. She felt infused with a sense of well-being and purpose. Gilles turned out to be a doting father, to his mother-in-law's surprise and joy. Isabel had worried that since he had been forced into marriage, he might not participate, and she was happy to be wrong.

Caroline started back to school in September 1985. She still longed for a career in health care. The best perk was that baby Matthew, now seventeen months, could be on-site in the college daycare. She was able to visit him between classes, scoop him up at a moment's notice for a breastfeeding. At nights Caroline carried Matty everywhere, perhaps to make up for lost time when he was not with her. With the breastfeeding, working nights and weekends, and now carrying a full course load, she was wishbone lean, a weight category she'd not experienced since grade two. Her first-term marks were excellent.

Then, in December, as the semester was ending, Caroline made a disturbing phone call to Rosalind. Caroline told her sister she had mailed a garter belt and sexy red panties to Darren, the singer she had been obsessed with on and off since high school. When Caroline began talking about Darren, her sister's internal alarm bells started ringing. Caroline didn't seem to realize that this kind of Christmas present was inappropriate to send to a male acquaintance; she said she'd even told Gilles about it. Caroline told Rosalind: "Darren and I are on the same wavelength. Even when we don't speak."

As her part of the family gift exchange, it turned out she'd also bought the same garter and panties for Peggy. Rosalind remembers trying to reconcile Caroline's actions. Was her marriage in trouble? Had she actually been in contact with Darren? Caroline didn't seem otherwise troubled. She was slim and fit, and radiated a happy freneticism. Perhaps too frenetic. When Gilles bought a Christmas tree from the Boy Scouts, she didn't sleep for three nights so she could decorate it in the brief hours when she wasn't working.

Gilles did not understand why his wife had sent such a gift to another man. He lost his temper and Caroline claims he pushed her against the kitchen wall. When she phoned Rosalind and then Sharon to tell them he had been physically abusive, she didn't receive much sympathy. While they'd had their doubts about Gilles, he had stepped up to take care of his son and he certainly didn't deserve to be treated with such disrespect by his wife.

Rosalind recalls asking Sharon, "Is this the end? I don't see how Gilles can move past this." But the sisters were also back to wondering what was fact and what was fantasy: had Caroline really sent the lingerie to Darren, or just thought about it and then wrapped it up for Peggy?

But before the marriage could hit the rocks, Caroline found out she was pregnant for the second time and they carried on. Had Gilles been willing to overlook Caroline's lapse in judgment with Darren, or did Caroline get pregnant to make amends?

———

Caroline had been euphoric while pregnant with Matty, at least once her circumstances were out in the open. Her second pregnancy was altogether different; she was dogged by fatigue and self-doubt about making ends meet. Gilles was only working part-time. Matty had become a handful, too, right on schedule. He threw epic tantrums. He wouldn't take a bath, refused all food except processed cheese slices or green jelly beans, and had no interest in potty training. Perfectly normal toddler issues, but Caroline felt manipulated by his wilfulness and had a hard time hiding her exasperation. She fell into crying jags day and night, and had trouble sleeping. She had been a mother who buckled up car seats and winter boots with fastidious care, and fed her child homemade vegetable purée free from chemicals and additives. But now she let all this drop. She was asleep as soon as she returned home from her classes, and had none of the energy that had been a hallmark of the preceding year.

In late April, when she was three months pregnant, she accused the daycare staff at her nursing college of sexual abuse of Matthew. First she sent an accusatory letter to the college's human resources department, and then she called her sisters and mother in tears about the terrible things that had been done to her son. Gilles was alarmed, of course, but all of them wondered whether this could possibly be true, including Caroline's parents. Arthur was even more doubtful than the others, reminding everyone that his daughter had been an aspiring theatre major.

The daycare responded immediately. Caroline was called into a meeting with the supervisor of the daycare and two social workers from the city. She told them her son had bruises, anal sores, and rectal bleeding. She alleged that a daycare worker had stuck plastic Lego bricks in Matthew's rectum. It was sexual assault, she insisted—he had been sodomized by that staff member. But Matthew showed no sign of injury. He was a bubbly little toddler who loved his routine at daycare. So where was this coming from?

The focus shifted to Caroline herself. The supervisor and social workers asked her extensive questions about her personal life, and showed genuine concern for her well-being as a student and young mother. They learned that she was working herself into the ground, and experiencing a tough second pregnancy. When the meeting was over, they basically wrote off her outrageous claims as the product of stress and exhaustion. This was true, but not in the sense they meant. Rosalind says, "Imagine if the social workers had recognized an exhausted, over-worked mother who was experiencing delusional psychosis?"

What is truly remarkable, Rosalind now realizes, is that nobody in the family had begun to correlate Caroline's state of well-being with such outrageous outbursts, and recognize that a pattern existed between the circumstances of her life and her offside behaviour. No one suggested counselling, or thought to send her back to a psychiatrist. Her mother didn't want to go there, and her father was in serious denial—or perhaps so afraid that she was following in his sister's path that he couldn't fathom the consequences. Her sisters were busy young mothers themselves with lives to navigate, and they were geographically at a distance, which made it hard to help out or keep tabs.

All four sisters chalked up Caroline's accusations to extreme fatigue, guilt over leaving her baby in daycare, and anxiety or depression. The big question they never asked was, why did their sister resort to lying in times of great distress?

The sodomization of Caroline's baby in daycare was *not real*; her tremulous feelings and anxious, racing heart about giving her baby to someone else *were real*. The dismissal of the allegations coincided with the end of term. Caroline was upset that the college daycare was exonerated, and angry that in the end neither her husband nor her family had believed her. She had the summer to get over it, though; finances were tight, and she worked as hard as ever. By the time school started up again, she had no choice but to take Matthew back to the college daycare. It was free, and they couldn't afford anything else.

Quite remarkably, Caroline had managed to score high marks in the semester when she made the accusations. After her first year of studies, she was near the top of the class in all six courses, despite sleep deprivation, pregnancy, and delusional thinking. But in her third semester, it was as if she ran out of gas. She lost focus and couldn't retain her lessons. The baby was due in December, and she had hoped to stay in school until she delivered, at least. But soon, in a teary phone call, she told her mother she had dropped out.

Isabel did her best to offer support. Arthur, however, continued to maintain a distance from the dramas in Caroline's life. But Rosalind believes he had to be wondering whether his daughter had some kind of genetic link to his older sister, and was unwilling to bring the comparison into the light of day. He ducked and covered, instead of learning from what had happened to his sister.

# 7

# The Stove

AFTER KYLE WAS BORN IN DECEMBER 1986, CAROLINE, not surprisingly, experienced postpartum depression. She was also overwhelmed by self-doubt and by the growing distance between her and her mother and siblings. Any closeness she'd once felt towards her husband was also gone. Gilles couldn't understand or even tolerate her eccentricities. The more she recognized her incompatibility with him, the more she was awash in discontent, and the more he found her insufferable.

Caroline did not exhibit the most common symptom of postpartum depression—a lack of interest in the new baby. Quite the opposite. She became obsessed with breastfeeding and baby care. But her bursts of energy were coupled with moments of dread and fatigue, and feelings of suffocation. Gilles could not reconcile how she could be full of energy one day and the next he would come home to find her asleep on the living room floor, with the baby wailing in his little bed and Matthew sticking army men into the electrical outlets. Yet for more than a year, Caroline managed to look after both of her sons and hang on to her marriage.

When Kyle was fifteen months old, Caroline called 911 from the phone in her kitchen and claimed that Gilles had physically and sexually abused her children and herself. In great distress, she described how her husband had pushed her up against the wall and hit her repeatedly. Four officers arrived in two patrol cars with lights flashing. Toys, Cheerios, and Lego pieces were littered across the floor. The breakfast dishes were in the sink. Two officers dragged Gilles into the back seat of their cruiser. The other two officers stayed inside to interview Caroline. The police were sympathetic, and Caroline seemed credible.

At the station, Gilles was quick to mention Caroline's unfounded allegations against the daycare, and when that story checked out, he was released. Rosalind recalls Gilles saying at the time, "I knocked up a girl and it ruined my life." He felt trapped by their seesaw marriage, and had no idea how to deal with his increasingly troubled wife.

Shortly after that 911 call, Caroline began to hear voices telling her to do things. She found it nearly impossible to differentiate between real and unreal. The voices were people she knew. Many times the voices were soothing, even congratulatory: they issued friendly reminders, endorsed how wonderful Matty was, and approved of the items she had bought with her hard-earned money, of her mothering. *You look beautiful. You are a good mother. You are the best mother. You are the only mother.* But they could also be degrading. They whispered insults. *You have no friends. Gilles only married you because you were pregnant. Darren thinks you are ugly.*

MRIs have shown that the same areas of the brain light up when a person hears an actual voice and when a person has an auditory hallucination. This explains why so many people who hear such "command" voices insist that the CIA, or some other secret agency, has implanted a bug in their brains. It's a plausible way to comprehend the experience, especially when no one else hears what is so clearly articulated to them. At times the voices made Caroline feel persecuted by Gilles. They also made her feel special: since she was the only one who heard the extraordinary commands, she felt she had been singled out.

We all hear voices in order to process our experiences. We lie in bed on a sleepless night and "hear" a steady stream of chatter that does not stop. We think our way through our problems with silent (insistent and often miserable!) internal conversations that mimic an automatic tennis ball launcher. Those balls keep coming. As exhausting as a sleepless night can be, most people start the next day with a renewed sense of purpose and fortitude. Rational thoughts help erase nocturnal worries.

Despite long stretches of hearing intrusive voices, Caroline had many ordinary days when she was free of the barrage of instructions, reprimands, and harassment. She could still be a loving and affectionate presence, and the photos she captured at the time with her Kodak camera show a young, earnest, growing family, a normal family. She baked layer cakes and let Matty dot the icing with colored Smarties and jelly beans and, for her own birthday, neon candles. Her sons played in the backyard among the maze of plastic pull toys, a teeter-totter, a blow-up pool that doubled as a bathtub, and the red swing set, Kyle usually plunking down among the toys while his brother ran circles around him. At night, she snapped photos of the boys in their matching dinosaur pyjamas tangled together on a plush sofa. None of these images captured the ugly thoughts that were threatening her safety.

At nineteen months, Kyle had just learned to crawl. He had never learned to roll over; he had none of Matty's agility. He was curiously overweight—already thirty-two pounds—which was strange since Matty was slim as a coat hanger. Caroline carried him to his high chair, to the car, upstairs to bed, an increasingly exhausting chore. It helped that Kyle was loving and docile, a contrast to Matty, whose childish exuberance made him contrary and often disobedient. He also liked to pick on and hit his little brother, who was an easy target.

Bad premonitions toyed with Caroline's brain and the voices reminded her that she, like Kyle, was not measuring up. At first she was able to resist when the voices, hypnotic in their potency, compelled her to discipline her elder son for hitting Kyle. Reflecting on her sister's situation now, Rosalind says, "Imagine trying to think or cook or play games with your boisterous children when you hear a steady patter from several people talking into each ear. Those voices were getting louder and angrier and gave instructions. Something had to give."

It did. Caroline began to hear a voice that told her, over and over, *You are a bad mother. Kyle is crying. It's your fault. Matty doesn't listen. It's your fault. You need to do something.* She was never alone, forced to share her space with someone who was making her feel bad about herself. The steady internal assault heightened her sensitivity to criticism, elevated her irritability, eroded her patience.

During that high-stress time in which Caroline was fighting against the instructions in her head, she left Kyle crushed into his high chair for hours and hours beyond normal mealtimes, his chubby baby body tightly nestled against a meal tray full of toys and rattles to keep him occupied. Caroline knew the high chair was a safe place for Kyle, away from his tormenting older brother. Matthew was a busy, normal four-year-old. He had been an only child for nearly three years. Baby Kyle was his competition. When Matthew was whining, misbehaving, not listening, the voice harassed Caroline to intervene. She didn't. She couldn't. She wouldn't. Her thoughts were so abhorrent she dared not share the voice-hearing experience with anyone. Years later, she told me, "I wasn't eating. I wasn't sleeping. I felt lost and alone except for the mean people I was forced to share my life with."

Caroline's voices were recognizable. Her mother. Gilles. Her brother Ian. Darren Fulton.

*Matthew is naughty,* they said. *Matthew deserves it. Matthew should know better than to misbehave. He is not sharing his toys with Kyle. Turn on the stove. Put the stool in front of the stove. Matthew needs to learn a lesson. Matthew needs to be punished. Call Gilles to come home. Don't hurt Matthew. Where the hell is Gilles! Put the stool by the stove, so Matthew can climb up. No! No! No! Go get Gilles. It's your fault. Get in the car and leave. Don't leave your children alone.*

One Saturday evening, after an exhausting day alone with her boys, Caroline snapped. Was it hot? Was she tired? Had Gilles been gone all day? Had she been up the night before, fending off demeaning voices?

The thing she knows is that she placed Matthew's hand on the burning element of the stove. The next few minutes have been expunged from her mind, although she remembers Gilles was not home and she made no calls for help. She remembers thinking her children weren't safe. She remembers thinking she was sick in the head. But the sequence of events is mislaid, buried deep in a place she has yet to revisit.

Peggy has a shadowy memory of seeing burn marks on Matthew's hand. She was in Montreal soon after the stove incident happened. Rosalind thinks it may have been a delusion—that Gilles might have come home to find the element carelessly left on, and may have lashed out at Caroline. Sharon has no recollection. Caroline herself remembers putting cream and Band-Aids on Matthew's hand because he had burned himself, kissing it over and over to make it better. Decades later, Caroline told me that Kyle put Matthew's hand on the burner by accident after Matthew had dragged the stool to the stove. But Kyle couldn't walk, so that scenario was as impossible as some of her other fabrications, likely invented to help her move past the abhorrent event.

At the time, none of the sisters realized that an acceleration of horrendous voices had been dictating Caroline's every moment. She'd been resisting all commands to punish her son, but did she give in for one brief, horrible moment? One fact is incontestable: Caroline was scared half to death by what she had done, or thought she had done, or intended to do.

Nobody will ever know how close Caroline came to permanently harming her child, but after that incident, however it happened, Gilles at last recognized that Caroline was not just a difficult, eccentric, stressed person, she was breaking down. Her non-stop crying verged on hysteria. Gilles took the two boys to his mother's house, believing at last that his wife was incapable of raising them. And Caroline agreed. Soon she signed over custody of her sons to their father, believing she was too sick to look after her children. By giving Gilles custody, she selflessly placed the welfare of her sons ahead of her desire to be a mother.

With great trepidation, Caroline began to make preparations to leave the little house they had been renting so that Gilles and the boys could return. It was too late for marriage counselling; Gilles was resolute—theirs was a rift he did not intend to mend. Once again, no one suggested Caroline needed professional help, even when the task of moving overwhelmed her. The house was littered with Tupperware containers, orange plastic Hot Wheels tracks, clothing, books, parenting magazines, a plug-in frying pan, an assortment of china figurines— all the things that had defined her life as a wife and mother and that she was supposed to put in cardboard boxes. She couldn't get organized. She couldn't stop crying.

When Caroline missed the deadline to move out of their house, a date determined by a court order, Gilles applied for an eviction notice. When it was granted, he called the sheriff. Gilles was beyond offering his ex any help; he had been far too upset by what had happened. Few people know how to cope with the crisis of an "unfit mother," and Gilles was no different.

The sheriff arrived and could have forced her out right then. Instead, he gave her a warning. After he left, Caroline called Peggy in Ottawa and asked for help moving her things to the tiny nearby apartment that Isabel had helped find. Peggy was more than happy to lend a hand. But when she arrived, all was still chaos. The disorganization was another symptom of Caroline's shifting mental state, but Peggy felt lied to, tricked into a situation that threatened to overwhelm both of them.

Peggy remembers that, while wandering about the bedlam, her sister spoke about resuming her relationship with Darren now that she was separated, an idea that Peggy might have laughed at had she not been so irritated. Peggy was in no mind to hear more farce, having driven from Ottawa on her day off to carry some boxes and now confronting the fact that absolutely nothing was ready to go. Furious, she drove back to Ottawa with the mistaken idea that her sister hadn't packed because she was unwilling to face the truth about her disintegrating marriage. In all the years since, Peggy has struggled with the notion of manipulation versus delusion. Both are terrible swords to fall on.

Caroline had been a homemaker who took pride in her matching curtains and had a designated place for each item, emulating her mother, who was also orderly and methodical. Her inability to pack was as upsetting to Caroline as it was to Peggy.

Finally, Caroline's older brother Donald stepped in to pack, drive, and unpack. Isabel showed up too, wrapping glass in newspapers, folding sheets. And she tried to brighten up the new apartment with African violets and new pillows. The family was unsure about visitation rights owed to Caroline, but two things were patently clear. First, Caroline was no longer capable of raising her boys. Second, she viewed the situation as temporary. She believed she had "lent" her children to Gilles while enduring a brief purgatory, and that after she was "fixed" she would get them back.

Everyone agreed that Gilles and his extended family would be the primary caregivers, given that Isabel and Arthur were spending six months of the year in Florida. Luckily, Gilles had three people to count on: his own mother, who had taken care of Matty when he was a baby and Caroline was at work, and a childless aunt and uncle who also stepped in.

It was especially hard for Isabel to see Caroline separated from her children when she had made so many personal sacrifices in order to be a mother. It was unfair, but it was completely necessary. Caroline's self-esteem sank to a new low as weeks of separation from her children became months. After three months of solitude and silence, she went to Home Depot and bought a screwdriver. She intended to stab herself in the jugular. It lay on the kitchen table for a week, and then another week, until she stashed it in a drawer. Maybe she couldn't imagine her boys motherless, or maybe she thought the method was too gruesome. She had already hurt her sons by leaving, a decision that meant she lived with chronic emotional heartache, as painful as if she had drawn blood—an agony softened only by the love of her sons. Every day, she called her sisters and her mother repeatedly until someone picked up, desperate for any kind of validation. Or she collapsed face down on her bed while the sense of her disgrace settled on her like dust.

Caroline told me she'd kept the screwdriver close by even after she had decided not to use it, because when she happened upon it, it was a concrete reminder that she had two boys who needed her, and sisters who hadn't yet given up on her.

The daily phone calls to family members became her therapy, her method of "fixing" herself. Unfortunately, everyone was still clinging to that single assessment by a psychiatrist who had said there was nothing wrong with Caroline. No one pushed for counselling. It just wasn't done.

For an entire year, Caroline was propped up by those calls. Rosalind had encouraged Caroline to return to the hospital as a nursing assistant. Sharon advocated as well. They took turns on the phone. Peggy admits there were days when she didn't have the energy to field her sister's calls; there was no caller ID, but when the phone rang persistently, she knew it was Caroline. Peggy remembers that, remarkably, Caroline could still laugh at herself during this time, the full-bodied, to-the-point-of-tears hilarity that made Peggy laugh too. When they laughed, at least, Peggy didn't feel as though she was being manipulated or deceived.

No matter why Caroline was the way she was, eventually Caroline's four sisters, Lorraine, Sharon, Rosalind, and Peggy, began to realize that they needed to offer sustained support. Caroline needed to be propped up in an ongoing manner, and by all of them. They hoped that, with their encouragement, she would get through the divorce and not be alone in her struggles.

# Aleks

Aleks's mother, Ljuba, is irrepressible. A Yugoslavian refugee, she and her husband arrived in Canada in 1952. At ninety, she still exhibits a Trojan work ethic undiminished by fifty years of cleaning offices, houses, and hospital wards, or by the long-term care of her mentally disabled daughter. She still maintains a fastidious three-bedroom house in Châteauguay, which is also home to two screeching parrots that own the kitchen when they are not in their cages. The constant noise is something Ljuba no longer hears, perhaps because her life has been nothing but one disturbance after another. She told me that her younger son caused her the greatest distress. Aleks has never been the ideal Canadian boy she'd hoped for. She'd wanted both of her sons to be hockey players, but when Aleks was too small to make the team, she enrolled him in figure skating instead, a compromise that felt second-rate, less masculine. She had been told that all Canadians were skaters.

She'd emigrated with the best intentions for her growing family, yet she brought with her two outmoded Eastern European ideas that shaped their lives in Montreal. The first: she did not believe in mental illness. To her, depression was a form of laziness, and hard work the cure-all for every emotional ill and setback. When her husband took sick leave for recurring depression, and subsequently lost his job, she divorced him, refused him access to their three children. She simply did not understand why he couldn't get up in the morning when people were counting on him. She was working three jobs without complaint, and had no patience for her idle husband's bedridden existence in a darkened room.

Second, she believed that homosexuality was not only unnatural but also criminal. When she realized that her fourteen-year-old son would be bringing boys home instead of girls, she gave him an ultimatum: either he changed his ways or he would be dead to her.

Aleks was desperately afraid of losing a second parent, so for five years he forced himself to live as a heterosexual. But in public washrooms and thickly treed parks, he continued to have sex with older men. Those clandestine, impersonal encounters caused him bewilderment and shame, and triggered his drug use. When, high on drugs that loosened his tongue, he told his mother he didn't know if he was a man or a woman, her reaction triggered his first psychotic episode. She thought he was overdosing on crack, locked him out of the house, and called the police.

Aleks, now fifty, is still uncertain of his gender identity. One breakdown led to another, and he has been diagnosed with schizophrenia, depression, and bipolar illness. He suffers severely. He is psychotic half of his waking hours, despite being heavily medicated. He has difficulty sustaining conversations, and for decades has been shuffled from one subsidized group home to the next in an effort to find the best fit— which hasn't happened yet. Because of his medication, he is always thirsty, and has become obese from the steady consumption of two-litre bottles of Sprite to combat that thirst, worsening the already persistent side effect of weight gain. Although he's unaware that his eyes and nose are usually crusty, that his tobacco-stained hands are repellent, he feels deeply stigmatized. Aleks wants two things in life: his mother's acceptance and the love of a single human being. He has neither.

In 2012, Aleks and I began to have coffee every second Tuesday. His blue eyes are the colour of the Israeli flag, he has more thick black hair on his head and arms than an affenpinscher, and it's still somewhat startling for me to see women's clothing peeking above his cotton pants and from beneath his flannel shirt. He often wears black combat boots but hangs a string of Christmas lights around his neck, even in summer.

His long, feminine fingernails are black with dirt, the nail polish chipped. He is almost always in a delusional state when we first meet, but the more Aleks is listened to, the more he can focus, and the more clarity he begins to exhibit. After an hour of intense one-on-one talking, he seems to shed his psychosis, and regains his intellectual capacity. When he feels safe, he can be eloquent, despite his heavily medicated state. For instance, he says of the people around him, "I can see them, but they pretend they can't see me. I am invisible to the world because people make a conscious choice not to go to the place that feels strange and poor and sick, and they close their eyes." The thread that connects Aleks to other human beings is gossamer thin; to him it feels nonexistent. The lack of visible links has all but erased his membership in society, leaving unfulfilled that precious need to be inside the cocoon of another person's care.

Once, he had a panic attack in my car as we were travelling over the Mercier Bridge to visit his mother, brought on by a combination of the inky, swirling water of the St. Lawrence River and his thoughts of how his mother would receive him. We stayed for one hour, and I saw with my own eyes that no bridge would ever be strong enough to connect them back together. Aleks was highly symptomatic, and his mother stiffened to see her son as unreachable as the moon. On the return to Montreal, I broke the speed limit as Aleks lay in the back seat so as not to see the menacing water of the river.

Aleks's despair is palpable, as is his desire to be touched. "I would like to enter someone's heart," he says. "Why can't that happen for me? I broke down a long time ago and now I simply don't exist. It's my fault. I hitchhiked to Vancouver and took street drugs. And now my life doesn't matter anymore." He goes on, "I have a memory of being in Vancouver and the sun was shining on my face. I was twenty-one. I had my whole life ahead of me. Look at me now. I sleep until noon. I eat something. I sleep some more. I have nowhere to go and nothing to do. We're forced to take sleeping pills. Back then, something cracked in my head. I was using bad drugs. From one minute to the next I knew I'd become different. I thought I was one with God. I said some pretty scary things when I thought I was God. People were afraid of me. I thought I could harm myself and be okay. I heard voices telling me what to do, but they weren't nasty like they are today. They told me I was beautiful. Men told me I was beautiful. Because I had no one else who loved me, I had sex with old men. It didn't feel right, but I said yes. My mother would have hated who I was with and what I did. It doesn't matter, because she stopped loving me when I told her I was a girl and not a boy. She stopped loving my father when he couldn't get out of bed in the morning. I heard he died.

"I thought I was being loved by those men, but it was just sex. It messed me up. The voices kept telling me I was a girl, so it would be okay doing what I was doing. I stole makeup and nail polish and mascara, but it messed me up more because of my beard. I'm not sure who I am. I took more drugs to feel better. Marijuana. Hashish. Stronger stuff, too. For a long, long time I wanted a sex change. Susan, do you think you can get those drugs for me?"

No, I tell him. Though I did agree once to get him some multi-vitamins from the drugstore, Centrum for Women, after which I instantly imagined that he might take them all at once, in his haste for results, and regretted buying them. I never did that again.

Aleks's muddled sexual and gender identity, whether he is gay or trans, is tied up with his mother's rejection. "I kind of still want a sex change," he tells me, "but more and more I've stopped caring so much about who I am. I don't think there is anyone out there for me. Back then, in Vancouver, when I was in my twenties, the voices became all negative and I felt bad about what I did with men. I had to check myself into the hospital. It was in there when I became obsessed about the drugs that would magically turn me into a woman. I asked for those kinds of drugs. They said no. When I was let out, I took more street drugs to hide from what I had done. I went back to the hospital. The doctor asked me if I heard voices. I said yes. Susan, do you think if I had a sex change I might find someone to love? Because no one wants me as I am."

Aleks's former intellect is painfully intact in these windows of lucidity. He speaks three languages: English, French, and Serbo-Croatian. "I don't believe in God anymore because He doesn't believe in me," he says. "Except I always change my mind. I fight with God. I ask Him, 'Is this my life? How can this be my life?' If I am going somewhere better, then at least I have hope. I have no purpose in this life."

I tell him that's not true. He is here to show the rest of us tolerance, patience, acceptance. Aleks has as much purpose as any of us. He is the face of diversity—not brown or black or yellow, skin-deep different, but a person with a set of challenges that makes it hard to know him. Somerset Maugham once wrote that tolerance is nothing but indifference. Aleks has been tolerated for far too long.

On one Easter weekend, he told me he wanted to mimic the sacrifice Jesus made for the love of his people. With Aleks, the sacrifice was for the love of his Catholic mother. He was going to hammer himself to the cross on Wellington Street, near the group home where he lives. Luckily, he didn't follow through.

At all times he yearns for love and companionship, and sometimes it occurs to him to behave inappropriately. Once or twice, he confided, he has exposed himself in La Fontaine Park, a vast, heavily treed green space in Montreal's east end. When he is caught for such behaviour, his medication is increased. Afterwards, he slurs more, and extra saliva gathers on his lower lip the way it does with a toddler.

During one of our coffee dates, Aleks pulls a dog-eared four-by-six photo of him in grade six from one of the many pockets inside his red ski jacket and hands it to me. He is perfection, with velvet skin and huge blue eyes, the side part of his hair straight as a knitting needle. I can see the collar of a pink shirt, the colour of a ballet slipper, underneath an argyle-patterned sweater vest.

"Are you sure you want me to have it?"

He nods. He takes a long look at the school picture, as though seeking evidence he is still that same boy. "My mother loved me when I looked like this," he said. When my eyes well up, he tells me he's not able to make tears anymore. I cry for both of us, and promise to take good care of the photo.

After months of meeting for coffee, walks along the canal, and visits to St. Joseph's Oratory on the mountain in Montreal, Aleks confided that he has been in a long-term relationship with Jennifer Love Hewitt, the Hollywood actress, though of course Love Hewitt is married, lives in Las Vegas, and has a young child. He showed me one of his love letters to her. It was the first time I had seen penmanship that clearly indicated psychological problems—densely packed, slanted, illegible letters.

After that, I helped him send Christmas cards and birthday cards to the address on her website. He would take a long time standing in the aisle reading the printed messages to make sure they were the right sentiment. It didn't matter to Aleks that she never responded—he was just happy he had a friend with him to help him mark those occasions and a person to reach out to who embodied his desire to be loved.

One morning, when I called the group home to confirm a coffee date, Aleks said he had spent the night with Jennifer. I said, "Wonderful. Hold on, and tell me everything when I get there."

At our usual table in a neglected coffee shop free of noise and other customers, I leaned in and asked him how the evening had gone. Where had they met?

Aleks seemed surprised, even a little worried for me. "Susie," he said, making direct eye contact, "I met her in the Ghost Garden. It's where I meet all the souls of the people I love."

I had to marvel. Aleks had just given me another gift: access to the hidden realms of mental illness. With that gentle correction, he'd shown me that a place of comfort exists for many who suffer from schizophrenia, an alternative world as real as Dorothy's Oz. So often we see the severely mentally ill as less than fully formed human beings, as ghosts of their "normal" selves. As ghosts, they can appear to be inanimate, unreachable, and frightening, but they, like all of us, tend an interior garden that is lushly alive.

# 8

# Evergreen

SOON AFTER SHE MOVED TO HER LONELY LITTLE APARTMENT, Caroline bought a second-hand navy-blue Oldsmobile Cutlass from an elderly couple who only needed a car to buy groceries. Afterwards, she went to the shops on their behalf, sympathetic to their diminished circumstances and lack of mobility. Her sensitivity to people in need came from her own identification with loss, coupled with a genuine desire to nurture others.

One month later, she drove the car into a telephone pole, crushing the engine like it was aluminum foil. She staggered from the car to the street, where a man stopped to help, then drove her to Lakeshore Hospital. Her car was totalled, and was towed away from the road for scrap. But Caroline's version of events did not match with the police report, which indicated no personal injury. Caroline insisted she had fractured her skull.

Deeply concerned, her parents wondered whether Caroline had been reckless or suicidal. Had she blacked out? Had she been smoking marijuana and lost control?

Caroline filed an insurance claim, and looked in the suburban classifieds for another second-hand car. She needed the car, she said, for her boys. Isabel kept her mouth shut.

Caroline had hired a lawyer to argue for shared custody, but the car accident played in Gilles's favour. In the final arrangement approved by the court, Caroline could visit her boys but there would be no shared custody, a painful reminder of her incompetence. Both boys were still too young to understand the terms of the separation. It helped that Matty was in school, and on occasion she was allowed to pick him up and drive him to Gilles's house. Kyle was always over-joyed to see his mother. To Caroline's credit, she made the best of the diminished parental time she had been allocated.

She was working once again, as a nursing assistant at the hospital, a situation that filled the long, empty days with productivity. Her next setback was a chronic back injury, the result of carrying heavy baskets of laundry. Despite several lapses, she had been able to keep the job throughout her studies, her pregnancies, and afterwards. Caroline filed for and was granted disability status. With that monthly disabil-ity cheque, she stopped working. From that point on, apart from visits to her children, Caroline had no place to be every day other than alone, absorbed by the clutches of her dark thoughts, her best inten-tions scattered like ashes in the wind.

The more discouraged Caroline became, the greater was her back pain, as though her bodily ills were a reflection of mental deteriora-tion. When the body fails, there are means and ways to recover. The loss of the mind seems far harder to grasp. Better to focus on a back-ache than try to catch the wind.

———

Arthur was paying for the divorce. When Caroline spent hours and hours with her lawyer, venting about the injustices that had transpired, the lawyer billed accordingly. When Arthur balked at the invoice, Caroline wrote the lawyer a ten-page letter accusing him of exploitation. The letter was articulate, detailed; she documented each appointment. Nothing in her presentation indicated she had any mental health problems.

The same week she chastised the lawyer, she sent another letter of complaint, this time to the manager of a Provigo grocery store, claiming she had slipped and fallen on his premises and hurt her back. She threatened to sue the store for negligence. She kept photocopies of both letters. Though they were written at the same time, they were radically different. In the legal complaint, both her thoughts and her handwriting were neat and concise. In the letter to the Provigo manager, she scrawled incoherently. She stored the letters of complaint in a briefcase with a coded lock, along with other writing and poetry, and accounts of Ian's abuses.

She also kept a single birthday card in that briefcase, signed simply, "Mum and Dad." Of all the cards she had received from her parents over the span of her life, she kept the one that was devoid of love or sentiment. There was no personal greeting, no expression of affection, and no indication of pride. When Caroline's sisters pored over the contents of that briefcase years later, looking for clues to her breakdown, they viewed the card as proof of Isabel's frayed nerves and exasperation. They understood why Caroline had kept it.


After a barrage of unsettling phone calls, Peggy drove from Ottawa to see her sister. She found Caroline with no food in the apartment. She had dropped a significant amount of weight, and had forsaken all grooming. She didn't smell clean, and gave her sister odd excuses for why she couldn't shower, or wash her clothes, or buy staples such as bread and milk. She said the shower head wasn't working. The grocery store had no detergent. She couldn't afford to put gas in the car. When Peggy looked doubtful, she said she was most upset that Gilles had been limiting her access to her sons. Without those visits, she had no reason to buy groceries or leave her apartment or wash her hair.

Peggy remembers that Caroline's place was so dirty, she didn't want to use the washroom. "I stopped at a gas station on my way home. As soon as I got home, I stripped down and jumped in the shower. Who do you know who does that after coming home from their sister's apartment?" Peggy admits that her sister's long stretches of normalcy made it difficult to rationalize a true incapacity.

In December 1990, Caroline decided to leave her tiny apartment in favour of a rented house in Beaconsfield that had extra bedrooms for her boys. Matthew was now six and Kyle four. The place was a few miles away from where her sons were living, but had more space for their toys, and a back garden suited to boisterous romping and building forts. She now owned a copper-coloured Pontiac Acadian, much pocked by rust, which meant she could ferry her boys to and fro.

She was able to afford the higher rent using her disability income plus her savings from past jobs. When she was able to put her mind to things, she was a workhorse of determination. And since she'd exhibited months of clarity, Isabel sanctioned the move. She wanted her daughter to have more time with the boys because it was evident her mental state improved in the company of her sons.

Her new address was two miles as the crow flies from where she had grown up. It was hard not to think that Caroline was trying to re-create her happy childhood on a similar leafy suburban street.

The brown-and-white house on Evergreen Lane, hemmed in by cedars, was a three-bedroom split-level with expanses of lawn dotted by mature trees. Best of all, it was fully furnished. She placed her beloved china figurines in each room: a bluebird on a tree stump, two fox siblings, assorted dogs and cats. She draped a woollen afghan that Rosalind had knitted and given to her as a wedding present over the back of a sofa. She stocked the boys' room with pyjamas and playdough, Mr. Potato Head, an Etch A Sketch, two water pistols, Meccano, Houdini's magic tricks, science experiment kits, and a dozen connect-the-dot colouring books for Kyle, who was still trailing behind other boys his age intellectually and especially physically. Rosalind says, "That intention to be a mother kept her from falling off the edge into depression or self-loathing."

She also hoped that preparing a new home would show her ex-husband Gilles and her family that she was no longer an unfit mother. If she couldn't regain custody, at least her visits with her sons would take place in a Mister Rogers' neighbourhood under a canopy of trees.

To avoid rattling around in a three-bedroom house by herself, Caroline soon invited a young homeless family—mother, father, and child—to live with her. The mother was only nineteen, her son was three and a half, and the father only a little older than his young bride. She had found them stranded near the Beaconsfield train station with a few ragged suitcases tied together with string, after they had been evicted from a low-rent apartment nearby. Caroline knew the parents of the young mother, an older couple who could hardly make rent either. Being a port in the storm for the young family filled a place in her heart that should have been occupied by her sons, a nursing career, and friends.

When Isabel paid an unexpected visit to Caroline a few days before she and Arthur were to head to Florida for the winter, she found them living in squalor. This was not the fresh start she'd hoped for. Isabel recoiled to see bugs in the sink and unmade beds, and when Caroline told a slew of outrageous "lies," Isabel lost her temper. After that single visit to the house on Evergreen, Isabel withdrew much of her emotional support from Caroline, saying to another daughter, "She's more trouble than she's worth." Peggy believed her mother reacted as strongly as she did because she found it too painful to see her daughter in such a filthy state. Had Caroline always been slovenly, her reaction might have been resignation. It was the abandonment of Caroline's standards that was so deeply offensive to Isabel. She asked Rosalind, "What have I done to deserve such punishment from God? What sin did I commit?" She felt sentenced by her own daughter.

Isabel and Arthur retreated to Florida, far enough away that they were not in the eye of every storm. For Caroline, the separation was unbearable, especially because her latest encounter with her mother had been so fraught with judgment. For Isabel, it was a welcome and necessary relief.

From mid-January until March 1991, Caroline's television set was turned on twenty-four hours a day. Saddam Hussein, Iraq's dictator, had ordered his army across the border into neighbouring Kuwait. All the eyes of the world were on the White House, waiting for a response. CNN covered the ensuing conflict, the Gulf War, live, from a Baghdad hotel. Caroline covered it from her living room.

New satellite technology allowed, for the first time, a bird's-eye view of missiles hitting their targets. From the outset, she watched the news without sleeping, engrossed in the personal messages being sent to her telepathically from the broadcasters. She became one with the mission, unable to eat, beset by irrational euphoria and frightening ideation. She kept the drapes drawn day and night because the FBI and CIA were watching her. Sounds of the wind whistling in the trees were whispers from international spies. Caroline felt the weight of all that she was responsible for. "I felt fear for the soldiers," she told me later.

The young couple who shared the house were drawn into Caroline's misbeliefs.

After two phone conversations during this time, Gilles cut off all communication with his ex-wife, and was too afraid to allow his sons to visit.

Over the phone, Caroline told her sisters that the part of the Middle East where the conflict was taking place was the geographical shape of a woman's ovaries, which was symbolic because of Saddam Hussein's misogynistic attitudes towards women. She told them, "I'll be able to solve the war." She paced in front of the television around the clock, mishmashing the real with the imaginary, convinced she was an important public figure. The television announcers jubilantly reported when smart bombs hit their targets. Death was not only sanctioned, it was being celebrated. Caroline found it terrifying to have been given the responsibility of ending the war. She was a peacenik. After she recovered from the shock of being personally selected by the government, she experienced the dawning wonderment that she was supernatural. Her sisters listened, distressed by their sister's derangement. They phoned each other to compare notes. Was it mania? Was it psychosis? Was it schizophrenia?

Caroline made more calls to various family members. Her speech, at times focused and persuasive, was otherwise choked with suspicion and fear. The unrelenting CNN coverage fed her obsessive anxiety. The fixation on the war bewildered her sisters, who knew her as gentle and accepting—certainly never political. Everywhere Caroline went, she told them, people seemed to be spying on her, including the once-friendly postman. She spoke of inky, black-coated spirits from hell that hid behind the cedar trees in the yard. She thought barking dogs were addressing her. She said she spoke dog, understood their complicity. Sharon tried to tell her there were no drooling, seething dogs on her tail. But reason can never penetrate deep enough to erase a psychotic certainty.

The calls continued. Caroline told her sisters small children on hot-pink bicycles were circling the neighbourhood, laughing at her with cruelty. The little girl who had clothespinned the king of spades to the front wheel of her bike sent out a rippling click of gunshots. She saw shadowy figures outside while standing at the living room window. She had panicky, unreasonable fears, worrying that her home was a poisonous environment and that the trees in her backyard were about to crush the house. Caroline revealed that she had phoned the White House and Parliament Hill claiming to know where Saddam Hussein was hiding. Nobody knows how the White House and Parliament Hill responded to more than thirty calls, which showed up later on Caroline's phone bill. It's curious that her outbursts didn't alert the police. She claimed the people gliding past the house were government officials responding to her phone calls, investigating the dangers outside.

In other moments, in a voice devoid of anxiety, she told them she had become the rescuer of the world. Rosalind recalls thinking that Caroline expected to be praised for these supernatural abilities. She spoke with utter sincerity; she believed her stories without a doubt. She had special powers, and she needed to share that news with her sisters so they wouldn't worry that the world was coming to an end.

Even as they worried, they also recognized that Caroline's grasp of the war was sharp, detailed, and full of intense colour and dimension.

She knew the names of the warplanes, of the generals in charge, of the towns being targeted. She knew the makes of the local cars in Beaconsfield, where they were parked, and which streets had spots where a car could sit and be totally concealed. If the delusion had not been so absurd, Peggy says, Caroline's vast knowledge might have carried weight. She had extracted dozens of details from the steady stream of reporting and repackaged them as an alternate truth. She believed she was a major player on the CSIS and CIA teams.

By inventing a relationship with these spy agencies, and Baghdad war plots, Caroline could rewrite the script of her life. Half the time she was scared out of her wits; the other half she believed she was impervious to harm. But she couldn't separate her feelings of invincibility from her fears of being persecuted by what was skulking outside her front door. The end result was a state of heightened, anxious anticipation shrouded in suspicion. When Rosalind called their father in Florida to tell him what was going on, Arthur said it sounded as though Caroline was having a psychotic breakdown.

All that had happened to Caroline before this episode were like chest pains that precede a life-threatening heart attack. Caroline was now shakily poised at the top of a huge and very steep slide.

Fern, the long-time family friend who lived in nearby Sainte-Anne-de-Bellevue, called Rosalind and her husband, Connor, to talk about what to do. "There is a quality of authority in her voice," Fern warned, "as though she really knows what she is talking about." Having never forgotten the time she threatened him with a knife, he was worried she would act on her thoughts. The family members who were available dropped everything—jobs, babies, obligations. Peggy, almost eight months pregnant, took the bus from Ottawa and got off in

Pointe-Claire. Sharon met the bus. They made a plan to arrive together at the house in a show of family solidarity.

Rosalind, Peggy, Sharon, and Donald met in the street, then rang the bell. When Caroline, wild-eyed and frazzled, answered the door, she was elated to see them. She hugged them all tightly, relieved to see friendly faces instead of the ones that had been plaguing her mind. Rosalind remembers that her sister's fingers sparkled with silver rings bought from a shop in Pointe-Claire village. "It's curious," she says, "the small details you remember after all these years." She had dropped so much weight that her once-fitted corduroy jacket overwhelmed her frame. Her thick blond mane was lank, clinging to her back like matted fur. She looked sleep-deprived and malnourished, overcome by agitation.

Caroline invited them into the kitchen, a room littered with garbage, dishes, clothes, mouldering food on the counter, cockroaches in the sink, and weeks of junk mail. She introduced them to the family she had rescued, who sat wide-eyed at the table while Caroline's sisters opened drawers and cupboards, the fridge, the stove. Very quietly, Sharon asked the young family to pack up and leave. She has often wondered since how her sister's behaviour might have affected them, especially their young son.

It didn't seem reasonable that Caroline could be oblivious to the mess. It was impossible to gauge when their sister had last had a shower, or brushed her teeth, let alone eaten something; her cheekbones almost protruded from her skin. There was nothing in the fridge except a package of decaying processed meat. A half-empty box of Cap'n Crunch cereal was on the counter. Light bulbs were missing from the fixtures. The garbage hadn't been taken away for months.

Caroline crumbled soon after her family arrived. She could see the worry and dismay on their faces, but mostly she saw judgment.

Donald began to pick up garbage, happy to lift and cart as his sisters did the emotional work. Rosalind tried to get Caroline cleaned up. Trapped body odour emanated from underneath her clothes, and her hair reeked of neglect.

Bug-eyed, Caroline would not enter the bathroom. She told them that spies were watching the house because she had first-hand, critical knowledge of the operation. "I can't. I can't," Caroline wailed, her capacity for logic non-existent. She was terrified to shower, afraid of being closed off in a curtained space, subject to a surprise attack. Worse, she was certain that the water contained toxins that would eat her scalp—she would not survive a shower.

Rosalind doubled down with kindness, but Caroline was distressed that her sister was oblivious to the poison spewing from the shower head. She panicked, afraid her sisters were in cahoots with the terrorists outside. Rosalind put her arm tightly around Caroline's back and steered her to the bathroom, turned on the water with one hand while gripping her sister with the other. She washed the crying Caroline as fast as she could, mindless of the shower curtain or the spray of water soaking the floor, trying to suppress her own mounting panic.


While Rosalind helped her get dressed, the other siblings gathered in Caroline's living room to formulate a plan. It was past the time for whispering, or couching their words to protect her feelings, or trying to untangle her ideas. Nothing made sense. She needed to be hospitalized—which they knew she would view as a betrayal.

When Caroline, dressed in rumpled but clean clothes, entered the living room, Peggy recalls that the front door of the house slammed shut for no apparent reason. Caroline was visibly startled, and said it was a sign from God. Sharon put her arms around her sister to stop her from shaking, and led her to the sofa. Caroline said to everyone, "Darren Fulton needs to be removed from this world." The siblings were dumbstruck. Since grade ten, Caroline had been a Darren devotee.

Now she said that Darren, the blue-eyed singing sensation, was evil come to life. Though he lived in a different province, she could hear sounds coming from inside his body. She had been given a new mission. She would need to travel to Toronto to confront him. He abducted small children, she said, cut up their bodies, and masturbated over their remains. Telepathic voices had given her the information. He needed to be stopped. She looked around the room for a paper and pencil. Somebody, maybe Sharon, handed her the writing materials and, with her eyes closed, she scribbled an image, letting the pencil zig-zag across the page. "See!" she said. The others saw gibberish. Caroline saw the evidence she needed to eliminate a child predator.

Peggy asked if she and Darren had been in touch on the phone, still trying to find reasons for the madness of the moment. Caroline nodded. "I can read his mind," she said. It's unclear when or if she spoke to Darren during those weeks in March 1991, or if she had dialed his old number hundreds of times with no response. Why had he resurfaced in her mind? What provoked the negative voices that condemned the man she had had a crush on since high school?

It occurred to Peggy that in previous periods of great distress Darren had entered her sister's mind as a saviour who could redeem the moment. It was an odd reversal that in the worst crisis of her sister's life so far, he had become wicked in her mind. She had turned on Fern once in the same way. It was sickening to consider who might be next.

The siblings tried to understand the tangle of her delusional accusations. Was this all because Gilles had rejected her? Or did she believe her children were defenceless against similar abuses? Had Caroline broken into a million tiny fragments because she was lacking Isabel's support? Why was this happening? They had dozens of questions and, sadly, no answers.

In the same way that Ian's bullying behaviour ended after Rosalind confronted him over the blue box, the plot to eliminate Darren ended Caroline's long obsession with her high school heartthrob. Perhaps she still thought about him, but the love affair was over.

I did contact Darren about Caroline. He prefers to keep the details of what happened private, but he says it was a terrible invasion of privacy to be stalked by someone he knew personally. It was a long time before he understood that she too was a victim—of mental illness.

As a victim, she had to mount her own solitary defence. In her history was a mix of real and imagined assaults: the episode at the daycare in which she felt she was the only one defending her son; Gilles's immediate release at the police station after her hysterical phone call citing abuse; no one believing her about the rape in Barbados; Ian's contempt; her father's alleged abuse; her miscarriage. Her intense sensitivity crowded out rational ways of coping with the damage. An accumulation of singular insults had gathered into a fast-moving, unstoppable, giant ball, and Caroline felt responsible for all that was about to crush her. She was the one who had placed her son in daycare and, worse, sent him back again; she had had too many drinks in Barbados; her pregnancy forced Gilles into a marriage; she deserved Ian's belittling, harassment, and name-calling because she had been too fat as a child. That sense of responsibility for unacceptable outcomes led to intense shame. Shame led her to fear she was unworthy of anyone's love. Fear led to a desperate need for self-protection. Self-protection led to thoughts of violence. Darren needed to be eliminated—it was a matter of self-defence.

Rosalind, Sharon, Peggy, and Donald undertook an intervention of sorts. Sharon, with her nursing background, said, "We don't understand your telepathic abilities, but we are worried about your health. We want nothing but your wellness and happiness. We think you should go to the hospital for help."

"I'm not sick. You're afraid of my capabilities," Caroline replied, in a voice laced with anger and suspicion.

"We're here to help you, Caroline," Sharon responded. "This isn't working for you. You're not eating or sleeping. You can come back home to Evergreen when you feel more like yourself."

Rosalind says some kind of steely resolve kicked in at this point, and all she could think of was getting Caroline into the car and to the hospital. Their sister was ill beyond anything they had witnessed before, and they would carry her out of the house if it came to that. Every incident from the past seemed pale in comparison. The siblings did their best to speak kindly; they offered love and compassion, not condemnation, united in their genuine concern for Caroline's well-being. But they had to get her into the car.

Sharon at last stumbled on the magic words: "Your boys need you to be well."

Caroline's anger dissolved into grief, and the muscles of her face softened in surrender. She was able to accept that she needed help for her children's sake, and when she did, she embraced her family's empathy as though it were the cocoon of a baby's receiving blanket. Unsteadily, as she was led out to the car, she cried out, "I've lost my mind."

The siblings made a hasty beeline, crashing red lights to get to the hospital emergency department. Caroline was admitted and interviewed alone by a psychiatrist. None of the details of this first crisis conversation, or of any others with the medical staff, were shared with the family; all those professionals were trained to respect patient confidentiality. Her siblings felt frustrated at being so roundly excluded when Caroline was having difficulty managing the simplest aspects of her life. Worse, she had spoken of killing Darren, although in truth not one of them believed she meant it, and none of them shared those threats with the hospital staff. In hindsight, Rosalind says, telling the psychiatrist about Caroline's violent ideas might have led to the hospital sharing more information with them. But it would also have meant tighter screws for Caroline, and none of them wanted her to be seen as a violent person. She wasn't. If anything, she was a victim. But they never got the chance to weigh in on the situation.

Within hours, Caroline decided she had been tricked, betrayed by her family. They had brought her to 4-East, the dreaded psychiatric floor at Lakeshore General. She choked out with unnerving intensity, "I won't stay. None of you understand. It's a prison." The sisters tried to reason with Caroline. She was lost to reason.

At that point they were navigating in the dark, unaware of the systems in place that protect the patient yet exclude the family. Rosalind says that if she were granted one wish she could go back in time and see fulfilled, it would be for more transparency, more sharing, more hope at the time of a first episode, when everyone is distressed and looking for a solution to a crisis. Peggy says that arriving in Emergency with a psychotic sibling and then being sent home as if Caroline was a stranger was like walking away from a burning car with the flames still licking the sky.

Then there was the matter of telling their parents the gravity of Caroline's situation. Arthur and Isabel cut short their winter stay in Florida to assist their daughter. When Arthur heard Caroline would be an involuntary long-stay patient on a locked ward, separated from the people she needed most, he cried. The medical system had not rescued his sister from her trauma-prone life, and now his daughter was in that system. Isabel was petrified.

As one month seeped into the next, Caroline remained in the hospital. The family remembers it as a time of frantic speculation about how best to help her surface from her breakdown. Oddly enough, they realize now, they thought less about what had led her to crack than about what could be done to fix the fissure.

Until that fateful day on Evergreen, Caroline's moments of inexplicable behaviour were short-lived, and were always tinged with the irrepressible humour that helped soften the landings. Caroline would refute her actions—"I didn't do that!"—and then she'd laugh. Her sense of humour certainly kept Rosalind, Sharon, and Peggy in the game for the long haul, because if you're not laughing, you're crying.

Arthur visited the ward without Isabel. She did not want to see her daughter in such circumstances, and she could not understand how her visits might help. For Caroline, Isabel's very noticeable absence created more shame and self-recrimination. But Isabel just couldn't force herself to go. When her children were growing up, Isabel understood that mishap was close by. Volatility was a rite of passage. But once they became adults, she expected her brood to take the reins and be responsible, resourceful, and, above all, independent. Instead, Caroline was unreliable, hostile, suspicious, told outrageous and hurtful lies, neglected her personal hygiene and her housekeeping. Each of these breaches was like a voodoo doll pin for Isabel. She had little tolerance for her daughter's inexplicable antics, yet felt the prickly pain of disgrace after each incident, as though she were somehow to blame.

Moving from one life stage to the next, from childhood to the teen years and then to an independent adulthood, is difficult, at times even traumatic, for everyone. Perhaps if Arthur and Isabel had been at Caroline's side anticipating every pitfall, she might have gone from one stage to the next without breaking down, but they had nine other children and their own lives to deal with. Also, Isabel saw Caroline's early manifestations of distress as incomprehensible, embarrassing, attention-seeking behaviour. She thought it would pass; she needed it to pass because she did not accept that a daughter of hers wasn't "normal." For their part, Caroline's siblings had never heard the term "early intervention." They had no idea that mental illness, like serious physical illness, must be tackled early. If knowledge is power, back then they had none.

According to Dr. David Bloom, chief of psychotic disorders at the Douglas Institute in Montreal, by the time psychosis presents, the illness is firmly entrenched. He believes psychosis is a misunderstood phenomenon, a symptom of loss of contact with reality. Still, he says, "with treatment, like other, better-tolerated illnesses, things improve." Life may never look as it once did, but he insists that a meaningful life is not erased.

Caroline's reality wasn't shared or understood by anyone else. When she spoke about her skewed experiences, she was shunned—which isolated her further. Then, when psychosis began to take root in Caroline's mind, she turned the key and opened the gate to a much harder, much less comprehensible, far lonelier landscape.

Rosalind now believes that Caroline had been "one of the pack," like all the rest of them, until age sixteen and that distressing final year of high school. No one then realized how deeply unworthy she felt, and how alienated, even when they discovered the accusations she'd confided to the pages in that blue box. The contents of those accusations had had the effect of shaming them all, rather than pinpointing a sibling who was being crushed under the weight of inferiority.

Only Arthur had an inkling of what might be in store for his daughter, but he couldn't look that thought in the eye. Would early acknowledgement of Marilyn's emotional upheaval have created a different bend in the road for her? Psychosis for Marilyn and Caroline, aunt and niece, was the product of a combination of genetics, stress, loneliness, feelings of failure, and a hobbled ability to construct a bridge to contentment—a lasting peace of mind untethered to external conditions or pleasure.

After Caroline had been admitted, Arthur continued to pay her rent on Evergreen. He was unsure when his daughter would be released, or what steps needed to be taken, but thought that keeping the house was a good enticement for Caroline to recover, given that she had put her heart into making it a home for her sons. Fern offered to walk over to the house and relocate her copper Acadian to Gilles's driveway, worried it would be vandalized.

Fern parked the car at the bottom of the driveway. For Matthew and Kyle, now eight and five, it was a daily reminder that their mother was in the hospital. They loved to play inside the car, taking turns being in the driver's seat, fascinated that a wasp had entered the trunk and begun to build a nest. Kyle, hands firmly on the steering wheel, soon splashed with spit from his made-up engine sounds, always drove to the hospital because his mum was sick. The effects of Caroline's condition had begun to ripple outward, with potential emotional consequences for her two boys. More yearning. More unmet hunger at the child level. Why isn't Mummy coming to see us?

• • •

# Andrea

The day I first met Andrea, at the Douglas in 2010, I was carrying a cardboard tray with four coffees and lots of packages of sugar. One was for Camilla, and the others were for anyone else who wanted a coffee. Andrea beetled over and said she would take one. Then she asked if she could have all three, but a nurse intervened and said one was enough. Camilla, who had been waiting for me on a stool nailed into the floor of the common room, came over and said to Andrea, "Susan is my friend."

"Well, some people have more than one friend," Andrea said, not unkindly.

"Not me," said Camilla.

"I'll be back," said Andrea, imitating Arnold Schwarzenegger, which made me laugh. Later, she gave me her phone number, and pointed to the patient telephone in a nearby alcove. She had written down at least twenty-five random digits on the scrap of paper she handed me, and I laughed again. As if I didn't know the hospital number by heart. When I next saw Andrea, it was in the underground tunnel that connects a dozen buildings on the hospital grounds. "Can I be your friend?" she asked.

———

Andrea, her two sisters, and her two brothers were educated at single-sex private schools in Westmount in the 1970s. She had once been among the sea of girls who walked to school in crested, box-pleated tunics hiked up with a sash, flashing bloomers, doing their utmost to dodge the headmistress's eye. A uniform signalled conformity at a time when Andrea's life was anything but conventional.

Her father was a wealthy banker who maintained an apartment in the Ritz-Carlton hotel to entertain clients, as well as the family home in Westmount. Montreal was still very much under the control of the anglophone establishment, and a financial hub for all of Canada; he was a player. Andrea's mother, a beautiful, willowy blonde, had been a heavy drinker before she married her husband. Her drinking became a problem after their fifth child went off to elementary school. (Andrea was the middle child.) After that, she was not able to rise in the morning and cook breakfast, or see her children off to school.

Their classmates began to notice signs of neglect when Andrea was in grade eight. She and her sisters came to school in fallen hems and torn stockings, greasy collars and unwashed hair. They smelled bad. Their torn blazers were either too big or too small. At home, there was swearing and name-calling, most of which could be heard far down the street. A friend of Andrea's younger sister recalls, "My parents remember hearing the screams of chaos when they walked the dog past their house. Now that we all look back, they were clearly in distress."

Andrea retaliated against the burgeoning scorn of her peers by living a fast teenage life, drinking and hanging out with older boys. There were times in grade ten when she stayed out all night, which her mother didn't notice but her classmates did, since she fell asleep at her desk. Andrea had a Catherine Deneuve type of beauty: perfect features, thick blond hair, a physique lithe from childhood ballet lessons. She also had a keen intellect, and was capable in all subjects, especially English literature.

One Christmas her mother put a small leather-bound diary in her stocking. She began to chronicle her life then, and didn't stop for forty years. She kept the diaries in two yellow crocodile suitcases, handmade in the 1940s, a gift from her grandmother, along with photographs of her privileged Westmount childhood. Also in the cases were seventy-five cassette tapes, music from the 1960s and '70s that reminded her of the days when all was well. Janis Joplin. Eric Clapton. The Doobie Brothers. And her favourite: the Rolling Stones. The cassettes still worked, but she had no "house" in which to play them. The same could be said for Andrea's mind. One black-and-white photo, secured in an album by four gold photo corners, showed Andrea and her two sisters wearing white mink fur muffs and matching fur hats, while a December snow falls upon their shoulders. The smiling faces hint at nothing sinister.

Andrea channelled her feelings into thousands of diary pages of poetry and lyrics that condemned every wrong that had befallen her, her handwriting varying according to her moods. "Andrea. DON'T DRINK," was darkly inked in her journals dozens of times, an admonishment from her mother not to fall prey to her own addiction. "I hate . . ." Fill in the blank. A sibling. A psychiatrist. A landlord. A drug dealer. "I love . . ." Fill in the blank. A social worker. A psychiatrist. A sibling. A drug dealer. Jasper Hollingsworth, a man who was, and is, and always will be the love of her life—a man lost to the streets but alive and well in Andrea's mind.

Andrea dragged those two suitcases to every place where she had a bed. The contents were irreplaceable, concrete evidence that she had intention, that her life had purpose. Without her diaries, Andrea was like all the other women who broke down from mental illness, who were forced to live on government handouts in tiny rooms, with nothing to show for the struggles they'd endured. Invisible but for the cost to taxpayers. At one point when she was hating her landlord and was on the move, the suitcases came to my house.

She and all four of her siblings, born into privilege but neglected all the same, have suffered with forms of mental illness ranging from schizophrenia to anxiety, depression, and alcoholism, and the resulting homelessness. A stressful upbringing of negligence and addiction robbed each child of their potential. It's hard to pinpoint who has suffered the most. One sister had a terrible fall and is confined to a wheelchair. Another sister lives on the streets, sleeping in shelters when the temperature dips below freezing. One brother has lived most of his life in a psychiatric facility. The siblings are not friends, for there is no solace in the shared experience of neglect. Seeing how far the others have fallen only presses salt into wounds so deep they are an incurable source of psychic pain.

Andrea had had more than one medical diagnosis: alcoholism, drug addiction, mania, anxiety, paranoia, schizophrenia. She was delusional and heard voices. But she had never had a single day of depression. She was kind. She laughed heartily, especially when she imitated her mother: "Flee thee from my castle. Don't any of you drink! It will ruin your life."

Children emulate their parents, and when Andrea did heroin the first time, she shot up with her younger brother at home. For decades, he and Andrea crossed paths in the underground tunnels of the Douglas Hospital, avoiding eye contact. They didn't look like siblings, their faces and figures ravaged by too many years of abusing their bodies. If ever there was a story of addiction colliding with a genetic propensity for psychosis and a lawless home environment, Andrea's family has written the textbook.

Andrea told me, "We all drank at home—the seven of us, five kids, my mother, my father. I think Ricky was ten when he started. He started drinking the earliest. It was horrific for the fights. It got ugly until one night Dad brought home some cocaine. That was a great night. We all loved each other." It seemed unfeasible to me that a parent could be that irresponsible, and I thought perhaps her memory was a delusion. But when I eventually met all of Andrea's siblings, and saw their dysfunction mirrored in mental illness and addiction, I decided anything was possible.

Andrea did not like to be touched. She resisted physical contact, a reaction to unwanted predatory touching that infused her with suspicion and negativity when her personal space was invaded. She lived, at times, in La Fontaine Park, the vast open-air garden of ponds and mature trees in the Plateau area of Montreal, and a haven for the homeless. She shivered when she told me how scared she was because of the number of times men approached her. To try to hide the fact that she was a woman, she slept under newspapers made soggy by the dew.

Place Émilie-Gamelin had long been a haunt too, a large green space at the corner of Berri and Sainte-Catherine streets notorious for homeless people, protesters, and drug dealers until it got a facelift in 2015 to mark the city's 350th anniversary. (The itinerant population stayed away for a while after the beautification, but they've now moved back.)

She once said, "You spend so much money on taking me out for coffee. Buy a jar of instant and we can share a cup in my apartment." I agreed. She had traded away the kettle I gave her, so we used warm tap water. At that time, she was living in a rooming house on the south shore, across the Jacques Cartier Bridge, off-island in Longueuil. For my visit she had made her bed and tidied her books, placed three ancient, threadbare teddy bears against a dingy pillow that had been coughed into who knows how many times. She bought no-name cigarettes in bulk from a guy who lived on a reserve. She offered me a cigarette every single time we met, something we eventually laughed about. I tried not to mind the streaks of mud on the floor, or the sink caked with bloody spit and toothpaste and hair, the cigarette butts ground out into candy wrappers, all of it unseen by her.

Six hours after I left her, I was called to Emergency. Andrea had drunk cup after cup of instant coffee until the whole jar, 170 grams, was in her bloodstream, a substitute for illicit drugs that had produced a high. She could have had a seizure, or worse. I blamed myself. After that, I brought yogurt and bananas, decaffeinated herbal teabags, raw almonds. To her credit, she never asked me to bring her coffee again.

At one time, Andrea must have been a real beauty. And even *in extremis*, she always brushed her teeth. That her full set of straight teeth is intact after a lifetime of mental illness and a hardscrabble existence on the streets as an addict is a minor miracle. I have seen her ask for free toothpaste at a drugstore. Something about the combination of her ravaged physicality, direct eye contact, and a genuine thank-you encouraged the staff to say yes. She had a beautiful smile.

Andrea had been in and out of psychiatric facilities for thirty or forty years. She had lived in more group homes than anyone I have ever met, from LaSalle to Verdun to Saint-Henri to Ville-Émard to Longueuil. Her stint at a housing resource in Longueuil was considered "the last possible placement," according to one of her psychiatrists, after she had burned every relationship with hospital-sanctioned group homes, but it didn't last all that long. That particular apartment is a rooming house with a sort of simmering illicit undertone, and for a time the proprietor was able to tolerate Andrea's midnight delusions, the most common of which was an assertion that Mick Jagger had come through the window and raped her. A more likely scenario was that a male resident had gone into the shared bathroom at the end of the hall in his underpants, or naked, triggering Andrea's sense of viola-tion. She admitted to having exchanged sex for money to pay for cocaine as young as age eighteen. This helps to explain why sexual predators were often at the centre of Andrea's delusions. She also told me that her father was one of her earliest violators.

She would call me in the middle of the night about Mick Jagger. I would say, "Oh God, Andrea, are you okay? Shall we call the police? What a terrible experience you have endured. How can I help you? Should we stop listening to his music?"

Being heard was usually all it took to bring her back to safety.

My first impression of Andrea did not change in all the years we were friends, especially her sense of fun. Despite her mother's inatten-tion, Andrea had flawless manners. She said "please" and "thank you" like a debutante. The roots of her privilege did not recede despite a lifelong battle with substance abuse and paranoid schizophrenia that propagated like Queen Anne's lace.

It was Andrea who explained to me how and where and when to get resources such as free food, metro tickets, and clothing from the various charitable organizations dotting the city, but she told me that I wasn't to tell anyone else. We often went together so I could drive her home. She was resourceful, resilient, funny, and loyal. And she was genuinely loved by the staff of those benevolent non-profits. She had worked the system for so long, she owned it. She had schizophrenia but was a visible member of several communities, at times notorious, but more often greeted with the same generosity she extended.

Remarkably, she didn't wish for another life. It was this spirit of acceptance that, in a way, gave her the keys to the kingdom. She had a severe mental illness yet managed to be unstoppable. It's so rare.

She called me every single day for six years. I would sometimes arrive home to twenty messages. Some days I wouldn't answer—then realized that the sooner we spoke, the sooner the calls would stop. It sounds unkind, but my family could do perfect impressions of Andrea's sluggish, post-antipsychotic-medication-injection phone messages, which she often left at two a.m., when all she needed was a listening ear. And a confirmation that Jasper, a man from her past who helped her live in the present, had loved her.

Her psychosis made her the enemy of most landlords. There were endless crises and evictions. Police officers in several boroughs knew her by name, she'd had so many confrontations with them, yet I imagine they found it hard not to smile when she was coherent enough to explain her reasons for breaking the law. For instance: "Réjean drank lighter fluid to get stoned, and I stole a six-pack of Pepsi to make him throw up. It wasn't for me. I don't drink Pepsi. His throat was on fire!"

"I should have had my own handcuffs," she once told me.

Andrea had twice-weekly injections of clonazepam at the hospital, a long-acting benzodiazepine used to treat panic attacks. She took antipsychotics and sleeping pills, and Kemadrin to help with the Parkinson's-like tremors. Some doctors view an excess of dopamine as the leading culprit in schizophrenia. The major antipsychotics block dopamine, and yet if the brain is deficient in dopamine, it sparks a neurological condition that mimics Parkinson's. It's a complicated balance to preserve dopamine in some areas and limit it in others.

Andrea faithfully took public transport to the hospital for her medications, and always knew the date and time of her injections. She was motivated to do so because she had private money that was doled out monthly by the hospital's patient accounts department, in pre-determined amounts. If not for the cash outlay, I wonder if she would have been as reliable about her injections.

She was a regular at Alcoholics Anonymous (AA) and Narcotics Anonymous (NA), mostly for the free coffee, she said. I went to an

AA meeting with her on Dorchester Street. She introduced me as Samantha, her long-lost daughter, and told everyone I was a recovering heroin addict. "Samantha" was also her alter ego, and at times she wished to be called by that name instead of Andrea so she could shed some of the horrors of the past. Drug busts. Being cuffed and dragged into police cars. Her mother's death from liver failure. Not knowing when her father died.

Andrea was a legend for her effect on legions of Montrealers, especially her caregivers—the doctors and nurses who never gave up on her. She was as notable for her screaming rants at police officers as she was for finding size-seven red cowboy boots to offer a social worker in thanks. She took, but she also gave. When my hair fell out—I underwent a stem cell transplant for a rare disease in 2016—she found the softest baby brush that would protect my head as my hair grew back. When I lost weight from chemo, she gave me second-hand cookbooks, with explicit written instructions to bake the cookies and the cakes.

A mainstay of hope for Andrea was her relationship with Jasper Hollingsworth, a street person, rooming house person, group home person—a man she hadn't seen in over ten years but who had once been her romantic partner.

They lived together, a situation that ended when spiralling addiction and psychosis meant doctors had to intervene, signing court orders to have her rehospitalized. Yet Jasper remained an ongoing part of her daily life, as useful to her as her arms and legs for what he represented. They met at a Narcotics Anonymous meeting, and Andrea always referred to him as the love of her life. "Jasper loves me. I need to get out of this shithole so I can find Jasper," she would say. He was an aspect of her past that kept her believing in a future. She had photos of him locked inside one of the yellow suitcases, a skinny bearded man who could as easily have been ninety as forty-five, due to the toll his own contest with mental illness and addiction had taken.

In July 2016, Andrea moved to a new housing situation near Cabot Square in Montreal, ten minutes from where she grew up. Her sister, remarkably, roams the same park. The two could have passed as twins: long, unruly blond hair streaked with white and the same sure-footed gait. The perils of procuring street drugs, trading small appliances and metro tickets for cigarettes, the ravages of sleeping on park benches, screaming run-ins with police officers, a permanent cough, lengthy stays at a psychiatric hospital—all had been phases of Andrea's infamous life, but her last housing situation was the best. She had support from a team of women who were trained to defuse delusion. They made room for every conceivable dysfunction, especially the imaginary, mythical Jasper. At last she felt safe.

Andrea would pick up the phone in the common room of Anne's House, part of the Nazareth Community, and call me to repeat her mantra, "Jasper loves me." I would agree and she would hang up. She needed the affirmation that she was worthy of love. She vetted most things through the imaginary Jasper: "Jasper wouldn't like me to talk to those girls. Jasper wouldn't mind if I had sex with Georgie, would he? Jasper doesn't like me to smoke marijuana. Jasper wants me to quit cigarettes."

Even if there had been proof of his death, Andrea would still have claimed their ongoing relationship. For her, death did not exist. Her parents were reincarnated; I was sometimes her sister, other times her daughter. She was in regular contact with her mother and father, long, long dead, but a further testament to the ghost garden, that special realm where all that can be imagined is true.

Andrea died in her sleep at Anne's House, curled up under a duvet, a rather gentle ending to a calamitous life, her two yellow suitcases neatly stacked at the end of her bed.

I miss her terribly.

# 9

# The Pink and Yellow
# Envelopes

A WEEK OR TWO INTO HER STAY ON THE LOCKED WARD
after the Evergreen incident, Caroline began calling her mother and
her sisters from the phone in the hospital hallway. Each call was a
relentless hurling of accusations and insults. "Why did you try to kill
my son? Ian tried to sell me for ten cents in the shack where we went
sliding in Saint-Laurent. Mum, why are you abusing the cleaning lady?
When did you stop loving me?"

The savage words crushed Isabel's spirit. Perhaps another reason she
wouldn't go to visit was that she felt she had failed her daughter. People,
including doctors, have been known to blame the mother for a child's
mental illness. That myth has long been overturned. Nevertheless, every
mother with a struggling child suffers ongoing, crippling self-blame.
*How could I have helped my daughter? What have I done wrong? Why is
she saying those hurtful, hateful things? If only I had done this or that.*

For six months, Caroline lived on the psych ward of 4-East, remaining aloof and difficult with her family. Nobody sends flowers after
a mental breakdown, and few send get-well cards to a hospitalized

person with a mental illness. Not a single friend came to visit. The family of the patient does not receive casseroles, or calls for updates. Being locked on a ward for the first time is supremely isolating. It's scary. It's daunting. It seems permanent. But most of all, it's hide-worthy.

When she was first admitted, Caroline had been administered high doses of lithium. The drug could not erase her past, but it softened the knifelike contours. She told me, "It creeps up on you. You don't know you are becoming more and more doped up until one day you wake up and you realize you can't remember where the bathroom is. You feel disconnected from your body parts. Disconnected from your emotions and feelings."

Caroline's verbal tirades, the indictments via telephone, ensured that Isabel did not change her mind about visiting. Nobody counselled Isabel. Nobody held her hand and said, "Don't take any of this personally. Your daughter will get better. You'll see." As Caroline felt increasingly abandoned by her most important lifelong ally, she escalated her accusations. She accused her mother of urinating on her, of attacking her sons—vile, unfounded attacks—yet Caroline needed her mother desperately, and craved her approval. She was the most needy of the siblings from her earliest years. That never changed. Isabel was still every bit a loving mother. That never changed either. But she went into self-preservation mode.

Arthur couldn't bear to see his wife torn apart. He encouraged her to cut ties with Caroline, at least in the short run. Isabel resisted, but Caroline's verbal lacerations were arrows that lodged in Isabel's heart, and when Arthur put his arm around his wife, eventually she let him lead her away.

Caroline was inconsolable over the severance.

———

In late spring of 1991, Arthur stopped paying the rent, and her sisters packed up Caroline's personal items from the house on Evergreen. Much was given away to charity—kids' clothing that was too small, bedspreads, toys, kitchen utensils. The rest was stored in Donald's garage. Among Caroline's personal treasures, Rosalind found well-creased pink and yellow envelopes containing locks of blond hair from her two babies, proof that she was a mother. Caroline pined to see her boys, who had been advised not to visit their mother in the hospital. The rules suggested that children be over the age of twelve.

After six months on the ward, Caroline had pulled herself together enough to control her emotions in front of the doctors and nurses who were assessing her, behaved as though her Gulf War breakdown had not happened. She mirrored this "wellness" with Rosalind and Peggy, who began to second-guess whether Caroline was sick or playing Snakes and Ladders, manipulating them up and down the spaces of her own board game.

"I *do not want* or need my family involved. I am well," she would tell the staff. "I *do need* my own apartment so I can be a mother to my sons." When she spoke this way, staff praised her for being a self-advocate, and for this, and a lot of other reasons, she preferred to interact with trained social workers and nurses rather than her family. The staff went out of their way to reduce Caroline's stress, exuded kindness and care, and did not pressure her or make her feel culpable for her shortcomings and her less than perfect behaviour as a mother. Rosalind, Peggy, and Sharon began to joke that it was as if Caroline were on vacation. In hospital, she had a warm bed, three meals a day, and no responsibilities. To be sure, it was respite for all of them.

While no one gave either Caroline or her family a formal diagnosis, from her history it was clear she had presented with psychotic symptoms in a deep depressive state. On the ward, there were good days.

There were bedridden days. The medications did not eradicate her profound sense of hopelessness, and left her slab-tongued and forgetful. When Caroline spoke to me about those weeks and months of heavy medication, she said, "Society needs to wait for people to heal instead of throwing meds at us. We are all fragile."

Still, she left the hospital with a measured dose of anticipation, and bottles of lithium to counter mania and lift her out of depression. Lithium's mood-stabilizing effects helped to minimize Caroline's feelings of being terrorized; it controlled her rushed speech, improved her judgment about her personal hygiene, induced sleep, reduced aggression, and curbed her anger—impressive for one drug that has been around for a hundred years. In addition, lithium has tolerable side effects compared with other psychiatric drugs. Caroline responded to it with only moderate aspects of weight gain, flat affect, cognitive impairment, nausea, and lethargy, and as her body assimilated the drug, the side effects seemed to lessen. Others taking the drug over a long period of time can suffer acute or chronic kidney disease. Lithium remains on the market because it works for some people; no one knows how it works, but it is sometimes the only drug that does. It worked for Caroline. In addition to lithium, she left the hospital with her first antipsychotic medication, Haldol.

Isabel's stance softened towards Caroline when she was released from the hospital. As the horrible incriminating calls had stopped, she felt she could help Caroline find an apartment in Sainte-Anne-de-Bellevue. Once again, Caroline could see her boys. She was overjoyed to have sanctioned, but unaccompanied, visits with her sons in the parks and streets close to where they lived. (The sisters had worried that Gilles would prevent Caroline from being alone with the boys; in fact, he welcomed the help.) The first time she saw them, after six long months, Matthew and Kyle raced into her open arms as though she had been gone a weekend, not half a year, soothing much of her anxiety. It was the start of the new school year, and she helped Matthew buy school supplies and new shoes with Velcro straps in preparation for grade two. Kyle held her hand as much as he could. Gilles, relieved to see she was in better shape, soon allowed Caroline weekend access, although he never let the boys stay with her overnight. Despite the long hospitalization, a sense of normalcy descended. Caroline was elated to have regained everyone's trust, notably her mother's. Isabel and Arthur felt comfortable enough to book flights to Florida for a late November departure.

Caroline's love for her sons, and their feelings for her, had not been corroded by time, distance, or deed. Purpose is the elixir of self-worth.

Perhaps because she had not seen them for a while, Caroline couldn't help but notice even more significant differences between Kyle and Matthew. At first she thought Kyle's lagging behind his brother was like her own struggles to live up to her siblings' example, and she told Rosalind that Kyle would catch up. But two months into the school year it was increasingly impossible to ignore the fact that Kyle, who was about to turn five, was not reaching the usual cognitive stages alongside his peers. He was obese yet always hungry, his hand–eye coordination was off, he didn't articulate words. It was hard to fathom how a young boy could carry so much excess weight.

One day Isabel confided her worries about Kyle to her hairdresser, who had a child with similar weight problems. The stylist told Isabel to look for two additional symptoms: testicles that do not descend and hypotonia—muscle weakness. The next time Isabel saw Kyle, she checked him over thoroughly, and suggested Caroline take him to the pediatrician. She did, and after blood tests, Kyle was diagnosed with Prader–Willi syndrome, a genetically caused condition whose key feature is a constant sense of hunger. There is no cure. There is, as yet, no medication to suppress the impulse to eat. As well, the rare condition is associated with poor muscle tone and physical, mental, and behavioural issues. The doctor, who knew nothing about Caroline's breakdown, told her to be ready for people to assume Kyle's excess weight meant he lacked self-control and that she was negligent.

Isabel was fearful that the gravity of her grandson's illness might undermine Caroline's tentative wellness, especially when they learned that the average life expectancy for a child with Prader–Willi syndrome is thirty years. Isabel offered to deliver the news to Gilles, sparing Caroline a potentially difficult conversation. When she spoke to him, Isabel downplayed the more sobering aspects for Kyle's future because she worried that this knowledge might invoke more stress, or volatility, between him and Caroline. They would have to live with whatever was in store for Kyle, after all. She didn't have to lay out all the sad possibilities so soon after the diagnosis.

As her mother had worried, the idea of her son's diminished prospects for normalcy and the likelihood of a shortened life slid Caroline into unstable territory.

Assuming responsibility for a child with such a serious condition, in tandem with her own setbacks, weighed her down like a fur coat in summer. The drugs she was on also heightened her feelings of suffocation. "I was in a tunnel," she told me. "You keep thinking the end is just over there. But it isn't." Caroline decided she could not help Kyle if she didn't feel fully alive, and so she decided to stop taking her medication.

At first she had a short-lived, blissful feeling of clarity and freedom. Five days, and five sleepless nights, later, she wasn't feeling so fine. Once again her phone calls to family turned accusatory. Caroline's abrupt withdrawal from her drugs or her sleep deprivation precipitated a second onset of psychosis, with accompanying nightmares, anxiety, sweating, and mood swings.

Rosalind recalls the phone conversation from this time that signalled Caroline was slipping. Instead of talking about Kyle, her sister claimed to be in constant contact with Mel Gibson. Gibson, she said, was Matthew's father. It mattered little that Mel Gibson was inaccessible, a Hollywood star, married, and a father of many children, none of them Matthew or Kyle. This fantasy was a grand deflection of the painful realization that her son had a disorder that was permanent and unfixable, and that he would die young. Even so, Rosalind did not realize her sister had gone off her medication.

Isabel once again became the target of a barrage of phone calls, recurring like a nasty rash, riddled with exaggerations, falsehoods, and accusations that were impossible to fathom. Her daughter said, "You don't love me. Why did you try and drown me on Lakeshore Road? You held my head underwater in the pool. I have brain damage. I'll never have another baby because of you. Why did you try to kill the dogs? Was it because they loved me more than you?"

Isabel felt sickened by her daughter's abrupt reversal, an uncontained finger-pointing outrage. She and Arthur were tired and retired. This was not how they had envisioned their post-parenting years. After a flurry of calls between family members, they all decided Caroline needed to be readmitted.

Against her will, she went back to the psych ward, driven by a white-knuckled Donald. While he was less inclined than his sisters to wade into emotional waters, "to his credit," says Rosalind, "he happily ran any kind of errand for his sister, including the purchases of Kotex, new underpants, and toothpaste." He was the only sibling who still lived in Montreal, and it was a godsend that he was such a willing chauffeur, day or night. On the way to the hospital, Caroline just buried her face in her hands and moaned, "My boys. My boys."

# Tamslynn

In 2017, I met a woman named Agatha at a peer support meeting for parents who need to know they aren't alone. I am not a counsellor, but I had asked to attend a meeting to see what kind of support was available for families. Agatha and I sat next to each other. It crossed my mind that she looked like an in-patient at the Douglas: messy, pale, and shaky. She seemed lost inside her clothes, a sweater and jeans that were too loose, as though she'd dropped weight suddenly. She had driven into the city from the Eastern Townships, ninety minutes away by car. I wondered if she was trying to be discreet about her situation or if there wasn't an English support group in her French-speaking city.

Agatha's daughter, Tamslynn, was somewhere on the streets of Sherbrooke, battling voices and feeling paranoia towards anyone who came close. Agatha told me she wished she could tuck a birthday card under her daughter's dirty coat that said, "I love you, Tam Tam." She wanted her daughter to know that their falling-out was never a question of not loving her.

For more than three decades at Christmas, Agatha had set up the town of Bethlehem on long sheets of white cotton batting—a crèche in a stable, the baby Jesus, Mary and Joseph, the animals and the Magi, and dozens of snow-topped houses and churches that she had collected since she was young. Two years ago, her teenaged daughter had flung the whole set-up at the window and stomped on the miniature lights. She didn't stop until the entire perfect village was destroyed. "There is no such place anywhere in the world," she yelled at her mother. "Stop pretending. There is no nirvana."

After Tamslynn ran to her room, Agatha glued everything back together. They cried separately. "The next day, I told her I was taking her to the emergency department of the Hôtel-Dieu hospital. My punishment for that decision is that she left and never returned. When she lived with me, it was hell, but at least I knew where she was, locked in her filthy bedroom on the third floor and talking to the walls, or the radio. I could smell the marijuana. Now I imagine ditches and alleyways, drugs, and her slipping and falling into the Magog River gorge."

She and I sipped our water and collected our thoughts. Then she whispered, "I'm paralyzed when the sun goes down and the night presses against my shoulders, my eyes, my temples, until the sun comes in through the window, and I get up and forgive myself, until night comes and I punish myself all over again. I open the drawers in her room. I look at her beagle pillow that says: *Love is a four-legged word*. I dream about finding her. I never learned how to detach myself. I couldn't cut her out of my life."

I asked Agatha to tell me three things her daughter loved. She looked me in the eye and said, "Tam worked at an animal shelter one summer. She took the dogs outside for walks. Some of them were bigger than she was." What else? I asked. There was a long pause, as though she was sifting through so many bad memories there was little room for good ones. "She liked buttons. She bought things at the Gap and Forever 21, then changed the buttons. Always trying to go against the grain." Agatha smiled, and I could see how pretty she was. She tucked her hair behind her ears and I saw three jewelled earrings in each lobe. And the third? "Maybe this doesn't count, but we looked a lot like each other even though I adopted her when she was two. She loved it when people said so. We both did." She absently touched the earrings.

In January 2018, my phone rang at midnight. It was Agatha calling to say, "Tamslynn died." There was a long, long silence from her, and then a deep, rattly inhalation as if she were in the final moments of her own life. "She died on the Epiphany. The Epiphany," Agatha repeated. "That's when the three Wise Men came." In the silence that fell, I knew she was searching for the significance. "I kept a calendar on my kitchen wall, glossy pictures of dogs. I ticked off the days with a black pen. I couldn't stop myself. I hadn't heard from her in fourteen months and five days. I know I was slowly going nuts. I should have tossed the damned thing out. My mind was a torture, but when a calendar of smiling dogs is the only thing that connects you, you can't. It's the hope that maybe today is different. Or at least tomorrow. I read Harlequin pocketbooks with happy endings, about love and peace and joy, so I can breathe."

I knew from many phone conversations with her mother that Tamslynn had been too volatile to live at home and too sick to adhere to treatment. Agatha had not found a doctor who could help, and had learned that unless a person was homicidal or suicidal, there was no place to go. She needed the parental support group as her own lifeline.

I think back to that meeting where we first met. The convener told us that the willingness of parents to self-destruct in order to help their child is the worst possible danger—two or three people fall to the ground instead of one. I couldn't help but think that, now Tamslynn was dead, Agatha was in even more danger. She was a single parent, an only child herself.

But when Agatha spoke again, some of the despair was gone. She said she felt lucky to have got the news, because her counsellor had told her some parents never hear.

And then she said, her voice cracking, "Dear God in heaven, please, please, please forgive me for feeling relief that it's over."

## 10

# Caramel Corduroy Jacket

BECAUSE OF PATIENT CONFIDENTIALITY LAWS, AS Caroline began her second long stay at the hospital in 1992, she was able to choose, once again, to limit the information passed on to her stricken family. However, they did know that going off her medications had propelled her into psychosis, and they could see with their own eyes that the new regimen of drugs was changing her for the better. She grew less combative, and made fewer hysterical phone calls, but her light had dimmed. Better dimmed than psychotic, is what they thought. As for Caroline, she recalls, "I got a few good nights of sleep because I had been clubbed in the head. You lose track of the days." The list of her medications had grown longer, and the dosage was increased. "I didn't care about what I looked like. It became easier and easier to bury my pain under layers of body fat."

Isabel was in Florida with Arthur, and did not come home. And she wouldn't have gone to see her daughter in hospital even if she had, for all the old reasons. Rosalind, Sharon, and Peggy kept their visits short. Caroline could not hide her anger, was silent, distant—her body language eloquently conveying her feelings of betrayal.

Caroline's weight had risen in proportion to the higher doses of medication she was now on, which dashed her self-image as Mel Gibson's perfect partner. The blunting caused by the drugs affected her ability to express her emotions. She described it to me this way: "Having a good cry makes me feel like I've weeded my garden. I feel clean again. There were times when I knew all I needed was a good cry, and I couldn't because the medication was suppressing all my outlets. That's when bad things grew inside me. The weeds. I was overtaken. If I can't cry, I know I'm strangled." Rosalind remembers that though Caroline was angry with them, on some level she was relieved to be under supervision, and insightful enough to say, "I went off the rails." Still, she was, as ever, emotionally crushed to be separated from her sons, and the medication did not touch her severe depression.

As a last resort, she agreed to undergo weekly, and then twice-weekly, electroconvulsive shock therapy, which gave her both short-term relief from the deep blues and noticeable memory issues. ECT, which induces a grand mal seizure by passing volts of electricity through the brain, has made a quiet comeback, though it still carries a stigma as an inhumane treatment because of the way it was practised and perceived in the past.

Though nobody knows why it works, some patients respond to ECT with near-immediate relief. Dr. David Goldbloom, senior medical adviser at Toronto's Centre for Addiction and Mental Health (CAMH), says that sometimes a quick fix, even a temporary one, is a godsend, especially for those with suicidal thoughts. Despite the memory loss and the cognitive side effects, some patients report a lifting of depression after a few treatments. Critics of ECT underline that once treatment stops, depression returns, because shock therapy cannot address unfulfilled longings, defeat, disappointment, loneliness, failure, poverty, and joblessness. It cannot fix homelessness, and refugee status, and divorce. It can, however, induce short-term memory loss, and perhaps that is enough of a tiny stopgap to give some relief.

Caroline accepted ECT without hesitation. She wanted *something, anything* that could rewire the connections that led to depression and alleviate her existential pain. "It was as though I had turned the lights off in my house," she says. "If the lights are off, my kids won't come visit because they think I'm not home. A good mother never turns her light off."

Despite her struggles, she did have some happy moments on the ward. She was able to connect with the other patients, as well as the nurses, social workers, and the staff who changed the sheets and washed the bathroom floors. This humanitarian side of Caroline is what kept some of her threads intact. She did not stop trying to find connections. At her core, Caroline is lovable and kind, funny and generous. Her depressions were greatest when she lost sight of those strengths. She sank even lower when medication dwarfed or deformed her purpose.

The sisters found it a relief to see Caroline washed and showered. When Rosalind brought Caroline's favourite moccasins and caramel corduroy jacket to the ward, dug out from a container in Donald's garage, Caroline stopped wearing the blue hospital gown. Peggy says, "I was so happy to see her dressed in her own clothes. People look so vulnerable in those gowns, body parts exposed in public ways meant to be private."

The staff worried about her apathy, especially because they also saw her warmth and generosity—unlike the sulky side she showed to her siblings. Another family crisis helped Caroline feel less alone. Her older brother Stuart had descended into addiction to the point that his wife was keeping their children away from him. Caroline was the first of his siblings to offer him comfort, perhaps because she recognized how much she needed it herself. Stuart's distress manifested as drug use rather than psychosis, but it helped Caroline see that she was not the only troubled sibling.

While at the hospital, Caroline picked up the habit of smoking. It was something to counteract boredom, an activity to fill ballooning time. She was soon up to a pack a day. Her parents were dismayed to hear she'd become a smoker, given that they had both quit. Another way, Caroline thought, that she had disappointed them. But she couldn't stop.

After six months living on the unit, she had been stabilized by a tailored cocktail of antipsychotics, ECT, lithium, and sleeping pills. She was calm, bored, and eager to get back into her life, and her doctors believed she was well enough to leave, although her family thought otherwise. Without a place to live, she would be as exposed as a spiderweb in a rainstorm. Where should she live, and who would assume responsibility for her precarious health? Her parents stepped in to help.

Arthur and Isabel now lived for the six months of the year they were in Canada at Creg Quay, an adult community on the waterfront in Lancaster, Ontario, twenty miles southwest of Cornwall. Moving in with them was not ideal, but no other plan seemed better. Arthur grudgingly agreed, though he asked, harshly, "Are we going to be stuck with this girl?"


After Caroline moved in, her father couldn't help showing how impatient he was to find a more permanent set-up for her, away from them. No one should judge them harshly; they were aging parents who were emotionally ill-equipped to deal with Caroline's ongoing issues, and had no support system for themselves. And, as Rosalind points out, always at the core for her parents were the shame and stigma of having a daughter with a serious mental illness.

The situation wasn't ideal for Caroline either. She was far from her boys, and afraid to drive to Montreal to see them because of her medication. In addition, she was vividly aware that her parents resented the burden of her instability. What saved them all for a time was the way Caroline used self-deprecating humour to release tension. "Nobody can call me boring," she'd say, and they'd all laugh, even Arthur, despite his gruffness. She also cooked and cleaned and planted flowers outside on the patio, doing her best to earn their favour. Peggy says, "I think my sister saw the shame they felt. It was unspoken, but Caroline had to sense that on many levels she was unwanted. Mum became tough on her, wanting more for her, not realizing the limitations the disease put on Caroline. Mum was on her about smoking, her clothing, her weight, her spending habits, not completing school. I think back and I realize she couldn't turn my sister away, but she made it hard for her to stay."

Because her sisters lived in different cities and provinces, and had young school-age children themselves, it was difficult for them to visit. Soon despair descended over Caroline like a cold, damp cloak. She knew that leaving the hospital had been the right decision, but living in Creg Quay was like living in an isolation cell with two people who disapproved of her. Negativity began to permeate her brain, pushing aside her resolve to do better and be better. Spellbinding voices once again plagued her day and night, speaking words so unacceptable she would not share them with anyone. She told me, "I was receiving unspeakable messages. I would sneak looks at my mother to see if she could read my thoughts, or hear what I was hearing." The medications she was taking did not seem to dissipate the dark clouds, or keep the negative voices at bay.

Arthur and Isabel did make an attempt to get help for themselves. A couple they knew had two daughters who suffered forms of severe mental illness, and the couple invited Caroline's parents to a support group in the basement of a church. Arthur and Isabel thought the gathering was only for parents. It turned out to be a rambling meeting for the highly symptomatic. They found it a terrible shock to see the exaggerated physical deterioration around them: people with weight issues, who were chain-smoking, who had Parkinson's-like tremors, vacant eyes, bedraggled Salvation Army clothing. They heard psychotic, delusional conversations that frightened them half to death, despite their experiences with Caroline. Half an hour into the meeting they felt as overwhelmed and hopeless as the forsaken men and women seated nearby in a loose circle of chairs. It was like a sneak preview of hell. They made a beeline for the door, and never returned or made any further efforts to get counselling.

But the experience led Isabel to accept the inevitable. There was no way home from certain mental illnesses, and this was a burden that had to be carried.

Neither of them could bear the idea that Caroline might lose her mind like the lost souls in the church basement. Is there any parent who is not engulfed by grief when a child shifts into territory that causes them to live a life of pain and persecution? Paralyzed by fear, and with no railing to hold on to, they continued to stumble blindly on, while inside Caroline's mind her voices were telling her: *What's the point? Why take the medication? You're not worth it. You have nothing to show for your life. Your mother doesn't want you here. Your father doesn't love you.*

Isabel had seen Caroline flourish when she had someone to care for. She and Arthur decided that living so far away from her boys was causing Caroline more harm than good. So the family banded together and helped her move into a little apartment in Sainte-Anne-de-Bellevue, the next village over from where her boys and their father lived. Isabel bought pretty cotton curtains, which Arthur hung. Caroline's meagre possessions were hauled out of Donald's garage, dusted off, and placed on counters and in cupboards. They arranged for a little dog on a trial basis. As a young girl Caroline was a devoted animal lover, gentle and affectionate. She was thrilled to have a pet. Maybe this would give her the unconditional love she sought, a creature to care for on an ongoing basis. And for a time, as Caroline's mood changed dramatically for the better, Isabel and the rest of the family felt that the situation might be looking up.

# Carl

The first time I met Carl, he was with a man named Larry, and they were greeting people on the grounds of the Douglas Hospital, unlikely ambassadors of goodwill. Carl shouted, "Every minute you're angry, that's sixty seconds less of happiness for you!" I had brought a pile of ten shirts, donated by my friend Alice, and Carl joyously accepted a pale-blue one. Larry took two, buttoned them both up to the top over his clothes, and thanked me by singing, "You can live forever in a cherry tree." It was Larry's hallmark phrase, and it made me smile. When he pulled his long white beard out from inside the shirt like Rumpelstiltskin, I had to laugh.

I met Carl again three days later at the wooden swing set outside the Moe Levin building, one of the hospital's long-term housing options for patients suffering from serious mental illnesses. He was wearing the pale-blue shirt. After that, I only saw him in a thick black winter parka with a hood, no matter the season.

Carl was unlike a great many of the hospital patients in that he was cheerful, a non-stop babbling conversationalist. The only downside to his loquaciousness was the occasional insult flung his way ("Carl! Shut the fuck up!"). And, unlike most of the patients on government assistance who hang out and smoke near the swing set, he didn't ask for money from the visitors and doctors heading for the building.

Carl and Larry, thirty-two and seventy-two respectively, were fast friends. On the swings together, Carl told me he also had a sister who loved him very much. I told him I had a sister who loved me very much too. He was slated to leave the Douglas and move to the same group home in LaSalle where I spent time with a couple of other people I knew. With his good nature and youthful exuberance, I thought he would be a good addition to the mix.

I saw Carl next a month later, after he had moved to the group home. He wore blue jeans, bright white running shoes, and a Tony the Tiger T-shirt under the black hooded down parka. I will never forget that parka, so out of place in late June. The beige faux fur of the hood was clumped together with some dark, unidentifiable, sticky goo. Maybe blood, but I never asked. Carl seemed much too chatty and charming to have a sinister side, although I knew, in the weeks leading up to the heat wave that struck Montreal that summer of 2012, that his medication had been increased; if a patient is doing well, there is no need to up the dosage.

Carl wore his down parka every single day in June and July. He wore it to bed, to breakfast, to the park bench, to the bathroom. He never took it off, and nobody noticed the inappropriateness of his attire. I know that he was very upset about the weight gain triggered by his antipsychotic medication, a side effect called a "psychotropic beer belly." Several times he asked me if he looked fat. His sunny disposition was a trick of sorts; he hid his dismay behind a giant smile and bright saucer eyes. I went out of my way to tell him how many friends he had, especially Larry. Nothing could dampen Carl's dismay.

I wish I had known more at the time about temperature dysregulation—that certain medications reduce the sensations of heat and cold, disrupt the body's ability to lower core body temperature. I wish the people who ran the group home had also been more knowledgeable. In the middle of the third night of a four-day province-wide heat wave, during which temperatures sometimes exceeded thirty-seven degrees Celsius, Carl suffered heatstroke and died. The LaSalle house did not have air conditioning. His devastated housemates found his body on the living room sofa the following morning, still in the hooded parka.

Caregivers in group homes are not always properly trained for these kinds of rattling experiences. They never thought to insist either that Carl remove his coat or that he drink extra water to compensate for his excessive sweating. Carl likely did not feel the brutal heat. He was his charming self to the very end. He had celebrated his thirty-third birthday two weeks before his death. There was a cake with candles, and ice cream and singing, and he'd been delighted to be the centre of attention.

Carl was happiest when talking. He chatted with both staff and strangers—anyone with the patience to listen. He once asked me if he could touch my lips and cheeks. I said yes. And when he gently touched me, I realized how starved he was for contact and not just conversation. His eyes betrayed how much touch meant to him. Then he asked if he could touch my breasts. Of course I said no, and he said okay, but I felt like crying, it was so sad. People need human touch, and the lack of it amplifies the loneliness of those afflicted by mental illness. Hugs strengthen the immune system. Carl's skin hunger is a special plague of the marginalized.

People with serious mental illnesses still have natural physical urges. They still have dreams of a long-term relationship, of marriage, of children. The medication suppresses much, but not all. It's a cruel aspect of schizophrenia. There's no privacy on a hospital ward, or in a shared room in a group home. Consensual sex happens on the wards. Non-consensual as well. It's a horrendous miscarriage when an assault occurs. Punishment is problematic. The perpetrator is already spending time on a psychiatric ward for deeds that can't be rectified by the usual legal interventions.

Carl was beloved by the staff at the hospital, not something that could be said about every patient. After his death from heatstroke related to his disrupted thermoregulation, the hospital made an impressive effort to inform all staff and support workers of this type of tragedy, and how best to avoid a future failure. His death was devastating for Carl's family, especially his sister, but was an eye-opener for caregivers who need to be aware of the fatal intricacies of the side effects of neuroleptics.

Larry doesn't understand that Carl is dead. He's been told, but because of his significant and cumulative cognitive decline, he's not able to take it in. One afternoon I was driving past the front entrance of the hospital and saw Larry sitting on the bench out front. He was picking things out of his tobacco-stained snowy beard. I lowered the window and shouted hello. He sprang up and bounded over to my car, opened the passenger door, and slid in. The incident caused a minor scene when a nearby social worker assumed Larry had jumped into a stranger's car uninvited. She ran after my moving car waving her arms and shouting, "Larry! Larry!" I hit the brakes, and when she caught up to us, I explained who I was. Miffed, she insisted Larry return to the Moe Levin building, where she could keep an eye on him. "Do you have more shirts for me and Carl?" he asked as he shuffled away from the car, smiling.

"Not on me," I answered, but I told him I'd bring more. Blue ones, I promised.

I used to think that never-ending delusion was a tragedy. Larry, who has lived at the hospital for decades and is chronically psychotic, waits for Carl at the swing set and sings his cherry tree song to people who pass by. Now I see it as a coping mechanism to counter the loss of his friend, and so many other losses I don't even know about.

# 11

# A Pill for Disappointment

IN THE HIGH HEAT OF SUMMER, AFTER CAROLINE HAD moved into the little apartment in Sainte-Anne-de-Bellevue, she rambled through town dressed in many layers of clothing—a coat over a sweater over a blouse over another blouse, unaffected by the thermometer or the humidity.

On a searing July afternoon, a day that withered impatiens and singed grass, Rosalind's mother-in-law, Mrs. Plante, invited Caroline over for lemonade. She was a woman who'd always been kind to Caroline, who knew of her troubling and ongoing circumstances and was generous with her time. It might have been the hottest day of the summer. Caroline rang the bell dressed in a dark-blue wool coat with giant wooden toggles, buttoned over a sweater, over a red turtleneck. Thick knee socks were tucked inside her suede moccasins. Peggy says, "She scared the bejeebers out of poor Mrs. P. It was well over thirty degrees. My sister was fortunate she didn't die."

After Mrs. Plante coaxed Caroline to remove her winter coat and the heavy sweater, she poured them each a glass of pink lemonade. They sat on the porch and began with the usual small talk: the weather.

That same hot, lazy July, Caroline was standing in a parking lot close to the main village of Sainte-Anne. She had been hearing voices but had told no one for fear of losing her apartment and her dog. She was having drinks at a bar with Fern, who now managed the Film Box, a tiny cinema frequented by West Islanders, and had just stepped outside for a cigarette when she had a vision of someone covered in blood—her first visual hallucination. Her scream shot like a firecracker across the empty parking lot, and she covered her face with her arms. Several people rushed to her aid, not realizing Caroline's pain was psychological.

At that point, even though she was on medication, Caroline was living with a turbulent riot of twenty different internal voices, male and female, all instructing, caressing, chiding, screaming, cajoling, and ultimately causing high anxiety and mass interference. But the bloody hallucination was a new terror and felt as real as Fern, who raced to her side in a panic. Caroline was shaking, and his reaction was instantaneous. He gathered her into his huge arms to help bring her back to safety. When the screaming finally stopped, he shepherded Caroline down the block to the Film Box, and took her inside. Never letting go of Caroline's hand, he phoned her brother Donald and asked for help. Isabel happened to be in town from Lancaster. They raced to the bar and parked in the lot where Caroline had had the terrifying vision, and waited, sick with worry, as Fern brought Caroline outside. As he and Donald tried to get Caroline into the car, she punched Isabel in the face, still caught in a frenzy of bloody hallucinations.

For the third time, Donald drove Caroline to the hospital, where she was immediately readmitted. Isabel went home to Lancaster engulfed in the now-familiar sorrow and anxiety, not knowing what terrible drama would come next.

Isabel also had the additional burden of Arthur's resentment at how the ongoing Caroline "crisis" was affecting their retirement. She was torn between looking after her mentally unwell daughter, who now scared both of them out of their wits, and spending quality time with her retired husband in Florida, away from the source of their pain. The desire to escape was acute—as strong as the need to flee a flame. The sense of having nowhere to turn was overwhelming.

In the past they'd found solace in Caroline's good nature. She went days and weeks where she was her old self. It was all so confusing— the dichotomy. When she was well, she was helpful, creative, hilarious, and good company. A screaming, punching stranger was anything but. A daughter who hallucinated bloody violence was beyond Isabel's realm of understanding.

Fern called Rosalind, and the sisters rallied. As usual, the questions resurfaced. Was Caroline bipolar? Manic? An attention-seeker? Had she stopped her medications? Or was she just plain senseless, as Donald attested after the crazy drive back to 4-East?

It was this third hospitalization that finally made Isabel break down and weep, no longer capable of doing what she did best, which was soldier on. No amount of wishful thinking would bring back Britches, her sweet, innocent girl.

It turned out that Caroline, once again, had gone off her medication, which led directly to the third long stay in hospital. The craving to feel normal, not to mention the galloping side effects that included massive weight gain, had overtaken her resolve that the medication was helpful. Perhaps Caroline understood that the secret to untangling her psychosis was not to tinker with her biology. Is there a pill to fix disappointment?

"It's too tempting to trick yourself into thinking that you are no longer sick," Rosalind says. "When the delusions and hallucinations disappear, you think you are normal." Once off the medication,

Caroline immediately plunged into psychosis, causing the family to wonder if the symptoms were a result of drug withdrawal. It was hard to admit that a long stay for Caroline on a locked unit was a holiday for all of them. At the very least, in hospital, Caroline would be incapable of inflicting harm, on herself or anyone else.

Each time Caroline walked through the emergency doors during a crisis, she was seen by a new psychiatric team. Her charts were there, but the relationships weren't, and it would be days or weeks before the new team was familiar with her basket of symptoms. As before, Isabel stayed away, burned by the devil's tongue. She coddled Arthur, miles away from the eye of the storm. Her grief could not have been greater if her daughter had been killed in a road accident, though she also placed some blame on Caroline. "I never wanted to see her like that," she told her other daughters. "Screaming at me. Hitting me. My thoughts bring me to such a terrible place of pain, that I could have raised a daughter like that." Isabel could not see that the illness was behind Caroline's behaviour.

The sight of their broken mother swayed Caroline's four sisters to circle the wagons around Isabel in order to protect her, and validate her decision to stay away from the hospital. They told her that she was burned out, that she had reached her own breaking point from the chronic stress. She was grateful for the acknowledgement. Arthur did go up to the ward to see his daughter, but Isabel always waited in the lobby.

Arthur, the medical doctor, had known what to do when eleven-year-old Lorraine had life-threatening kidney disease. He had no idea what to do about Caroline. Her invisible disease seemed to him as ephemeral as the air from a burst balloon. He did know that psychosis is an edgeless, unknowable state that no one regimen will fix.

Caroline's sister Sharon was her steady and most trusted contact during her third hospital incarceration. Sharon tried her best to reassure

139

Caroline that all was temporary. She made her feel less marginalized and, most importantly, still loved.

During this third hospital stay, Rosalind began to chart Caroline's wellness, or lack thereof. The hodgepodge of medical assistance, the timing of each breakdown, the psychotic episodes, the lies, the verbal battery of abuse—as much as possible Rosalind tried to keep track of the rock pile of Caroline's crumbled life. Rosalind was beginning to see into the future—that the burden of Caroline's care might last a lifetime. She also began to realize that compiling the data would be essential to help other families, if not their own. To compensate for a wretched feeling that perhaps it was too late to help her sister, she kept track so that others wouldn't falter as dismally as they had.

As far as Rosalind could see, after Caroline was medicated, she would have a period of tranquility when she was stable enough to take her drugs. How come the medications were unsustainable? Would Caroline ever have a modicum of sustained independence? The sisters had lives to live, babies to nurture, jobs, spouses, and mortgages. During the worst of times, some of Caroline's nine siblings went missing; not all family members have the stomach to sustain a roller-coaster ride.

They had no plan. No map. It was scary. There were no answers. It was anything but sparkly clean. It was menstrual blood, maggots, dirty sheets, dental havoc—all this from a girl who had grown up in a wealthy suburban family, the daughter of a well-known doctor.

In July, it was Caroline's birthday. Since she was in no condition to leave the hospital, her sisters decided to take the party up to the unit. Isabel was against the idea, and told them she would not visit, no matter the occasion. She wanted Caroline out of the hospital as soon as possible, and argued that any little celebration might be construed as a reason to stay longer. The sisters asked, how bad can it be to laugh and sing and eat chocolate cake? Rosalind says, "Always there was the baggage of shame and stigma. She clung to Dad's reputation as the former director of that very hospital." She worried over any aspersions being cast her way. She, like so many others, viewed Caroline's break with reality as a crumbling of character, a state of disgrace. And Isabel did not want Caroline's struggles to become her identity. At some level, she refused to give up on the idea that Caroline was entitled to her little corner of the planet, rather than a life that rendered her a shadowy ghost. Isabel would not, could not, and did not ever say that her daughter had schizophrenia. To her it was nothing but a label that would deepen into permanent disability and downgrade any recovery.

Though she didn't go to the hospital, for a time she did pick up the phone. But the longer Isabel stayed away, the worse the verbal onslaught from Caroline. Rosalind remembers the tirade: "You ruined my life. You never loved me. You have never been my real mother. I hate you more than the dirt that is swept into the garbage." It seemed that Caroline was sawing off the branch on which she sat, because the more she attacked her mother, the harder it became for Isabel to show any kind of affection for her daughter. The telephone's call display feature became Isabel's friend. When she saw her daughter's number, she didn't answer. Eventually, she disconnected the voice mail.

Caroline's grief knew no bounds. Though Rosalind tried to step into the breach, there is no substitute for a mother, especially when that mother has been the cornerstone of the child's upbringing. Of course, it's possible to have a meaningful life replete with solid attachments without a mother, but a loving mother offers her breast while she cradles her baby and looks into its eyes. A young child, or even a kitten or puppy, that is loved and knows it is loved will believe it must be lovable. It is this unconscious sensation of feeling worthy of love that gives every creature self-esteem.

As a child, Caroline had had Isabel's love. It was intolerable for her to see her mother retreat. It allowed Caroline's illness to root and bloom in her subconscious mind so that she lost that sense of being lovable. The old saying about loving yourself before loving others was turned upside down. She felt she could love herself only if Isabel extended her love.

During the third stay on 4-East, Caroline had more electroshock therapy—proposed by the hospital but sanctioned by Caroline. Her sense of options must have seemed meagre, or non-existent. As before, the family was not consulted, though they were deeply troubled by the gnawing realization that her cognition and memory were being permanently affected. It was harder to have in-depth conversations with Caroline, and her attention span had been compromised. She had trouble following the plot of TV sitcoms and movies. She couldn't recall important past events. When she couldn't remember which elementary school her sons attended, she covered it up by saying they must have been home-schooled. She wasn't reading books, not even magazines, which had been a go-to purchase since high school.

She had a love-hate relationship with treatment. Medication allowed her to live outside the hospital, and saved her from the spy agencies in the backyard and suicidal thoughts. It likely saved her life. Yet, as she put it, "It makes me feel like such a less than. I know I am missing out when I have a pillowcase over my head."

The voices told her she was worthless, obese, unlovable, and the proof was reflected in the mirror. Why continue on the road to better health?

On the unit, she was truly broken. There were not enough staff or volunteers to provide Caroline the kind of companionship she needed to suppress her panic. The doctors, nurses, and social workers were compassionate, and genuinely wanted to see their patients improve, but they were simply spread too thin. Medication was their first line of therapy.

"Having two children kept her alive at that low point," says Rosalind. "She still had one reason to carry on. Even though my sister wasn't able to be with her two boys, having them in her life kept her alive. The idea of motherhood was somehow always there. So too, the idea of being mothered."

At last, Caroline agreed to let her family join meetings with the psychiatric staff. Arthur and Isabel declined, saying they'd been on the receiving end of too many insults and accusations and some things cannot be unseen or unheard. Rosalind, Peggy, and Sharon rushed to attend, and though Caroline had consented to their presence, seeing them in meetings sparked nothing but her rage. She'd hiss, "I fucking hate all of you." What she was really saying was, "I needed you then. I need you now. I will always need you." But Peggy says they had no interpreter to help them deal with her attacks, so they all retreated again. Caroline's release was postponed.

# Eliot

When Eliot, a musician who teaches guitar, hears voices, he pays attention to the messages in order to keep his family safe. It's a Biblical responsibility, he says, akin to that of Saint Christopher, who carried the disguised Christ across the stream, feeling the weight of the world upon his shoulders. Just as Saint Christopher made it safe to travel, so too Eliot must persevere on behalf of his father and mother, Lucas and Carmina.

Eliot has a stillness—a detachment—that is almost unnerving, until he responds to my greeting, surprised I remember him. He seems timorous, yet his eyes dart and glint as though my hello has touched a nerve. He is shy and withdrawn, but when he sits down and plays the guitar, he is able to channel his unspoken thoughts into music that is haunting, fluid, and resonant. It's an emotive sound, refined from years of solitude and thousands of hours of teaching and practice. While playing the guitar, Eliot can access an inner realm of deep comfort and shelter.

His father, Lucas, an Episcopalian priest in the Albany area of upstate New York, says, "It all began with a first episode when my son was twenty-eight years old. He had built a career in music. It was

2008, and the year of the financial collapse. Voices began to harass him with specific threats of harm toward his family and friends. He refers to the voices by name: Hitler, Rommel, and Himmler. Sometimes the people speaking to him work for the CIA or FBI. He believes the voices are a malevolent force that controls the lives of himself and his family. Eliot thinks it necessary to engage in a constant dialogue with the voices to protect us from harm. He must do this because he does not believe he has an illness."

Lucas feels that his son's particular thought patterns stem from a time in Eliot's life when he did not feel safe. "I do not think Eliot's psychosis is based in biology. It comes from trauma. The highly sensitive have a lower set point for coping with distress. Eliot almost lost his mother to illness when he was three years old. When he was seven, I was going through a tough time at work. Eliot worried incessantly that we would lose our home. Without being aware at the time, I brought that anxiety into his life. He has scoliosis, a curvature of the spine. The doctor gave him a scary prognosis that included complicated back fusion surgery. Eliot passed out in the practitioner's office upon hearing the news. That operation never happened, but the fright is still there, a pending sense of future suffering. The voices may have begun when Eliot was a child. In my opinion, his label of schizophrenia is actually the genetics of temperament. Other people's pain is too much. Normal situations that are not injurious to others cause Eliot to become psychotic. He is more vulnerable than most of his peers."

And so, during the recession of 2008, when, one by one, Eliot lost all his music students and was not able to support himself, he felt such emotional pain that it led to a psychotic breakdown. His thinking became enmeshed with Nazi horrors. He could not shake the dread that evil was all around him. "After that, it was impossible for Eliot to flourish," his father says.

Eliot, now in his forties, has always lived at home. Lucas experienced years of heartbreak as he tried to come to terms with the frightening changes in his son's temperament, his conversations riddled with delusion. "Carmina has more patience than I do, and is far less perturbed by Eliot's psychosis," he says. "She is sustained by her gardening, and her deep faith."

Along with music, rock climbing and running are two other activities that help Eliot cope. Whippet-thin, he runs along a path in Cherry Plain State Park. With his flowing auburn hair and full beard, his friends tell him he reminds them of Forrest Gump clocking miles across America. For Eliot, the charm of running is the weightlessness, a pure endeavour with no expectations or responsibilities, and no end goal. Exercise can improve resiliency at virtually every level of physiology. It's freedom therapy. And it costs nothing except the impetus to begin, which can be hard to find for someone who is medicated.

Exercise (especially a heart-pumping activity like running), direct sunlight, and human touch all elevate serotonin. Less well known is that serotonin is abundant in the gastrointestinal tract, which produces 80 to 90 percent of the body's supply. A healthy diet, exercise, and music have all helped Eliot, but they haven't cured his psychic pain. Eventually, when the burden on Lucas and Carmina became too overwhelming, he began to work with a psychiatrist.

"We came across a woman," says Lucas, "a doctor. She started a clinic to help stabilize the mentally ill, and, like most of her peers, she was prescribing antipsychotic medications. Eliot was medicated as per her instructions. In an unexpected turn of events, the doctor had an episode of psychosis herself. The hospital where she sought treatment used restraints on her. She was given the same medication that she had been scripting. When the psychosis ended, she said she could no longer prescribe antipsychotics. She told us, 'If I hadn't taken them literally, rather than symbolically, my practice would not have evolved.'"

Lucas has one message for other families: do not lose hope. "This condition my son shares with others will take you to the bottom of yourself, and you will fail. You can't swing it. You lose patience. Without the help of other people and caregivers, you can't cope. Eliot does take some medication. I refuse to call the pills antipsychotics—that's a misnomer. They do not eliminate psychosis. One set of symptoms is exchanged for a second set, and perhaps the feeling of being less anxious is better than the voice-hearing experience, but neither one is good. The medication helps Eliot sleep and eat more. For that, I am happy. I do know that, unfortunately, people can get lost in psychosis, and for that I wish the current treatment model were flipped. Less medication and more supportive talking. One of the doctors we consulted told us it's biological. 'Get used to it. You'll never get your son back.' It made me feel dead. You go numb. I accept that not everybody recovers, but I always default to hope."

With encouragement from his psychiatrist, Lucas began to seek out organizations that embrace alternative methods of treatment. Open Dialogue is a social network developed in Finland in the 1980s whose first aim is to create a shared understanding about the causes and the difficulties of psychotic behaviour.

The principles of Open Dialogue helped Eliot understand that his language, thoughts, and deeds were constructs of the events or relationships that had occurred in his past. Psychosis and its presentations are merely ways to survive trauma. With communication therapy, all of Eliot's thinking is validated, regardless of the delusionary aspects.

Trauma tends to go underground, to go silent, because it hurts to talk about loss and failure and disappointment. But unaired wounds never heal. Open Dialogue gives Eliot a platform where he can be heard without being judged. Everything he thinks and says is unconditionally accepted: embrace the ridiculous, the impossible, the implausible. The constraint of Open Dialogue is exactly that of other cognitive behaviour therapy (CBT) models: it's time-consuming. It requires people on the ground with the expertise to further these conversations, a seismic shift in resources. It's so much easier to suppress the tidal wave of a panic attack with an injection rather than spend the time to talk someone down from a frightening illusion.

Lucas is resigned to the merry-go-round of his son's delusional thinking. He also believes that early traumatic emotional experiences leave lasting traces, in the form of mental disturbances, but also can lead to cancer and diabetes, physical ailments. If true, the greater the number of emotional upsets, the more likelihood of a breakdown later in life.

If trauma is locked in the body, what techniques might help a person let go of those events to achieve better physical and emotional health? Might there be alternative pathways to surviving mental and physical illness? Resilience. Connection. Love. Hope. Mindfulness. Meditation. Exercise. Positivity. Yoga. Solfeggio frequency (the sound frequency of the Gregorian chant that is thought to raise vibrational energy). Religious faith. Could any of these have helped Eliot early on? Lucas and Carmina are resigned to Eliot's ongoing psychosis, but yearn for ways to cope.

Regarding the impact of his son's illness on his own ministry, Lucas says, "I think it has given me greater patience. The understanding that strange behaviour is probably rooted in trauma makes it easier for me to not take things personally.

"The biggest contribution is the sacrament of failure. Every parent travels that road. Trying to support an actively psychotic person is impossible without lots of help, and even so you will routinely be brought to the limits of your endurance. There come habitually moments when you just can't cope. You don't know what depending on God really means until you get there. Give us this day our daily bread."

# 12

# More Losses

IN OCTOBER 1994, ISABEL HAD A CAR ACCIDENT IN Jupiter, Florida, and was charged with and convicted of reckless driving. Arthur decided to sell their Florida home, and in March 1995 they came home for good.

His daughters thought that Arthur seemed to be both detached and in great emotional pain: he was sullen and distant, and avoided making plans to see his children or grandchildren. In hindsight, Rosalind says, he must have known something was physically wrong: "On some level your body and mind are aware even if it has not yet reached the surface. He knew something. He was seventy-two, had not touched alcohol in years, but I think he was worried about unfinished business. It was a sad moment of reckoning. Alcohol came back to haunt him with a cancer that migrated quickly from the liver to the lungs. By the time he got a diagnosis, it was too late for treatment." He likely had kept it to himself in order to safeguard two fragile people: Isabel and his struggling daughter.

Caroline was released from the hospital again two months after her parents moved home, and she went back to live with them in Lancaster at Isabel's insistence. With that single generous act from her mother,

Caroline felt forgiven and she felt loved. Isabel, on the other hand, found herself living with two unbalanced people. Arthur was withdrawn and bitter, caught up in his health crisis. Caroline was skittish and temperamental, fretful that the negative voices would come back. Isabel would not abandon either of them.

Caroline was aware of her parents' doubts. Of course she was. She says, "The people in our midst are the mirrors reflecting back who we are. I saw my own reflection on the faces of my mum and dad. They were afraid of me. I used to see disgust and fear in the eyes of those in front of me. My siblings. My dad was unhappy and all I could think about was that I wished I had hugged him more, been a better daughter, and radiated more love in order to mirror a kinder state of mind."

In the early days, living with her parents once again brought out the best in Caroline, a small silver lining. In moments of clarity, she recognized her capacity to drain her closest allies: "There are times when I don't deserve anyone's love. But love is a tap that is never turned off. It keeps running. As long as I still need to be loved, I think I'm okay. Sometimes I don't care about anything. That's when I become unlovable." But she easily picked up on the fact that Isabel was scared of what she would or could do next. Isabel slept fitfully. Caroline had uncanny radar for her mother's moods. The voices began, despite the medication. She did her best to ignore them.

In September, prompted by her sisters, Caroline registered for a nursing course at a local college. Sharon felt certain that having a purpose would help Caroline offset some of her other disappointments. Most importantly, she would have something to do that would provide meaning. When she was accepted, she rented a room from Monday to Friday in nearby Cornwall and commuted back to Lancaster on weekends. Isabel was obliged to drive Caroline to Cornwall on Monday mornings and retrieve her on Friday afternoons, which caused Arthur high anxiety. After Isabel's car accident in Florida and Caroline's crash into the pole on Lakeshore Road, he didn't want either of them driving short or long distances.

Isabel remained devoted to her duties as mother and wife, but she was miserable with the situation. She was harsh with Caroline. Arthur also felt the sting of Isabel's simmering wrath for making his displeasure so obvious. It was a lose-lose situation. He wanted things to be different. He was aloof with Caroline, an attitude that said, "Please don't stay long." Still, he would or could not throw his daughter out.

Caroline tried to paper over the fissures with humour. "If we weren't meant to eat ice cream at midnight, there wouldn't be a light in the freezer," she joked. She made breakfast, cleaned the oven on weekends, and tried her best to lighten the mood. She blamed herself for her father's lack of sympathy and her mother's agitation. Caroline says, "The little girl who needs the most love will always ask for it the most damnable unloving way." She was endearing and grateful, and deployed an endless arsenal of small acts of kindness that she herself wished to receive. The gifts given are often the ones most needed.

After a fully medicated Caroline had been attending school for six weeks, she began to have grievous thoughts that her classmates were spying on her. Snippets of overheard conversation turned into indictments of her weight, her behaviour, her right to even be in school. It began with one calm voice: *You should think about quitting.* At that point, had someone coached her about the impact of the newness of being back in school and living in Cornwall, the age disparity between herself and the younger students, and how friendships take time to develop, perhaps she might have succeeded. She still wanted to be a nurse. She craved to rise up and meet the expectations of her parents. But her mounting dread that she was on the cusp of another failure heightened her anxiety, which triggered voices. When she saw two nursing students give her a sideways glance while they were chatting, Caroline concluded they were plotting her expulsion. She lashed out at them with accusations that sprang from her imagined suspicions. She went back to her basement apartment under a weight so heavy it made it hard to breathe.

When Arthur was finally diagnosed with terminal cancer, his oncologist told him to go home and settle his affairs. His cancer had already spread from his liver and lungs to the bones. When he was given a scant three months to live, he finally spoke to everyone about his illness—everyone except Caroline. No one else told her either, attempting to protect her, but as a result she blamed herself for her father's gloomy distance.

Isabel took the news hard. She had done her best to ignore his weight loss, his low appetite, his surly mood, attributing them all to his corrosive worry over Caroline. Isabel's was a consummate grief; she wondered if she could go on. Her love for Arthur had shaped her entire life. Rosalind remembers being shocked at her mother's frailty after Arthur broke the news. It emphasized how much she needed Arthur's support. And he hers.

After a few more weeks at school, Caroline couldn't concentrate at all. In a panic, she fled a classroom, called Isabel from a pay phone, and insisted she needed to be picked up. The voices were harsh: *This is all your fault. Why did you move here? They didn't want you. You are a failure. You will never be a nurse. Dad is unhappy because of you.* Isabel, unable to cope, called Rosalind.

Rosalind drove to Cornwall, hoping to prevent an escalated breakdown. From there they drove to Lancaster to be with Isabel. Lorraine, the second-born of the ten, had flown in from Vancouver to spend time with Arthur. At the house, Isabel broke down, and Caroline, who had no idea of her father's mortal illness, was able to extend extreme empathy towards her, was magnanimous, nurse-like, fuelled by compassion. Rosalind knew that Isabel was crushed by the prospect of becoming a widow and even more afraid to be Caroline's sole caregiver.

When Arthur and Isabel left the house for an errand, Caroline told Lorraine and Rosalind that she had met a man in a bar. They had had plenty of drinks, she said, spent several hours together, but then he drove her to a remote field near the edge of the woods in Lancaster and raped her. Lorraine was aghast and bombarded her sister with questions. "What did he look like? Did you get the licence plate? Did you call the police? Shall we call the police right now?"

Rosalind, on the other hand, had been down this road before, and was unsure of what to believe. When Caroline's answers changed directions several times, Rosalind recognized the delusionary aspects and took pains to help Caroline feel safe. Caroline's true violation came from a situation occurring inside her head. The fear of disappointing her parents was transferred to delusional stories of harm. Caroline ended the conversation with tears in her eyes, told her sisters the man had said she was a kook with a capital *K*. That he'd called her a moron, and told her she was ugly and fat. How many real barroom encounters had there been over the years? Rosalind wondered. How many drunken men had used her sister before casting her off as a liar, a loony-tune, an escapee from the bin?

In those weeks when Caroline could no longer concentrate on her nursing, she wanted to be living with Isabel. Despite her sharp tongue and chronic impatience, Isabel represented safety. Without her mother, Caroline was an untied rowboat, adrift in waves that moved her farther and farther from shore. But Isabel put her foot down: Caroline's issues were so persistent, so all-consuming, that Isabel could not be a caregiver to both her daughter and her dying husband at the same time. Caroline would need to be cared for and live elsewhere. All three of them were emotionally distraught. Unfortunately, third-party caregiving for the mentally unstable isolates the person most desperate for connection.

Better one go down than everyone. Best if no one goes down.

Rosalind negotiated Caroline's withdrawal from classes, based on her mental state, and brought her to Ottawa, where three of her sisters were now living.

The sisters found Caroline a room in a shared apartment near Algonquin College in the Nepean area, miles and miles from anybody she knew. The house rules did not permit smoking inside, so when she wanted a cigarette, she sat shivering on the front steps inhaling smoke and exhaling resentment. The sisters felt guilty, knew it was a Band-Aid of sorts to place Caroline with two girls who had no experience dealing with someone like their sister. The second the ink was dry on the lease, they had misgivings. Caroline was marooned without support, miles away from them. No services. No job. In their defence, Isabel had crumbled, and they had to keep Caroline at arm's length so they could all meet Arthur's final days with their full attention. No one seemed to think it was unforgivable that they hadn't told her that her father was dying.

Caroline made frantic calls to Rosalind about a creepy man who had lurked in the back garden and dragged her into the woods, where he did unspeakable things. More fabrications. Crazy is doing the same thing over and over again and expecting the response to be different.

They were rescued by the Salus organization. Friends of Rosalind helped introduce them to a programme for people with serious mental health issues, an independent organization offering support to adult men and women just like Caroline. The psychiatry department of the Lakeshore General Hospital provided Caroline with a referral.

In November, the Salus team found another living situation for Caroline, a shared three-bedroom house on Creighton Street in Ottawa. "Salus was a gift," Rosalind says. "We felt rescued, even though it was Dad's final days." Rosalind remembers being told by Caroline's assigned caseworker that her sister was ill but that she had responsibilities and choices. "It was a godsend to hear those words. It meant that the weight of her care was not entirely on our shoulders. We were told that Caroline was still a capable person, even if there were dire moments when her competence seemed non-existent."

Salus told them that psychosis is not a permanent state. When not under stress, Caroline could be a thinking, rational person. For the sisters, it was like being reminded that roses have thorns, that beauty and pain can exist side by side.

The family was advised by the Salus team to put a court order in place that would allow the police to act on their behalf when a situation seemed beyond their abilities. That decision required a hasty trip to an Ontario courthouse, accompanied by the caseworker from Salus who had been designated to oversee Caroline's progress. Rosalind signed Form 3, a Certificate of Involuntary Admission—documentation to admit a person to hospital against their will. The certificate would allow the police to physically remove Caroline from her home and bring her to Emergency. A precaution, Salus advised, given that Arthur was deathly ill, rendering Caroline more vulnerable, more unstable. It was also important to have the court order in place because each new psychotic breakdown, the team warned, could be fatal.

———

Arthur died in November 1995, surrounded by several members of his family.

Afterwards, Peggy and Sharon went to the Creighton apartment and with great care and empathy told Caroline that their father had passed away. She was stoic. Rosalind told me, "I remained behind with Mum. Of course, we all knew Dad was dying weeks earlier. We didn't dare tell Caroline. I can't help but know his passing meant something different for each of us, especially for her. I remember that hiding his condition added a surreal layer to those last visits. Dad had always been so grief-stricken about Caroline's mental illness, and I don't think he ever totally resolved those feelings, stopped blaming himself, his genes, couldn't escape from the thoughts that plagued him. He was still wrestling with his memories about his sister, and boarding school at Brébeuf. Years later, when I could finally talk to Caroline about Dad, she said he never had the right filing system. He never learned how to put his stuff in the right drawers. I think she was right."

Rosalind recalls feeling relieved when Caroline's doctor prescribed some extra medication for her during that emotional week. Sedatives. The family needed to be sure that the news, and the upcoming funeral, wouldn't tip Caroline into psychosis. Nobody could bear to have those final days, when the entire family had gathered, turn into a crisis leading to the psych ward.

The funeral was a bittersweet service for the man they had all craved to know and love, and to be known and loved by. It was a family reunion of shared stories about past holidays, hot summer nights at the cottage in Saint-Sauveur. The gathering was a healing of sorts, to pay homage to a patriarch who didn't profess to have all the answers. Arthur's children were circumspect; they honoured their father, saluting his many triumphs, and allowed anything that wasn't worthy of praise to fade to black. They judged Arthur as a man who had tried his best—a lonely intellect who felt he had won the sweepstakes when he found Isabel.

As much as Rosalind took comfort in seeing her brothers gathered together, she was disturbed by their attitudes towards Caroline. Some of them viewed her as simply troubled or difficult, and refused to believe there could be genetic reasons for her psychotic episodes. She had fallen on her own sword, said Ian. It was clear that support for Caroline would remain on the shoulders of the four sisters.

"At that time we didn't have a definitive diagnosis," Rosalind says. "Over many years, we had been told she was a depressive, had mania, delusional thinking, grandiose ideation, anxiety, paranoia, and who knows what else. She had a form of separation anxiety at not being with her sons, needed my mum's approval, and always her life was tinged with guilt." The family gathering was a lonely moment of reflection for Rosalind. "On that day I knew I would carry the greatest responsibility for my sister." She had already been on the front lines of her sister's troubles for so long. Four of her five brothers lived too far away to be able to count on for any heavy lifting, but she had hoped they would be more available in a spiritual sense.

When they all went back to Ottawa, the sisters watched over Caroline, and with Salus's help Caroline did not disintegrate after their father's death. Although it was worrisome that she wore the same caramel corduroy jacket every day for months, it must have been a comfort for her.

The calm was short-lived. On New Year's Eve, Caroline rushed to Emergency at the Ottawa General Hospital and told staff she was going to walk across the semi-frozen Ottawa River. The staff took her in, listened to a hot streak of words about her dead father, and pieced together that she was having a delayed reaction to his death. They administered more medication. A kind team of compassionate medical professionals let her cry herself to sleep. She felt she needed to make amends for the turmoil she had caused her father, and she felt responsible for his truncated life. "My own life would have been over then too, if not for the help I got from two social workers," Caroline says. "I was talked back into my life."

She spent one night in Emergency and was released the following morning. She felt proud to have navigated the crisis on her own, that she had not worried her sisters or her mother while they grieved for Arthur.

# Chantal

I volunteer with a woman who is an identical twin. She and her sister are university-educated, articulate, and trilingual. Both are accomplished musicians and have travelled far and wide, but only Chantal is psychotic and delusional, suffering from both schizophrenia and what the psychiatrists call "lack of insight," which means that she does not recognize that she has unfounded beliefs.

On a busy Montreal street last summer, we came upon a public piano near Côte-des-Neiges. Chantal sat down and played from memory a nocturne by Québécois composer Alain Payette. The people at the pedestrian intersection came to a standstill. I had to turn away so she wouldn't see me choke up from the beauty and poignancy of her performance. Imagine if Beethoven, who suffered severe depression, had been drugged and hospitalized in perpetuity as Chantal has been. There would be no Symphony No. 7.

It squeezed my heart to hear her perform, and to know that on the ward where she lives, there is no piano and as a result Alain Payette's composition lies dormant in her memory, with the other classical pieces she has memorized and performed. To play a composition with such feeling requires access to the limbic system, the brain structure that controls emotion. I realized then that music, and the great well of connection it springs from, was a part of her untouched by malfunction.

If genetics were wholly responsible, both Chantal and her sister would have the diagnosis of schizophrenia. But her sister, a successful lawyer, is unaffected by mental illness. As children, our lives are shaped by genes to some extent, but also by where we are, by who is guiding our choices, and by the interests and impulses that lead us to our destiny. Chantal began to have unusual experiences in her twenties. Now twenty-seven, she believes she is eleven months pregnant with twin girls, and is engaged to a member of the CIA, who is their father. Sometimes one baby is dead.

Delusions? Yes. But not meaningless, though I still have no idea where her trauma resides. Her lack of insight means that any attempts to dissuade her about the reality of her pregnancy are ineffective. Rather, the babies represent something altogether different—perhaps her earliest memories of being connected as a twin. My response to her is to validate her experience, not try to snap her out of it. No treatment she has encountered yet has held up a mirror in which she can see her delusions. When Chantal has her monthly injection, her psychotic symptoms do not go away, but she feels less upset about not having regular ultrasounds to monitor her unborn babies. Without the drugs, her distress is overwhelming.

But as she played piano on that street corner, she showed me how much joy she finds in music—what a trauma-free zone it is. I couldn't help think that each hour of musical practice was an hour less time of feeling distressed over her false pregnancy. Music may be the key to Chantal's future.

There is an uncanny closeness between identical twins, and who can calculate the burden of separation as those twinned babies grow to adulthood? My mother-in-law was an identical twin. Her sister died at age twelve from a blood-clotting immune disorder. It was 1942, a time when emotional upset, even over the untimely death of an innocent child, came second to the drama and needs of fathers, brothers, and uncles serving overseas in the Second World War. My mother-in-law, who died in 2015, suffered with severe bouts of depression for most of her life. I have long thought that the loss of her sister, and the pressure to soldier on through that devastating grief, had a profound effect on her.

My own son, Reid, was born from a twin pregnancy in which one baby died before I gave birth. Reid asked, as he was learning to tie his sneakers, "Does my twin know how to tie his shoes?" He was four years old.

In 2018 I was asked to be a guest speaker for Yom Kippur at the Temple Emanu-El-Beth Sholom in Westmount by Rabbi Lisa Grushcow. As a way of saying thank-you, she donated a piano from the synagogue to the psychotic disorders ward at the Douglas Institute.

Chantal has agreed to give piano lessons.

# 13

# Call Display

IN FEBRUARY 1996, CAROLINE MET OSCAR FIELDING AT a bar. Fielding, who worked for the Department of National Defence in Ottawa, was a burly and gregarious alcoholic who spanned two places at a table. Caroline was drawn to him as a moth to a flame, and he loved her easy laugh and endearing generosity. If Oscar paid for the first round, Caroline paid for the second and maybe the third, something she was able to do because her father had left her a bit of money, plus her disability income. That first night, they closed the place down.

Oscar was at least a foot taller than Caroline and older by more than twenty-five years—a divorced father and grandfather with bushy grey hair and a beard. But when he put his big bear arms around her, she melted into the sensation. Desperate for physical touch and longing for a home where she could once more build a domestic life, she moved in with him all too quickly, according to Rosalind. Oscar even had a spare room where Caroline's two boys could spend the night, and a backyard with a gate that opened onto a local park. And soon he was buying baseball bats and gloves for her boys, as he'd done for his own kids, and inviting them over for afternoon visits.

Caroline claimed to love Oscar, and he too seemed enamoured of his plucky young girlfriend. But the people at Salus were alarmed that Caroline had left a stable housing situation all too quickly. The family was rattled too, and also fretted over the fact that Oscar was a big drinker who they thought would encourage Caroline along that path— all types of inhibitions could be loosened by alcohol.

Despite everyone's reservations, there were lots of positive signs. For the first time in ages, she exercised regularly, walking herself down to 125 pounds. She wasn't working but she signed up for corre- spondence courses in health and nutrition four months after she moved in. Trouble was, the correspondence courses were online, and she had no computer experience; she wasn't able to navigate or manip- ulate the documents. By mistake she deleted her homework, which meant she had to do it all again, triggering a tiny fissure in what she felt had been a perfect little setup with Oscar. The fanatical walking slowed, then stopped, and soon she had trouble getting up in the morning. She and Oscar were drinking in the evenings.

With encouragement from Salus, Caroline returned to the Ottawa Civic Hospital for a short stabilization. Oscar was supportive, express- ing sympathy for Caroline's precarious mental health. Some days she baked muffins, filling the house with the scent of cinnamon and apples, and other days she couldn't get out of bed and despair clung to her like yesterday's perfume. But Oscar, at work every day, carried on unaware of the many daily trials that Caroline did her best to cope with or hide. She wanted the relationship to work; when her thinking spiraled out of control, she tried hard to make corrections.

Eventually Oscar couldn't look the other way: his girlfriend had begun to make fantastic claims. *My sister Peggy started the Salvation Army. My sister Rosalind is married to the prime minister. My brother-in- law Gavin gave my mum six million dollars.* With encouragement from the Salus team and Oscar, she checked in for another short stay on the psychiatric unit. No one was more congratulatory than Oscar when she sought help on her own; he saw it as a sign of responsibility. He rode out her first two short hospitalizations with a kind heart and genuine care. He thought she deserved a second chance. Her doctors adjusted her antipsychotic drug regimen to help her subdue the grandiose ideation, which dulled her down. "I came home with a hood over my head," she says. But the voices could now cut through the fog. Home alone during the day when Oscar worked, Caroline used the telephone to keep them at bay. She called Peggy several times a day, then Rosalind, Sharon, Lorraine. And her sons, which often caused her more worry. Kyle was now in grade two, after repeating grade one twice. He was eating so much his bowel movements were uncontrollable and he was often sent home because he'd dirtied his pants. It was hard on Kyle, eyeballed by classmates who found him disgusting, and tough on Gilles, who needed to leave work to pick him up. Those days when her younger son was sent home from school, the distance from Montreal to Ottawa seemed infinite to Caroline.

With call display, it was easy for Caroline's family to ignore her calls. "I made a promise to myself that I would do my best to pick up," Peggy says, "or get back to her if she left a message." But sometimes she didn't have the strength to do her best. If one person didn't answer, Caroline lit another cigarette and tried someone else.

Salus kept checking in on Caroline. Workers encouraged her to take an eight-week course to build her self-esteem. They persuaded her to swim at the local YMCA, a pastime that had given her endless joy as a young girl. If she wouldn't walk, she needed some form of physical exercise in order to offset her chronic rattly smoker's cough.

Four months after they met, Caroline and Oscar went on holiday to St. Petersburg, Florida. As far as anyone knows, the trip was peaceful.

They walked the beaches, swam in the warm ocean, held hands day and night. Floating in the salt water, Caroline experienced an easy freedom that unexpectedly reset the dials of her mind. In the evenings they had drinks and dinner with another couple, which enhanced Caroline's forgotten sense of being normal. She returned home tanned, fit, confident, and as mentally balanced as anyone had seen her in years. She also came home with plans about how she would step into her future, secure in Oscar's love, which also seemed to have been enhanced by the sun-soaked days and starry nights.

Upon her return from Florida, Caroline stopped taking her drugs again, on a weekend in which Gilles had driven her boys to Ottawa for a special sleepover. It was the first time he'd trusted the boys to her overnight.

"I don't need meds anymore. With Oscar, I have all my ducks in a row. I want to be normal and normal people don't take these kinds of antipsychotics," she wrote in her Hilroy notebook, capturing her thoughts while sitting at the kitchen table. Out the window and through the open gate, she could see her sons tumbling on the grass in the park with Oscar nearby. It was as though she had forgotten every conversation she'd ever had with every nurse, doctor, family member, Salus worker, and her own sometimes rational mind. In Florida she had reclaimed something vital. Not only did she love Oscar, she loved herself, a feeling that had been elusive in the fog-bank of drugs.

She did remember the words of one social worker from her third long stay at Lakeshore: as long as she was still loveable, the social worker said, she would be okay. Loveable people didn't walk through life numbed by a handful of little coloured pills. She did not remember that, every time she'd flushed the drugs down the toilet, her symptoms had come back in full force.

Oscar left for a business trip three days later. The night before his departure, she begged to go with him, but he refused, which pierced the bubble of her joy. The next morning, she watched his Oldsmobile skid around the corner and disappear, taking with it her feeling of safety. Caroline's mood slid off a precipice. The brightly hued psychedelic sky of initial withdrawal turned a sickly grey.

She was alone in the house and began to have ominous thoughts. She smelled noxious fumes and called the gas company to report gas billowing from every electrical socket. She put Scotch tape over the plugs. When she ran out of Scotch tape, she used Band-Aids. The company mobilized, and the gas technicians undertook a meticulous search of the townhouse but found nothing. They left, scratching their heads. Caroline didn't sleep, spent the night in a frenzy of worry and dread.

At seven a.m. Caroline called Sharon and asked if she could come over. Sharon heard the panic in her voice and said yes. Caroline hurried outside with a bus ticket in her hand, having been awake for thirty-six hours. As soon as she was safely through Sharon's door, she told her sister there were dead babies in the basement of Oscar's townhouse. When Sharon tried to dissuade her, Caroline leaned close: "But Sharon, I've seen them." After many cups of tea and much hand-holding, Caroline took the bus home, calmed by her sister.

The following day, she called the gas company again. She spoke to several people, with ever-increasing alarm, about the deadly potential of the extreme buildup of poisonous gases in her house. She was utterly convincing, because to her the delusion was real. Her voices said, *Call the gas company or there will be an explosion. People will die.* On the phone she insisted that the company would be responsible for her death. Once again emergency workers hurried to rescue a customer from impending disaster and found nothing. The next day she called again; the company came a third time and again found no leak. Caroline threatened to sue if the problem wasn't rectified. Nobody had any idea that Caroline was psychotic or that she had not slept in three days. While her own mother had blocked Caroline's number, the gas company couldn't do that—it had an obligation to check out every report of trouble.

When Caroline called Rosalind to tell her that the townhouse was a death trap, Rosalind realized what was happening to her sister. Rosalind called Sharon, and the sisters rushed to Caroline's place. She opened the door to them, looking worn out, skinny, exasperated, jumpy—a combination they had seen many times before. They coaxed, cajoled, and begged Caroline to accompany them to Emergency for a consultation, and when she finally agreed, they drove to the hospital in grim silence.

At Emergency, at first Caroline paced and then, while her sisters were handling the paperwork for her admittance, she fled. Unseen from the check-in desk, she hurried down a hallway and out a side door, with no plan other than to escape the mounting swirl of inky liquid in her brain that had drowned out the last vestiges of rational thought, consumed by anxious reminders of a lost husband, lost children, lost Oscar, lost friends. Loss. Loss. Loss. *What recovery?* she wanted to scream. *What does recovery mean if nothing is left?*

When they realized she was missing, Rosalind and Sharon did a frantic floor search, and then a grounds sweep. No luck. They gave up trying to find her on their own and went to Rosalind's house, where they rummaged around to find a recent photo. Then they drove to the police station to report Caroline as a missing person. Though she hadn't been missing for long enough to trigger an investigation, the police finally agreed to open a file. The sisters left the station feeling queasy and apprehensive. When they got home, they weren't sure if they wanted the phone to ring, afraid to hear what might have happened to her, wandering Ottawa in that precarious sleep-deprived state. In the early evening they drove around to the coffee shops and bars Caroline and Oscar frequented. Still no luck. They went back to waiting.

Rosalind described it as hours spent in a terrible state of suspended animation. For the first time she and Sharon discussed the possibility that Caroline had committed suicide. Given that they found the thought of another long hospital confinement nearly intolerable, how must Caroline be feeling? Rosalind's mind churned with thoughts of Caroline's memory loss from shock therapy, the horrid phone calls, the hysterical crying, locked doors, isolation.

Near midnight the phone rang. It was Caroline, calling from Oscar's townhouse. At last she had returned home, at wits' end, spewing incomprehensible and unlikely scenarios about where she had been all day, and with whom. She'd been raped and abused in the woods, she said—her standard imaginary construct of personal violation. Her manic incoherence was so disturbing that Sharon and Rosalind sent the police to escort her to hospital, for the first time activating the court order that allowed the police to act on behalf of the family. It was a sombre moment. The sisters felt as if they were sending a lamb to the slaughter. They knew Caroline would panic and resist, which would intensify her psychosis. It seemed an indefensible action to send the police because they had been incapable of dealing with their sister. Their one fervent hope was that the police intervention would speed up medical care.

When the officers rang her bell, Caroline sprang up to open the door, certain it was Oscar coming home early. Upon seeing the grim faces of two large men in uniform, she ran into a closet in her bedroom and hid, shouting for them to leave her alone. She clawed her way to the back, pulling pants and shirts off hangers to barricade herself under layers of Oscar's clothing. The officers, empowered to physically restrain her, were forced to drag her out of the closet and pin her to the ground. In their report they described a woman experiencing a "full-blown manic psychotic episode." She spewed verbal venom and spit on them, resisting with every bit of her strength.

Incarceration was like a death sentence. She was certain it meant the loss of another relationship, and knew she faced months of drug-induced stupor. A room with a single plastic mattress on a steel bed. Sturdy chairs and tables bolted to the floor in the common areas. White walls. Locked doors, zero privacy, institutional food, and distance from family. A place that screamed, *Leave as soon as possible. We don't want you.* No door handles in the bathroom from which to hang oneself, rounded chairs and rounded tables that couldn't be flung. The one refuge was a smoking room, but how could a cigarette possibly compensate for human connection?

The police officers had no choice but to handcuff Caroline. She was so determined not to cooperate, she ended up with her feet shackled too. After the officers had carried her to the cruiser, they drove as fast as possible, siren blaring, to the emergency wing at Ottawa General, slowing down only when Caroline finally let go of her anger and began to cry like a wounded pup. She still remembers that when she started to cry, the officer in the passenger seat blew his nose, cleared his throat—a little moment of empathy she still clings to.

Rosalind and Sharon stayed away from the ward for a few days until the sedative aspect of her treatment could take effect. They were learning to protect themselves. In the hospital, Caroline had to be restrained in a giant leather harness that held her fast at the shoulders, thighs, and ankles. "Thank God I didn't see her in that," Rosalind says, her voice cracking. "It's too heartbreaking. Another cliff. How do you crawl back up?"

The restraints soon came off, but the psychological damage was done. Caroline says, "The panic comes back and you happily swallow the pills, because you invite the fog. It swallows up the feeling of being tied up. Otherwise you smother."

Those pills were an assortment of medications—sedatives and anti-anxiety drugs, antidepressants and antipsychotics to attenuate the symptoms, sleeping pills at night. Most psychiatrists view such drug regimens as the most expedient route out of an intrusive psychotic experience. Drugs go a long way to soothe the family, for sure, but not necessarily the patient, says Dr. Pierre Etienne, a psychiatrist who practises in Montreal. "The drugs make people less disturbing but still sick." He embraces the idea that therapeutic relationships and empathetic listening should come first. He believes those methods, not drugs, guarantee the fastest route off the ward for a person who arrives in Emergency subsumed in psychosis, alone with the person they hate most—themself.

But on the psychiatric front lines, defensive practices are in place to guard against self-harming activities, violence, aggression, and suicide. The staff is tucked inside a glass-partitioned station, removed from the people they are there to heal and protect. No matter the intent, the ruling impression on a locked ward is that patients are bothersome and volatile, even dangerous. No other hospital unit assaults a patient's self-esteem so thoroughly as the locked ward, given that its whole purpose is to separate the individual from society, as if someone like Caroline didn't already feel the Gulf of Mexico between herself, her friends, and her family.

——

Slowly Caroline's anxiety lessened. As she reflects now, "Mental wards are the toilets of the world, but the kind and caring nurses and psychiatrists are somehow able to put the pieces back together when we arrive off the street, completely broken. Because of them, there are days when I feel quite normal."

A psychiatrist new to her case advised the family that Caroline would be better served not on the locked ward at his institution but at the Royal Ottawa, a whole hospital dedicated to the treatment of mental health issues, and one of the most highly regarded psychiatric facilities in Canada. Though beds were scarce, he offered to make a referral. Caroline's sisters had a euphoric moment of hope that help was on the way, even if it would take more time to implement. That same psychiatrist, looking at Caroline's history with fresh eyes, used the word *schizophrenia* as a possible diagnosis. Rosalind and Sharon had long suspected this was what was happening to Caroline, but until that point no professional had used the term. Schizophrenia is the most highly stigmatized of mental illnesses: insensitive or ill-informed people automatically associate the condition with violence and aggression. Isabel especially resisted the label; it was her chronic nightmare to have a daughter unfairly cut off from life because she was "a schizophrenic."

The doctor described what Caroline had as a slow-onset form of schizophrenia, which meant she had long stretches of stable behaviour pockmarked by delusion. He told them that Caroline still had access to proper reasoning and rational thought, and that the notion of psychosis as a permanent state is a public misconception.

As he pointed out, Caroline was quite rational when it came to acquiring cigarettes. She knew the minute they were dispensed from the nursing station. (Even now she knows exactly how many cigarettes are in the Ziploc bag that is never more than three feet from her person.) Nicotine hits the nicotine receptors and releases the chemical dopamine, which is necessary for survival; therefore nicotine is a survival mechanism. Caroline smoked to stay vital.

When Caroline again had a clear mind and was told by her clinician that she was suffering from schizophrenia, she asked to have her tubes tied. "It would be irresponsible to have another baby," she said. In the end, she changed her mind, but her initial reaction signalled to her sisters that Caroline had returned to sanity. When Caroline speaks now about the idea of bringing another child into the world after that diagnosis, she says, "I remember walking on the hospital grounds and staring up at the perfection of an apple tree. I saw a blue cloudless sky. I realized there was nothing perfect in my life. I didn't have enough to offer another human being."

# Maureen and Jean-Pierre

The first thing I did with Maureen and Jean-Pierre on a sunny Monday in June was to exchange a twenty-dollar bill for quarters at the Super C discount grocery store. That gave us eighty chances at Petites Pelouches, a vending machine in the store that dispensed keychains, tiny furry animals, and plastic jewellery. It took fifty-six tries before we scored two plastic wedding rings.

The couple met on the psychotic disorders ward at the Douglas Institute. Maureen, who spoke only English, was a long-stay patient on the third floor of the Moe Levin building, and Jean-Pierre, who spoke a Quebec dialect called *joual*, was on the second floor, a unit reserved for mood disorders. They sat together on the wooden swing set in the grounds to smoke cigarettes, come hail, wind, or blinding snow. Somehow they had each other, though their communication took place beyond language. Two lonely souls seeking connection.

I went on outings with Maureen for a year before she was moved to a group home in LaSalle. Within days she was angling to have Jean-Pierre move from the Douglas into her bed at the group home. Staff tend to discourage relationships between patients because such partnerships don't often work out. But after much prodding and cajoling on her part, Maureen won them over. It was a brilliant and humane decision on their part.

Maureen had schizophrenia. Jean-Pierre's underlying disorder was masked by decades of medication, but he'd been robbed of much brain function. He was no longer curious, but he had a permanent disarming smile and was exceptionally tolerant and calm. Maureen was smitten. There was nothing violent or aggressive about either of them, which likely cleared the way for their unique living situation.

Their fondness arose despite the rougher, dirtier side of each other's physicality: the unpleasant side effects of medication such as dry mouth, body odour, apathy about cleanliness, and weight issues. They would sit together, their shoulders touching, in a gentle familiarity that marked them as a couple. Maureen had more French words than Jean-Pierre had English, so they spoke a mangled Franglais. I often saw him grinning at his *blonde* as though they had somehow cheated the system. Whole days would go by without any meaningful verbal communication between them, but that was not the point. They had each other's backs.

They had both suffered. Jean-Pierre was married and had three children. Maureen had been in two bad relationships with men who were abusive alcoholics, as was her father. She was the first to acknowledge this pattern: "You choose what you know." They were no longer connected to anybody from their past, which helped explain their desperate need to be together and the solace they found in each other.

Jean-Pierre told me without any embarrassment that he hadn't had an erection in years. But sex wasn't what brought the two of them together. When so much of life had been lived on the fringes of society, they found unconditional belonging with each other, maybe for the first time. Marriage had been on Maureen's wish list before her battle with psychosis, depression, and drug addiction meant years spent on or under the benches in a park in the east end of Montreal, before she ended up a regular on the third floor at the Douglas.

She and Jean-Pierre shared cigarettes, money, french fries, and other snacks void of nutrition. Maureen would walk to the gas station next door to the group home to buy the two-litre bottles of Coca-Cola that Jean-Pierre craved. Every night they'd sneak into the bathroom around three a.m. for a quick cigarette, although it was strictly forbidden to smoke inside.

Jean-Pierre was obese and had diabetes. Maureen was gaunt and had untold health issues she refused to mention to her doctor: heart arrhythmia, daily diarrhea, low appetite, and a smoker's cough so loud that every time she erupted, it threatened to tilt the neon-toned picture of Disneyland off the living room wall of the group home. She endured much in order to stay out of the hospital, but after she and Jean-Pierre became a couple, she was able to eliminate most of her medications, her schizophrenia under control. The drugs had been replaced by her connection to another human being.

Maureen saved her food for Jean-Pierre—toast, hotdogs, doughnuts brought to him wrapped in paper napkins. Her weight went down by a few pounds every week as his went up. Jean-Pierre was grateful to be further nurtured and nourished, and Maureen was happy to be needed. On the stoop they sat together on white plastic chairs, in front of a paint can swimming with rainwater, loose tobacco, and soggy butts. The zipper on Jean-Pierre's ski jacket had broken the previous winter from the strain of his belly. We found a bigger coat at Walmart. When that zipper broke too, my tailor replaced it with a two-way zipper that opened at the bottom.

When I was with them at their group home, I would hear the snap of a lighter and watch as Maureen placed the cigarette she'd lit into his mouth. Their casual intimacy was so touching. "*Maureen est ma belle blonde*," Jean-Pierre would call out to anyone he thought needed to know.

I can't remember when they first began to speak about marriage, but between them they couldn't afford a licence, let alone the rings. They both survived on welfare, handing over to the group home $740 of the monthly allotment of $900 they received. Still, Maureen wanted a ring to make it official. And so we had driven to the Super C as if it were the grandest jewellery shop on the island of Montreal. As the wrong items came out of the machine, Jean-Pierre gave them to mothers with children, who were mostly reluctant to take anything from him until I beamed my encouragement. Eventually the staff began to root for us. And we all cheered when our mission was accomplished.

I offered to host their reception in my dining room. Maureen's dream day included party sandwiches with the crusts cut off. No one set a date. It wasn't necessary—the idea of a wedding in the future was more than enough to satisfy Maureen's dream of a walk down the aisle in a satin dress with daisies in her hair.

One pre-dawn November morning Jean-Pierre was unable to wake Maureen for their usual cigarette in the bathroom. He called me at five a.m., crying; he told me he needed help to wake her up. He didn't realize she had died from a heart attack. Her medications and her addiction to cigarettes had made her extremely vulnerable to heart disease, and the earnest simplicity of his love had kept him ignorant.

I called the police, who called the coroner. The coroner needed proof of who she was, but Jean-Pierre was incapable and neither staff member on duty would go into Maureen's room and sift through her things to find some ID. I knew she didn't have a health card or a social insurance card, a birth certificate or a driver's licence, but I had seen her powder-blue faux-leather wallet many times and knew it held two plastic gift cards for Tim Hortons, an STM Transport Adapté card with her name on it, and a burgundy ID card from a local hospital.

I went in. Maureen lay peacefully on her side, her mouth open, dentures in a pink plastic holder a foot away on the bedside table. I ran my finger down her cheek, which was still soft. Her hair! She had asked me to dye it, and I'd done so on the Friday night nine days before she died, in the common area of the group home. *The Price Is Right* was playing on the TV while I used my blow-dryer to style her hair. Maureen laughed and pointed to the TV, but no one else except me caught the joke about how my price was right for her new hairdo.

I remember how Maureen stood in front of the bathroom mirror later to appreciate her new look. Styled hair is a luxury beyond the reach of people like Maureen. She once told me she had used paper towels from McDonald's to deal with her period, because she couldn't afford the cost of pads or tampons.

When I saw her on the morning of her death, I realized that she had not washed her hair since the blow-dry. It was still smooth and sleek as it lay on the pillow. I was so sad for her, but I knew she hadn't been afraid to die. We had recently gone to mass at St. Patrick's Basilica, where she wanted her funeral to be held, she told me, and then coughed so hard she almost fell over. As I looked at her lying so peacefully on her queen-size bed, I wondered if she had known where she was going and who she would be meeting next.

Jean-Pierre mourned her loss for several months, but he finally adjusted, aided by his low cognitive function. If Jean-Pierre had been the first to die, Maureen would have suffered greatly. He had been a healing salve for the damage she'd suffered in life.

To love and be loved is an irreducible need. Without it we ache, we hurt others, we fall ill. Loving another person means we belong.

## 14

# The Cold, Clean Water
# of an Irish Spring

AFTER BEING RELEASED FROM OTTAWA GENERAL IN 1997, with a referral to the Royal Ottawa pending, Caroline returned to Oscar. He told her how much he had missed her, which was music to Caroline's ears. She convinced him that she would never fall ill again. If Oscar had been more astute about mental illness, he would have realized that Caroline's certainty was something like insisting water wouldn't evaporate on a hot sidewalk. Still, he wanted to believe. He'd missed the woman who baked her famous Black Forest cake for the smallest of celebrations and left love notes under his pillow.

Oscar's sense of reality was probably blurred because he worked all day and drank all evening. Since in his experience Caroline had many "normal" days, it was likely hard for him to imagine that she was suffering from anything truly chronic or incurable. Or maybe he had a well of empathy that ran deep, allowing him to accept her numerous idiosyncrasies. Gilles had given up, but Oscar wouldn't. At least not yet. Oscar kept his motivations to himself, but he was still in the game.

And why wouldn't he be? Caroline still made him laugh. She cooked his favourite roast beef and smashed potatoes on Sunday evenings, just as Isabel had done for Arthur for five decades. On weekend afternoons they walked to Baskin-Robbins for ice cream sundaes, she in tawny moccasins and a hippy-dippy dress, he in an ironed button-down shirt, his pants cinched by a leather belt, never far from his military roots. Caroline reached for his hand as often as possible, and she didn't expect perfection of him. On a good day Oscar thought Caroline was the dearest person he'd ever met.

A year of relative calm passed, despite lots of nightly drinking. Though they rarely visited, Caroline's sons called her regularly, especially Kyle. She was mostly symptom-free, taking her drugs, keeping the voices she heard at a distance. One of her many social workers taught her that the voices were emanations from her mind that could be challenged, even sidelined, and that stress was the usual culprit that caused them to hiss the insidious messages that devoured her confidence and purpose. She tried to keep her life calm and level.

At the end of October 1998, Oscar announced he needed to go to Halifax on business the upcoming week. Around the same time, Caroline's sisters were organizing an event to mark Isabel's seventy-fifth birthday in early November, and they did not invite Caroline. After much discussion, taking into account Isabel's grave reservations about seeing her troubled daughter, the sisters had decided that a successful birthday party for Isabel was more important than Caroline's feelings. Although Rosalind explained their decision tactfully, Caroline was devastated. She couldn't take on board that she was in the penalty box for past behaviour and that she needed to earn her way out over time. She didn't even try to plead her case—to remind them that she was faithfully taking her medications and that there had been no incidents for a year. The rebuff stung as much as the time she'd been ostracized from her mother's sixtieth birthday dinner, after she'd revealed she was pregnant and unwed.

Nobody knew that the exclusion would drive Caroline to a sort of retaliation.


Caroline asked Oscar if she could travel with him to Nova Scotia. He felt sorry that she'd been excluded from the family celebration, and agreed to bring her along.

Before flying to Halifax, she flushed her medication, deciding that she needed to be "normal" when she accompanied Oscar on his business trip. She tried to rationalize that decision to me: "I did not want to feel heavy, exhausted, cloudy, mushy. I was walking with a heavy blanket over my head at all times. I could no longer sleepwalk through my life." The feeling of being over-drugged was causing her emotional pain, and sexual dysfunction. Her weight was creeping up and her blood sugar levels were precipitously high—all drug-related. Her clothes didn't fit. Her belly fat spilled over the front of her underwear. There was chafing between her thighs. She had the odd shooting pain near her knees from stress on her joints. But more than all that, normal people did not take drugs, so she would not take drugs. It made perfect sense to Caroline.

Perhaps alcoholics reason the same way when they fall off the wagon. The damaging behaviour is mistakenly seen as a solution to a bad situation. Or maybe psychotropic medicines that muffle your sensory experiences are too much for anyone to sustain over the long haul. Once again Caroline's need to be fully awake had overtaken her judgment, which had been weakened by her many psychotic episodes. Each bout of psychosis causes a little more damage to the brain, more loss of grey matter, although drug critics are quick to say that antipsychotics may be the reason for the brain shrinkage, rather than the psychotic episodes. No one knows.

For whatever reason, Caroline said, "Enough." She viewed the trip as an opportunity to spend three sensual days with Oscar in a hotel—a re-enactment of their romantic Florida sojourn. "I wanted my thoughts to flow like cold, clean water in an Irish spring," she says. "I wanted to be able to move freely, like a leaf in the wind." (She still wants that.)

Two days before the trip, Caroline phoned Peggy. "Dad is not dead," she told her sister. "After his death he descended to become a botanical garden. He is once again earthbound, with things to take care of before his final crossing. He needed to be seen as a thing of God's beauty. He needed peace. He never had that." Given that Caroline had given them all a year of much-needed calm in which her sisters had been able to relax and get on with their own lives, Peggy listened with only half an ear, assuming Caroline was in one of her philosophical moods. Caroline's words were positive, so no red flags went up; to Peggy, Caroline's psychotic breaks meant unleashed vitriol. This was far from that, especially given that Caroline ended the call with "I love you, Peggy."

For another twenty-four hours Caroline felt the usual galactic euphoria she always experiences when she first stops taking her meds. And no sleep whatsoever. "That was the best decision I ever made," Caroline told me. She flew with Oscar to Halifax, fizzing with anticipation, freed from numbness. The hotel room was small but clean, and after they checked in, Oscar wanted to jump under the covers with her and she wanted that too. Mission accomplished.

The bubbles began to pop on day two, as her wakefulness gave way to anxiety and fear. On day three the full unravelling took place, against a cityscape that was raw with the first blast of winter. When Caroline looked out the window, she saw that clouds had rolled in off the ocean to coat the maritime city in fog, mirroring her mood.

Caroline began talking a mile a minute to Oscar. She became suspicious of the hotel staff and told Oscar they were plotting against the guests. She claimed that poisonous fumes were escaping from the hot-water faucet in the bathtub and that the air vent was spewing carbon monoxide. She angrily complained to the hotel manager over the phone. He sent maintenance, who found nothing amiss.

In a matter of hours, Caroline went from being Oscar's amiable little partner to a liability. His sympathy dissolved completely when Caroline banished housekeeping because she thought the bathroom was a chamber of death. He had another day of the conference to get through and he couldn't do it with Caroline in that condition. He snapped, throwing her clothes into a suitcase, dumping her at the airport, and telling her she had to fly home alone. It was an impossible challenge, given her disorganized mental state, but Oscar was overcome by impatient rage and not thinking straight himself. Somehow Caroline managed to change her ticket. But by the time she stepped on the plane, she was so agitated that the two female flight attendants saw an unruly, intoxicated problem instead of a passenger in a heightened state of mania and psychosis. She was escorted off the plane.

Completely freaked out, with nothing to do and nowhere to go, she found the airport bar and drank until she was obliterated. The RCMP were called. Caroline was rude, and when the officer grabbed her wrist, she became unhinged, shouting every profanity that had ever touched her ear. "Get your hands off me, you fucking pervert! You touch me again and I'll scratch your eyes out!" She was arrested, charged with being drunk and disorderly, and jailed downtown to await an arraignment.

On that same night, the rest of the Evans family gathered to celebrate Isabel's birthday with a cake and candles and many poignant toasts. Isabel revelled in the loving attention of her adult children and extended family. There were fifteen assembled, some of whom had travelled from the west coast to mark the occasion. Someone recalled that Caroline had announced her unwed maternal status at the last gathering they'd had to celebrate Isabel's birthday. They felt they could safely laugh about it, assuming that Caroline was in Halifax with Oscar.

Then the phone rang and Rosalind picked up. It was a Halifax police officer, calling for Isabel at Caroline's request. Aghast to hear what had happened, Rosalind explained her sister's long history of mental illness to the officer.

"We will put her on another plane," he said. "I'm sorry to be the bearer of such unfortunate news. Don't worry, we will get your sister home." The officer's swift offer of support is something Rosalind won't forget, and it still brings tears to her eyes. It was a rare kindness from a person in authority, laced with empathy and understanding.

The next morning, two young officers drove Caroline from the overnight lockup to the airport, a long way from the city centre. Humour was her crutch, and she managed to put them at ease with a self-deprecating story of why she'd been in the bar—too much at ease. She asked to use the bathroom inside the terminal, and when they let her go by herself, Caroline disappeared. The two men didn't know about the "flee factor" when it comes to people in the angry grip of psychosis. Full of chagrin, the officers called Rosalind to report that Caroline was missing.

She resurfaced in downtown Halifax, thirty-six kilometres from the airport, despite having no cash. She still does not remember how she did it; it's possible she boarded a free shuttle bound for the downtown hotels. Her suitcase was on its way to Ottawa, and she had nothing but the clothes on her back and her purse.

On Sunday morning, two officers in a patrol car spotted a naked woman walking along Kent Street in the business district of Halifax. Her lips and limbs were blue from the cold November breeze off the

Atlantic Ocean; her long blond hair whipped her face. Caroline was bone tired and red-eyed from her night on the street, a night her sisters still don't like to imagine.

Caroline's aunt had also walked naked down a busy Toronto thoroughfare in 1947, her mind brimming with self-recrimination, incapable of dealing with the trauma of being pregnant, unwed, and Catholic. Dr. Ridha Joober, director of the Prevention and Early Intervention Program for Psychosis (PEPP) clinic at the Douglas, says that when people in the grip of psychosis can't get rid of their distress, they sometimes feel that the only release is to shed their layers of clothes. It's as much of an emotional shedding as it is a physical one.

Caroline, in a semi-catatonic state, was taken by the police to the emergency room of Victoria General Hospital. Worried about hypothermia, the staff warmed her with thick preheated blankets and subdued her with potent drugs. No one in the family called Oscar; they didn't know where the conference was being held or which hotel he had booked for the stay. And after Caroline had managed to tell them how he'd dumped her at the airport, they didn't feel he would be receptive to her plight. At Isabel's urging and expense, Rosalind and Sharon flew to Halifax to take their sister home, grateful for each other's company. On the flight there, they agreed between them to listen to Caroline without judgment. That way they might have better access to her state of mind, her delusions, her fears, and the provocations that had brought her to a hospital so far from home.

The sisters waited at the gate, radiating nervous energy. They had been told that Caroline would be monitored and checked through security under tight police escort. They imagined a prisoner returned from captivity. The same flight attendant who had ordered Caroline off the plane was on duty, remorseful and apologetic. "I'm so sorry. I didn't understand the magnitude of your sister's problems," she said to Rosalind. "My main concern was for the safety of the other passengers." The airline was paying for Caroline's flight home and offered to reimburse the sisters' fares, too, a gesture that added a touch of humanity to a humiliating situation.

The officers handed Caroline into the arms of her relatives, dressed in clothes from a welfare box—a shapeless sweater and pants, slip-on running shoes without laces. Caroline was so drugged as to be unsteady on her feet. She'd lost her purse, so she had no proof of who she was, but it was more than enough for the police and the airline that Sharon and Rosalind were there to vouch for her. Rosalind remembers thinking, *My sister is a homeless person.*

The officers were delighted to learn that Sharon was a nurse, and grateful that family members had come to the rescue—they spoke of similar incidents where no one had arrived to show support. The two officers even offered to accompany them back to Ottawa; after they were turned down, they stayed with the three sisters while waiting for the flight. Moments before they were to board, they led a stumbling Caroline outside so she could smoke a final cigarette, watching like hawks as Caroline took each inhalation. They weren't going to lose her again.

Just before they were to take off, the flight to Ottawa was cancelled because of an engine malfunction. Another airline offered to accommodate the passengers on a flight leaving shortly. With no time to lay groundwork with the new airline about what had happened with Caroline, the officers agreed to stay in the background until she was safely on the plane, so they wouldn't raise alarm bells with the other travellers. On board, slumped against the window, Caroline was heavy-eyed, sluggish, and had trouble speaking—worrisome details not overlooked by their flight attendant, who pressed her sisters for an explanation. When they were bringing Caroline home after a psychotic episode in Halifax, the inflight staff became terribly upset that they hadn't been informed of the situation before Caroline boarded the plane. "We would have insisted she fly with police escorts," one of them said.

Police officers, hand-picked for their experience with persons in crisis, met the plane in Ottawa. Rosalind recalls that the female lead officer was compassionate, knowledgeable, kind, and caring. After the uncomfortable interaction with the irate staff on the plane, it was a welcome relief to be greeted in a way that didn't cause more shame. The officers drove them to Ottawa General. Caroline cooperated, largely because she was in no condition to do otherwise.

That was the last of Oscar. When Sharon called him after he got home from the conference, she blasted him for being so irresponsible. How could he have abandoned Caroline when she was clearly psychotic? He'd seen her in the grip of her illness on other occasions, so why had he been so clueless as to what was going on? In his defence, Rosalind now realizes, Oscar had not fully grasped the speed with which Caroline's mood could deteriorate and a delusional state arise after she stopped taking the drugs. And she points out, too, that Oscar had given Caroline another stab at being normal—and as a consequence had also given the rest of the people who loved her a much-needed space in which they could get on with their own lives.

For her part, Caroline had provided a home for a divorced, alcoholic older man. Oscar had made room for a woman with a fragile mind that was subject to periodic invasion. For a time, each had been able to see past the inadequacies of the other. Caroline adored him unconditionally, as was her inclination. I wasn't able to talk with Oscar, as he has passed away, but Rosalind thinks he behaved the way he did in Halifax because he didn't really believe Caroline had schizophrenia. He thought she had too many good days to be "crazy," which, like many others, he viewed as a permanent condition. Like Isabel, he may have felt that Caroline was being histrionic, emotional, and attention-seeking. For a time he'd made space for those eccentricities because of her limitless capacity for love, but he wasn't ready for full-on schizophrenia.

Caroline said to Peggy later, "When you are a prisoner of your mind and your body, a solid relationship to another human being becomes a pipe dream. Without Oscar backing me up, I lost all my bearings." To me she says, "He wasn't mine. I had to let him go. My illness was too much for him. Oscar was wonderful until he wasn't."

# Georgie

Georgie called me at seven p.m. on a Friday, asking if could I bring him shoelaces. My first thought was that he wanted to hang himself. For two weeks he had been missing from his rooming house in Longueuil, Quebec, his room an eight-foot-square space with a single bed, a sink, a dismantled stove, and a low-wattage light bulb that dangled from a ceiling of water-stained tiles. Still, I was relieved to know he was alive. His depression had resurfaced weeks earlier, something that has plagued him along with schizophrenia.

"I'm on Burgess," he said, barely audibly. Burgess is the psychiatric emergency wing at the Douglas Institute. "More than anything, I need a cigarette." Over the years I have bought many items for the people I volunteer with: coffee, groceries, clothing, boots, stationery, greeting cards, Tampax, chocolate bunnies, penny loafers, snow pants, belts, CDs. I have never bought anyone cigarettes, though I have given them money, which I guess is the same thing. I had the idea that if I bought them cigarettes I would be actively participating in their decline, even though I have seen the comfort that cigarettes bring them. I have not yet met a person with schizophrenia who has managed to quit smoking.

I got the shoelaces and headed for the hospital.

"I'm here to see Georgie Paperman," I told the security guard on duty. From my purse he removed my car keys, a short golf pencil, iPhone ear buds and a small silver nail file—weapons for stabbing and strangulation. He held the shoelaces up to the light for a few seconds, as though determining the hidden power of black cotton. Then he set them on the little pile of dangerous items.

The guard unlocked the elevator, waved his blessing. He had a resigned look about him, as though he had seen too much. Over time, bearing witness to repeat hospitalizations can become overwhelming and sad, even for staff who are a few steps away from first-line care. A silver crucifix half-hidden in his chest hair caught the light as the elevator doors shut.

I found Georgie slumped in a blue plastic chair in the waiting room by the glassed-in nursing station. He was as thin as a garden hose. Years earlier, he'd decided that if he ate a tablespoon of powdered laundry soap every day it would counter his substantial weight gain from antipsychotics. It worked—or something had. Then that dose of soap became his personal form of chemotherapy, a protection against parasites, cancer cells and Ebola. His voices tell him he is particularly susceptible to Ebola. He says he's cured himself of an Ebola infection three times. His teeth have been equally affected by his antipsychotics. He once told me he had ten teeth, but then he passed his tongue over his greying gums and corrected himself. Nine. Certain foods, such as meat and apples and crunchy salads, have become unmanageable.

When he saw me, he stood up and tried to smile, then beckoned me to his room, a curtained area he shared with one other patient. Tilting his head towards his rumpled bedding, he whispered that he was safe-guarding five million dollars that had come from Syria. I knew right away he had gone off his medication, even though his drugs are administered by the caretaker of his rooming house, which has ninety residents—mostly the disenfranchised, either poor or mentally ill or both. When I asked if he had quit the meds, he said no. I wasn't convinced.

The tongues of his battered Converse running shoes lollygagged to the sides. "Did you bring me the laces?" I shook my head. "Confiscated?" I nodded. He scanned the mottled linoleum as he let out a resigned sigh and then said, "It's for my own safety." I noticed the bits of tinfoil collected from cigarette packages crumpled into his ears to block messages from the CIA. Months earlier, he'd confided in a whisper that an android from an international spy organization had placed an implant in his brain. He didn't want surgery to have the implant removed, because more things could be inserted in his brain when his skull was open. But he wanted the voices to stop.

One hand was jammed into the pocket of filthy white jeans that rode so low on his tiny hips they exposed his backside. From the rear he could pass for a prepubescent boy, and it's impossible to imagine that he once had weight issues. "My belt was taken too," he apologized when he noticed me noticing. With the other hand he pointed to his newest possession, a Panasonic radio he'd found in the recycling bin behind the rooming house, placed there by God, he said. He was carrying it with him when he went to Emergency.

"Does it work?"

"Yes," he said. Furthermore, the singers on the FM channels sent him cautionary personal messages through their lyrics. Balled-up scraps of those warnings formed a doorknob of crumpled paper in a back pocket.

Georgie once told me he had done something terrible when he was young. It's hard to imagine this gentle waif of a man committing a crime so heinous it created an ocean of distance between his old life and his current life. But his mind clamour is a reminder of those awful days, voices that impersonate people in his life so accurately that it becomes impossible for him to differentiate between the real person and the version in his head. "There are six voices," he told me. "They suggest ways for me to kill myself. I was seventeen when I first began to hear voices. The person was very quiet and used the 'you' voice. *You are going to lose your job. You are going to fail math, and Mr. Framingham is going to give you the strap.* I was smelling disgusting things, and when I looked for that smell, I couldn't find it. I would smell dog shit and vomit and the sick horses in Old Montreal. I smelled rot. I was smelling myself. I was putrid." Georgie said that back then he had checked himself into the emergency department at a psychiatric hospital. There are two conditions for immediate admittance: posing harm to self or harm to others. I decided not to ask more about what had happened. He had lived a long time with suicidal and homicidal thoughts, and more important than my excavating his past was being a friend to him.

Georgie is highly intelligent, up on current events, and reads ancient history; he knows and can discuss literary devices and can draw accurate outlines of small countries with a pencil. His best two traits? His humility and his deep sensitivity. He is grateful for every gift, every word or kind gesture that comes his way. Unlike many others, whose emotions are completely blunted by drugs, I have seen him cry several times. He told me he's lucky to have that outlet.

That night on the ward, he thanked me again for coming, Then he said, "Janet left me; she took all her things. And I put my hands on her neck—loosely. Very loosely. She screamed at me that I should go back in."

"Do you miss her already?" I asked. He and Janet had been on again and off again for more than a decade, two struggling people looking for love. He nodded, tears slipping down his cheeks. He and

Janet both lived in the rooming house, sometimes together but more often not. All he wanted was the simplest of things: a relationship with Janet, work, a modest income.

His eyes, as grey as a neutral country, often gaze off into the distance. Being on the medication, he explained, "is like being half-awake in your life." It's a form of blunting that strips away motivation, reduces libido, and increases cognitive impairment. He takes olanzapine and Haldol and another drug, Seconal, in order to sleep at night. He cherishes the memory of what it was like when he didn't take medication. The nurses have told him over and over that adherence is the only way to keep his symptoms at bay. But, just as Caroline does, he finds the idea of feeling and being "normal" too seductive. The answer lies in finding the lowest dose possible that permits the highest degree of function. For many, that perfect level is elusive.

He got deeper into the tension with Janet. "She traded my leather jacket for three five-dollar bags of marijuana. I've had that coat since high school." He kicked the bed a few times. The poor trade stuff to get whatever will make them feel better. The market for stolen goods on psychiatric wards and in group homes is brisk, although there are limits: few will exchange snow boots for street drugs in January. For the most part, in cities with plunging mercury, winter clothing is out of bounds.

For a while I honed my donations to make sure there was less of a chance they would be traded away, but after a time I stopped thinking that way. Who am I to judge when I can easily afford my own pleasures— a glass of wine, Lindt chocolates, a gym membership.

Georgie lay on the bed and pulled his knees up to his chest. He told me he and Janet had broken up three weeks ago, maybe four—he'd lost track of time. He hadn't meant to hurt her. "I had sex with Andrea," he confessed. "I told Janet just to get even."

He's told me more than once that he uses sex as a way to feel alive.

It's not an addiction, he insists. The physical response is not unlike the hit from nicotine, increasing dopamine in the brain. "Okay, maybe I'm a sex addict. I told Janet about Andrea *after* she sold my jacket. She's gonna scratch Andrea's eyes out of their sockets."

"Would you like me to find you another leather jacket?"

He nodded. Except that it's never about the jacket. It's about unshakeable loneliness, the sickening feeling that something important has been lost and may never come back.

"I'll be released tomorrow," he said. Georgie does not have a psychiatrist or team that follows him on a regular basis, but he readily admits that's because he does not have the discipline to maintain that continuity of treatment. He shows up for help only when he's in a crisis.

As I went back down the elevator that night and picked up my confiscated items, I wondered when Georgie would return to the hospital.

## 15

# A Disposable Paper Cup

AFTER THE HALIFAX DEBACLE, SHARON FILED THE
paperwork to declare Caroline incompetent. Without such an order,
she could be held against her will for only seventy-two hours. Her sisters were not going to take any more chances. Sharon was so worried
that Caroline's psychosis would prevent her from accepting the benefits
of hospital care, or that the hospital wouldn't think she was sick enough
to keep her, she admits she even contemplated exaggerating her sister's
behaviour, adding more terrifying details. It was far from necessary.

Sharon and Caroline's psychiatrist accompanied Caroline to a hearing at the hospital where the facts were put before a review board. A
committee that included a lawyer, a psychiatrist, and a layperson listened to Caroline's case and agreed to sign the order, which meant that,
at last, the Evans family could participate in all decisions related to her
care and that Caroline was no longer able to make unilateral decisions
about her life. Caroline became frantic, undone by what she viewed as
treachery. Sharon bore the brunt of Caroline's verbal outrage, a searing,
hurtful public accusation of betrayal that was difficult not to take personally. Sharon has perspective, but she concedes that the day of the
hearing was among her toughest in the long trajectory of her sister's

illness. She also admits that she has not been able to forget the cruelty of her sister's words. She has forgiven but not forgotten.

Caroline's brain had become a blender that mangled delusional ideas with partial truths and fragments of memory into a soupy slosh of ideas. "John Glassmeyer was a leper but he was cured," she told a nurse on the ward. John was a high school classmate, orphaned when his parents were killed in a tragic accident. "Donna's father is Ben-Hur. She must be sad that he lives in Hollywood." The father in question did have an uncanny likeness to the actor Charlton Heston. Then there were the total fabrications: "The Oklahoma bomber was sexually abused by unhappy employees from Walmart." She made, and still makes, such assertions with utter conviction. And they are not lies: delusional thinking erases the idea of lying, replacing it with unbelievable truths.

Caroline was once again afraid to shower, and despite heavy medication she was still exhibiting delusions, hallucinations, and racing thoughts. "I am so sick. I am full of cancer. This morning the nurses wheeled my bed to the grassy common area outside the cafeteria. I removed my clothes and lay on the ground. When I was nude, the ayatollah of Iran came and removed my cancer. I was in the Garden of Eden. If I had not been so thoroughly cured of cancer I was going to end my life." Caroline rarely spoke openly about suicide, although she may have been thinking about it during her many depressive episodes.

Peggy remembers that day. Caroline actually had danced naked on the grass in full view of those having a meal in the hospital cafeteria. "In years past I would have been mortified about a situation like that," she says, "but I think I became desensitized over time. And I always had Rosalind to talk to. We could commiserate together. We could even laugh about it. We reassured each other that it was just the illness. It's never just the patient drawn into the madness. Believe me, it was all of us."

What concerned the sisters, and Caroline too, was that she was still delusional despite the drugs. Emerging longitudinal studies indicate that antipsychotic medications do not eliminate or reduce the frequency of psychosis in schizophrenia in all people, yet they are the cornerstones of short- and long-term care. A subset of patients relapse, despite full adherence to their antipsychotic drugs, a phenomenon called "psychosis breakthrough." Perhaps when that same subset, which includes Caroline, does not see an improvement in their life, the temptation to flush the medication down the toilet becomes irresistible.

Dr. David Bloom says, "Often it's necessary to try different types of medication. Switching medications several times causes the consumer, and their family members, to lose faith in the drug therapies, but when the right diagnosis is finally matched with the correct medicine, a leap forward towards recovery can occur. It would be wonderful if mental and physical disease could be prevented by caring relationships, but we're not there yet. Love and humanity alone will not do the job." Bloom suggests that a better life starts with accepting what's happening without embarrassment and fear, with accepting the symptoms of mental illness. People suffering from other debilitating illnesses, such as diabetes or cystic fibrosis, seek help without a second thought. The shame and lack of understanding of psychosis complicates the act of reaching out for aid.

Without a doubt, medication reduced Caroline's acute distress. But with this hospitalization, she had ever more trouble orienting herself and swung from delusion and paranoia to apathy. Her feelings were subdued, yes, but struggling for air rather than extinguished. "When I'm fuzzy, the voices don't go away, but they seem less scary. When it's bad, it's like I'm having a nightmare but my eyes are wide open and I can't close them. Some days are so terrible to face I welcome the chance to disappear. Please, please, give me more medication."

Most, if not all, of Caroline's breakdowns were driven by a crushing disappointment, the loss of someone dear, or feeling severed from her sons. A breakdown is a response, a crucial bid to signal that something is going desperately wrong and to reclaim emotional health. A crisis reveals the mind's need to fix something that has been damaged. Psychosis is a sign of that need for repair, just as a fractured bone can be a signal of insufficient calcium. Without a psychotic break, there is no indication of the problem, and so no opportunity to address the issue. But when the breakdown is treated only with medication, the person suffering has no chance to dig into what's going wrong.

It's hard to know if Caroline's crash in Halifax was prompted by her sudden drug withdrawal or a resurgence of schizophrenia. Those kinds of distinctions have yet to be determined by science. When powerful drugs are used to influence brain chemistry, a sudden withdrawal from them will cause the brain to attempt to readjust. Antipsychotics are, true to their name, drugs that suppress psychosis. Whenever Caroline withdrew from her powerful drugs, she plunged back into severe psychosis in short order, but perhaps the drug was the actual spur. The majority of doctors and scientists believe that both the resurgence of schizophrenia after drug withdrawal and the drugs' side effects are the price tag for management.

Scientists have assumed that schizophrenia is a neurodegenerative condition in which brain volume loss is associated with the pathophysiology of the condition. Past research hypothesized that antipsychotics act as a neuroprotective agent, slowing neurodegeneration among men and women with schizophrenia. A long-held claim is that schizophrenia is progressive and that the eventual cognitive declines are due to advancement of the illness. But more and more professionals are wading into the conversation with the idea that some people might recover without medications. The reality is that medication simply does not work for some patients, and that non-adherence to these heavy drug regimens is a worldwide dilemma.

Two weeks into Caroline's stay she had yet to be stabilized. She told Rosalind and Peggy, "The nurses lifted me off the grass and placed me back in my wheelchair. My father put a bouquet of flowers in my hands. I was healed. Pop has finally transcended this life and works from a heavenly garden filled with roses and daffodils and delphiniums. My mother will be reincarnated as Evelyn. It will be good to see her again, as I haven't been with my family for thirty-two years." The sisters had no idea who Evelyn was.

It was months before Caroline achieved stability. When her release was finally at hand, her social worker and a member of Salus sought to find a new housing situation, since even Caroline understood there was no way she could go back to Oscar's. She called him, though, and they exchanged teary goodbyes. Rosalind thought it best that she collect Caroline's things from his townhouse. They had secured a bed at provincially run Watford House, Caroline's first group home. She was willing to go there—relieved, in fact, especially because once she was out, she could see her boys again; she never wanted them to see her when she was on a locked ward—somewhat ironic given that her own mother's absence on the unit caused her such emotional distress. She was starved for their physical presence and to be reassured that they hadn't been permanently damaged by the latest upheaval.

As ever, thinking about the boys helped her focus on wellness, but it also exacerbated her fear of being overly drugged for their visits. She was afraid that her lethargy would dwarf her ability to demonstrate her love to her sons. "Being over-medicated makes me feel expendable, like a Tim Hortons paper cup. I think about the day when my boys will throw me out. My heart constricts."

For a monthly fee that her family paid from Caroline's disability allowance and inheritance income, she had a bed, meals, laundry, and other people to talk to. Activity, sports, card playing, and walking were encouraged. It was as if she had roommates, except the people weren't chosen, and all of them were also maladjusted in some way or another. No matter. It was far better to live in a supervised environment than a hospital. Caroline was more than cooperative.

Rosalind recalls with poignancy that, with this move, her sister no longer needed her furniture. Sofas, the rocking chair she'd used for breastfeeding, kitchen stools, sewing basket, china platters, silverware, bed linens, toys, curtains—all her things to make a home were given away. The few items she kept were packed into two small trunks. Those two trunks, one brown and one blue, represented the sum total of Caroline's losses so far.

For Rosalind, the sight of the trunks was visceral. Caroline would never return to the starting line. She would never wear cashmere sweaters or designer shoes, or throw a dinner party in a home where paintings graced the walls and music played from an invisible sound system. The hardest part was the surrender of long-held dreams, dreams that were once viable. But Caroline's salvation now lay in her ability to see life as it was, not what it could have been.

For a time Caroline fought the good fight, monitored by Salus. She was subsidized to take swim classes at the local YMCA. "I was so happy to be swimming again," she says. "It helped me believe in myself. And when I believe in myself, the spaghetti doesn't fall off the plate. It's about getting the tilt right." She made two new friends and happily shared her cigarettes, her bus tickets, her pocket money, her sense of humour. Weeks turned into months.

But it began to wear on her that the managers of the group home would not permit Matthew and Kyle to sleep over. Eventually she began to slip out at night to find solace in bars nearby, downing inexpensive drinks that helped numb her disappointment and deadened her sense of being alone in the world. Caroline was soon back to drinking heavily, running up bar tabs and mixing alcohol with her antipsychotic medications. Yet since she showed up at mealtimes and was in bed before the front door was locked, she managed to fly under the watchful radar of her caregivers.

Somewhere during this stretch, Caroline met a long-haul truck driver. Their dates, Caroline told me, took place in the cab of his big rig as he made deliveries to Canadian and U.S. cities. He taught her a new language—the citizens' band system of communication from driver to driver about the locations of fuelling stations, speed traps, and weigh stations. Her CB radio handle became "Blue Beaver"—for the cornflower colour of her eyes, she said, but also likely for something a little more vulgar. It was exciting, she said, to be travelling and seeing Canada, especially the Maritimes, from the safety of a vintage eighteen-wheel Peterbilt. He called her "bucket mouth" when she talked too much. Caroline loved every minute of the attention.

One week it ended, or he just stopped calling or Caroline was too needy or his wife caught him, if he had one—who knows what happened? Caroline may have told him her sister Rosalind was married to the prime minister, and she would have delivered the line with such certainty he might have believed her for a few seconds. When Caroline was delusional, she had conviction.

Then Caroline heard that Isabel, wishing to be closer to her daughters, had purchased a three-bedroom bungalow near Rosalind. Caroline was ecstatic; she asked if she could move in with her mother, presuming that they would both be less lonely and her sons could at last stay over. But Isabel could not hide the fact that she was afraid to be alone with Caroline, especially at night. Rosalind admits now that her mother was also mortified by Caroline's obesity and her poor personal hygiene, drinking habits, and cigarette stench. She said no.

Caroline took it hard, and the rejection set her off. She phoned Rosalind to say that her old flame the truck driver was reaching out to her telepathically; he had instructed her to meet him at a restaurant 250 kilometres from the airport of St. John's, Newfoundland. She had seen the name of the rendezvous village on the "TV screen of my mind." Rosalind was used to Caroline's fabrications and mangled semi-truths, so she didn't pay any attention. How many times had her sister planned to fly to California to rendezvous with Mel Gibson? Newfoundland was two thousand kilometres away, and Caroline was being monitored by a Salus team, had a good group-home setup, and was in regular phone contact with Matthew and Kyle.

But flying to Newfoundland to meet her old darling became a fixation. For two weeks after her mother told Caroline she could not move in, the manic calls to Peggy and Rosalind built up. (Isabel did not answer the phone.) When Peggy stopped by for a visit, she saw that Caroline had stopped showering and was wearing a shapeless black hand-knitted sweater, although she hated the color black. Over time, her sisters came to see that sweater as a benchmark of Caroline's moods. Exchanging the caramel corduroy jacket in favour of the sweater meant she had physically crossed over to the dark side. When the Salus team visited Caroline for her weekly checkup, she refused to let any of them into her bedroom.

It didn't register on Caroline when the truck driver cancelled his phone number so she couldn't reach him. Unlike her other dis-organized thoughts, which were malevolent and self-destructive, the idea of meeting him was happily exciting. It was also unstoppable—her soulmate was beckoning. Caroline booked a flight through a travel agency in a nearby shopping mall, using her debit card to pay for the ticket. The agency did not suspect that anything was amiss, even suggesting a few motels she could book for her stay.

When Caroline did not return for dinner or to sleep at the group home that night, they reached out to Rosalind who called Peggy and said, "Oh my God, I think she might be trying to get to Newfoundland." Rosalind struggled to recall as many details as possible. She knew that the trucker's first name was Russell. (Caroline had once taken him to meet her mother and sisters at Rosalind's house. Isabel had disliked him on sight, calling him "a dishevelled hulk of a man with frog-pond teeth.") She didn't know his last name or where he lived, or what trucking line he worked for. Peggy called Air Canada to see if Caroline could be located on an outbound flight originating in Ottawa, citing mental illness as a reason to breach passenger confidentiality. Yes, she was told, Caroline had flown to St. John's, Newfoundland, and the flight had already landed.

Peggy spent the day tracking Caroline's whereabouts via her automated-teller withdrawals. Peggy worked at a bank and, although she did not have clearance to view her sister's activity, she thought it was a breach for which she'd receive absolution, given the danger her sister was in. She saw that Caroline had used her debit card to withdraw cash at various ATMs, including three hundred dollars at a 7/11 convenience store in Ottawa. At that time, there was no limit on Caroline's withdrawals and she had thousands in the bank. Her ceiling was the amount the machine would dispense, which really worried Peggy.

Next she saw that Caroline had booked a motel room. From what Peggy could gather, it was close to the airport. She phoned the motel, but Caroline was not there.

From the motel, Caroline travelled more than 250 kilometres in a taxi. She'd given the driver the name of a remote place Russell had spoken about: Glovertown, a village one hour from Gander. She withdrew another wad of cash from a bank machine in Glovertown after the taxi driver left her there on Main Street. Caroline did not have a cellphone, so there was no way to contact her. Her sisters simply had to wait for the inevitable wreck.

After the cab dropped her off and she'd withdrawn more cash, Caroline walked into a restaurant bar on Main Street and ordered a rum and Coke. Animated and full of expectation, she befriended the bartender, who happily listened to her tale about why she was in Newfoundland and the man who was about to join her.

Peggy called the motel a second time and spoke to the manager. She explained, "My sister is unwell. She's delusional and hears voices." The manager was supportive but said there was nothing he could do, given that Caroline had not yet returned. Then, to Peggy's enormous relief, Caroline used her debit card to pay for several drinks at the bar in Glovertown. Peggy called the restaurant and explained the situation. The bartender summoned Caroline to the phone. Peggy tried her best, but it was the sympathetic bartender who ultimately persuaded Caroline to take the 250-kilometre cab ride back to the airport in St. John's. His attitude and care helped Caroline retain her dignity in a situation that could have devolved into panic and police officers. She was devastated, humiliated, angry—and intoxicated—but as a result of the barman's kindness she was able to muster up the will to leave.

Caroline flew home on her return ticket without any assistance. Obtaining more cash from an ATM when she landed, she took a taxi to her group home. Then Rosalind called the police to take her back to the hospital. Caroline complied, but in the back of the patrol car she was weepy, confused, and dejected about being stood up. The situation was as real to her as if she had been left at the altar like Camilla in her Goodwill gown. She crawled into a dark tunnel of rejection where no one could see her, and where she couldn't see herself either.

# Andrew

Antonio Moretti is a lifelong friend of a high school classmate of mine. Through my friend I had heard many stories of Antonio's exceptional son: his academic brilliance, his great marriage, how beloved he was as an English teacher. But then I began to hear different kinds of stories. His divorce. How he lost his job. His disconnection from his immediate family.

Antonio is a successful defence lawyer and litigator. His wife, Poppy, is a busy realtor in the Oakville, Ontario, area. They have two sons, Andrew—the one I'd heard so much about—and Brendan. Andrew embraced academics, attended Western University and the University of Toronto, gained a master's degree, and planned to ascend from teacher to professor of literature. Brendan, a high school athlete, had been more of a worry for his parents, who believed he lacked direction. But it was Andrew, not Brendan, who threw a television over the balcony of the Robarts Library at the University of Toronto, where he held a part-time job. And it was Andrew, in the highly stressful end-of-year exam period just before the TV incident, who accused a professor of wrongdoing. His father had believed him without reservation. If Andrew, whom his father trusted and respected, said a professor was persecuting him, Antonio would help him fight for justice. It was a chilly dawn when he realized his brilliant son's claims were unsubstantiated. And then Andrew threw the television.

With their connections, the Morettis were able to secure a speedy appointment with a psychiatrist at the Centre for Addiction and Mental Health (CAMH) in Toronto, a remarkable feat, given how difficult it can be to find professional help at the time of a crisis. More often there is a delay in which an emergency can escalate. The doctor gave Andrew olanzapine, a second-generation antipsychotic, to cope with his delusional thoughts, which had first focused on the wrongdoings of his professor but later expanded to include those of his mother, his uncle, and his brother. After several months of medication and ongoing appointments with a psychiatrist, Andrew's thinking at last changed, but he hated the fact that the drugs made him feel less creative, unable to write and think with clarity.

Antonio and Poppy insisted that he maintain the regimen of antipsychotic injections no matter how he felt. For a while Andrew listened to them and complied, even though his parents were often the targets of his delusion. Eventually, though, he became extremely angry about his diminished capacity, which led to more psychosis.

Antonio looks back on this period with regret. He and Poppy didn't know where to go or what to do or how to approach a brilliant son whose thoughts had become incomprehensible to them. They hung their hopes on the medication, and when Andrew refused that path, they lost him. Andrew began to see his parents as a locked door standing in the way of his happiness. "I wish I had sat with him in the early years and talked," Antonio says. "I wish I had been a better listener. Eventually I wanted him to be happy, nothing more."

But it was so hard to listen. Andrew's vitriol was frightening. They found it devastating when he ranted that Poppy had acted on a twisted incestuous lust for him, that she was the queen of the defilers. It was soul-crushing for Poppy to be the subject of her son's delusions. She was grief-stricken, and found it little consolation to be told that schizophrenia is an illness like hypertension or diabetes, treatable with prescribed medications. The truth was that Andrew preferred the illness to the cure. The gap between his delusions and his parents' hope for a return to normalcy became bigger and bigger.

"Each time he went off his medication it scared the shit out of me," Antonio says. "All I wanted was for him to get back on the drugs. But that was not what Andrew wanted. He saw us as the prime antagonists to leading life with the mind he was given. We were unspeakable rapists and pedophiles. How do you reconcile that? It was agony for my wife, so much harder for her because his attacks on her were so personal. In my line of legal work, I have seen much tragedy. It has helped me see that life goes on. Your son is lost to you, but you have another son who needs you too. You can't let it take you to the floor." Antonio has been better able to withstand the nonsensical insults. Poppy has an unmendable broken heart and deeply mourns the loss of her loving, caring son.

Andrew has never seen himself as someone with an illness. To him, his brain is different, not broken, rendering him lonely and greatly misunderstood. "I'm a misfit," he told me. "It's not easy to admit I'm not in the right human container." On some level, Andrew does not feel that his authentic self is good enough for his parents.

The last time his parents saw him was in 2017, when he had relapsed into psychosis. "The verbal abuse was terrible," his father says. "We said to ourselves, 'He's not coming back this time.'" Sadly, the illness has made Andrew a stranger, but the bigger tragedy is Andrew's disconnection from the love and support of family members. To his family he is a missing person.

Antonio and Poppy sought counselling in the early years of his illness, but with Andrew gone, they stopped going. Poppy has a circle of supportive friends. Andrew's doctor is in the wings, ready to help whenever Andrew is ready to step forth from the shadows. Is it like a death? I ask Antonio.

"No, it's worse, because at the back of your mind he's out there and you don't know where to find him, and when you do find him, you can't reach him. It's taken me a long time to make peace with all that has happened," Antonio says in his gentle, articulate manner.

Knowing that other families have suffered in similar ways is small comfort. The couple endure both guilt and shame over the fate of their son and can't help but feel they have failed him. Moving beyond such emotions is a Herculean step in the right direction for all families that have an affected son or daughter. Antonio and Poppy did not cause their son's illness, yet they, like every family, bear the burden of feeling judged.

The most puzzling, hurtful thing for the couple is that Andrew is lost only to his nearest and dearest: his ex-wife, his parents, and other family. After our first conversation, he began to call me periodically from his cellphone. We talk about books and authors and philosophy. His conversation is usually way over my head. He talks; I listen. There are times when I can't follow his logic, especially when suspicion and wariness are threaded through his theories—devious plots, government intervention. He feels deeply connected to Mother Nature, addressing her as "Divine M" when they are in conversation. Divine M, he says, told him that all global issues of climate change and disruption have been orchestrated as lessons for humans who refuse to respect the earth. In the same way that Andrea had Jasper Hollingsworth and Aleks had Jennifer Love Hewitt, Andrew has a deep love for M that seems to offset some of his loneliness. After he asked me to send him a book and I agreed, he gave me an address in Newfoundland. I sent it, but a month later it was returned to sender.

Although Andrew is unmedicated, he has made several personal choices that will continue to serve him well. He is devoted to exercise, runs, and has at times been a regular at the YMCA. He is a vegetarian and does not smoke cigarettes or take any drugs, prescription or illegal. Those clean lifestyle choices will keep him alive longer than other schizophrenics, who lose an average of twenty years of life expectancy to the impact of their drug regimens and the persistence of the illness. He has long stretches of intense intellectual curiosity during which he can dig deeply into the areas that interest him. But his delusions persist.

Though he has cut himself off from his family, Andrew told me, "In order to thrive, face-to-face socialization is a vital necessity to fight off depression and anxiety." He knows he needs connection. Antonio and Poppy retain a sliver of optimism that he is wrapped in the warmth of another human being. If not them, then someone.

For many conventional psychiatrists who say that recovery hinges on the patient's taking medication, Andrew is a kind of guinea pig. How long his symptoms will last is anybody's guess, as is the trajectory of his psychosis. Will his delusions peter out? Will he benefit in the long term from not having taken medications? Will he carry on oscillating between periods of wellness and psychosis, and be able to recognize the difference? Will he teach again? Only time will tell. He wishes to be accepted for the way he is.

He's not entirely negative about antipsychotics. At the onset of his delusions, he admits, the drugs helped him sleep. For some people, he says, "It keeps them from jumping off bridges." He acknowledges that a drug called quetiapine, taken occasionally, was acceptable. "It's the only drug that didn't steal my every function," he admits. "When you cannot connect to the world on a spiritual level, why bother? There have been times when I was psychotic and I conceded that robbery of myself, and I took the drugs."

It's been suggested that highly creative people and schizophrenics have a lower density of dopamine receptors, making them more prone to mood swings. With fewer receptors, it's possible that the brain does less filtering of information; therefore all ideas are good ones: the risky, the preposterous, the untried. Antonio said that Andrew used to write long essays expounding his theories about science and anthropology. He still writes, and some might consider his work groundbreaking, for his vast knowledge is keenly evident. A special kind of patience is required to sift through Andrew's originality to remove the delusional weeds that are choking the fruits of his imagination. I learn something exceptional every time I speak to him. I can't help but think of the mathematician John Nash, who won the Nobel Prize for the Economic Sciences in 1994, despite his lifelong battle with symptoms of schizophrenia.

Some medication resisters such as Andrew have been shown to recover from the symptoms of psychotic delusion. Many of these people assert that rejecting mainstream psychiatric treatment was their salvation. The terrible dilemma for Andrew's parents is how long they can wait to see if wellness will triumph over psychosis. Years or decades?

What does schizophrenia mean to you? I once asked Andrew. He took a long time to answer. From such a studied silence I expected something profound or nuanced or riddled with complexity. He eventually said simply, "I'm a searchlight for a friend." Alone and lonely, he craves to rejoin humanity, but as yet no one has seen his signal.

# 16

# Santa's Elf

IN 2000, CAROLINE WAS DISCHARGED AGAIN. THE SALUS team found her an apartment in a large multi-storey building on McLaren Street in Ottawa. The building housed a number of residents challenged by mental illness, as well as a mixed bag of lower- to middle-income folks. It was close to the Greyhound bus station, too, which meant her sons could come from Montreal and she could visit them. Matthew was sixteen and Kyle was thirteen.

On the ward, Caroline's weight had spiralled into dangerous territory, and Rosalind noticed that, for the first time ever, her sister had stopped making plans. Peggy remembers the day Caroline threw all her clothes over the balcony. They didn't fit, and she had nothing to dress up for.

That had been an exceptional burst of energy. Caroline had asked Rosalind for new pillows to replace the dirty, lumpy ones she had cried into one too many times. Six months after they were delivered, the pillows were still in their original package, inside a Sears bag on the floor beside her bed—seen but unobtainable because of the effort required to remove the plastic. Zyprexa, her current antipsychotic, managed the symptoms but also induced a form of defeat the sisters were reluctant to admit was both a curse and a blessing. Caroline's docility meant they could relax, although it was heartache to know that her spirit had drifted away.

The essence of Caroline—the energetic little elf whose eager eyes danced with glee—was lost. But that day so long ago, when the helicopter landed on the hospital grounds, was a touchpoint still. She told me, "I remember that day so clearly. I loved my costume and the little bells on my green felt shoes. It was the most exciting day of my life until my dad took me on the wards to hand out the presents. I saw bald, ghostly white children with tubes in their noses and down their throats. I wanted to cry, but how can you cry when Santa Claus is holding your hand? All I could think about that day, and for months and months afterwards, was death." Caroline's deep sensitivity had been already evident at age nine.

Her knees were a constant source of discomfort. Although her apartment was on the eleventh floor and she could use the elevator, it was agony even to walk on flat surfaces. It hurt to pull up her pants, to sit to pee, to make her bed. Green-furred food on the counter went untossed, bowls full of cigarette butts weren't emptied, exhaled smoke darkened the paint on the walls, and the apartment was permeated by the smell of decay. Her malaise grew so deep she spoke as if Matthew and Kyle were somewhere off at an unbridgeable distance. "I have no family in this country. I grew up in Poland where the first male scrotum was found. I was raped by Poles. It's why I'm so blond," she would mutter. When the Salus team advised her to spend more time with her sisters, she said, "How can I? I don't have any." It was her way of saying "I do not want to live."

When smoke began to billow along the hallway of one of the upper floors of Caroline's building, someone pulled the fire alarm and the elevators automatically shut down. The building had no sprinklers.

Residents knocked on doors, raced down stairwells, alerting everyone that the pulsing alarm was not a prank. Caroline had to walk down eleven flights as fast as she could, knees on fire, shaking from panic, and winded from years of smoking.

In the lobby, a shoeless older man hurried over to Caroline, held her by her quivering shoulders, then grasped her hands. "Are you okay?" he said. "You're shaking. Don't worry, it's just Wally Deakins. He fell asleep and burned his dinner again." He told her he lived in the building too. They went outside and waited on a bench near a bus shelter, smoking, while a small army of firemen extinguished a grease fire that had been made worse with water. Other firefighters canvassed the multitude of stairwells and searched for stragglers who might not have made it to safety. Ancient Mr. Deakins was encouraged into an ambulance to get treatment for smoke inhalation.

"I'm Simon," the shoeless man said.

"I'm Caroline."

When the firemen gave the all-clear, Caroline invited Simon to her apartment. He accepted, but first went to the beer store for a six-pack. Simon's kindness during the evacuation was enough to instigate a friendship, especially given that Caroline's affection was sparked by the smallest gestures of goodwill.

Rosalind and Peggy came to know Simon as a good-hearted, sometimes homeless wanderer who flitted among low-rent rooming houses—a speck of humanity who took up very little space. He soon became the June bug to Caroline's porch light. She paid for most everything. Peggy said, "In the beginning he probably glommed onto her for her money. It wouldn't have been the first or last time Caroline was taken for a ride." Caroline's mission in life was to share everything she had; helping others propped up her sense of worthiness.

Her apartment became a kind of refuge for lost souls—men and women in the building who wanted to sit around and smoke. Simon was emaciated, a dishevelled drunk with a bulbous, spider-veined nose. He was dirt poor because of his addictions to alcohol and cigarettes, which he paid for from his monthly welfare cheque. He drank whenever he had a dollar in his pocket and smoked as if it was sacred. He wore a thin gold chain with a Madonna medallion that he had pawned and redeemed three times. Caroline joked that the pawnshop owner was the only banker Simon had ever known. She soon grew to love the runty castaway, who seemed impervious to heat and cold, in the summers wearing a stained wife-beater undershirt and jean shorts that may have been Caroline's. In comparison to Simon, Caroline was pasteurized milk. In his company, above all, she could be herself.

Oscar had been invited to Evans family gatherings, and even the truck driver was asked to come to dinner once, but Simon never was. Like Caroline, he was the parent of two children, but somewhere along the road he had lost them or been disowned by them. Caroline's deep sympathy for Simon's failings came from her own experience of not being a "fit mother." Simon had slept over warm street vents and on benches in parks; he was a fixture in public places where he panhandled for money to buy cheap alcohol, a classic example of what happens when mental illness, addiction and poverty come together in a misshapen dirty ball. But he was cheeky and resourceful and managed to bolster her spirits, no small feat on some of her darker days. Where her sisters saw a shifty low-life, Caroline recognized a man familiar with mortal despair.

Simon did as much for Caroline as she did for him. Theirs was an unspoken camaraderie that transcended class, social standing, and education. They laughed together over shared beers in the local pub. "Sometimes when you are completely emptied out of all the things you think you need, you can be ready to receive," Caroline says. She became Simon's unconditional lifeline, and in return he shouldered the responsibility of her instability. He was a port in her storm, an ally, a trusted friend, an overnight kindred spirit.

# Milly and Hogan

One steamy August afternoon, Milly, Hogan, and I went for ice cream cones at the local Dairy Queen in LaSalle. It was a nice change from maple-glazed doughnuts and coffee with three teaspoons of sugar for Milly, four for Hogan. I had pangs about Hogan's choices—he was diabetic—but in my role as a volunteer, I had long ago made the decision not to police any of my friends. Hogan, like so many others who take antipsychotics, struggled with his weight and cholesterol and had high blood pressure; everyone he knew admonished him about his cravings for junk food, which he went to the gas station every day to buy. Hogan craved Coke and sweets and fatty, salty foods like potato chips and oversize bags of Cheezies that turned his hands orange. He did not crave salmon and arugula. He couldn't see the tips of his toes, even when he leaned over.

On this particular day, Milly's hair was standing straight up from her head, stiff and yellow, the colour of a box of Shreddies. Scars from a car accident gave her lumpy forehead a shiny, ethereal luminescence. She wore a vivid orange and turquoise quilted jacket suitable for January, its sleeves black to the armpit. She didn't feel the intense heat and humidity, a side effect of medication. Milly saved everything—cards and their envelopes, gifts of clothing, pens, matchbooks, the Sunday order of service from church, candy wrappers. It was a form of hoarding, and it came from a dark place of deep deprivation. She gratefully accumulated clothing even if it didn't fit, an attempt to fill a bottomless pit of need. We were regulars at Dollarama. For Milly, roaming the aisles was almost as good as buying stuff.

We left the Dairy Queen and both Milly and Hogan had one last cigarette beside my car before climbing in. Milly was in the front with me and Hogan squeezed into the back, his giant belly making it impossible to fasten the seatbelt. His feet were swollen from a combination of poor diet, high blood pressure, and the day's intense humidity. The only footwear he could manage to tug on were oversize black winter boots with silver buckles; at a quick glance they looked like ski boots. Since it was hot, he wore navy shorts and a giant T-shirt.

We were making a turn when the light changed from yellow to red. I heard the short blast of the police siren before I saw the cop car. I pulled over, rolled down all the windows, and waited for the officer to come to my side of the car. He peered inside. I told him that I had two psychiatric patients from the Douglas hospital with me and that I was taking them in for their injections. Milly and Hogan stared straight into his eyes with deadpan faces and didn't say boo. The cop scanned the car: Hogan in undersized shorts and oversized ski boots and Milly the "before" picture of a hair makeover, wearing a filthy neon winter coat in blasting summer heat. He stared at us for another few seconds and then, with a huge wave of his raised arm, he dismissed us, saying, "*Allez, allez! Dépêchez-vous!*" Go, go! Hurry up!

We laughed all the way back to the group home. Convulsive laughter. "That was rich," said Milly, guffawing and coughing at the same time. I often think back to that day. Even Milly would admit that the endorphin rush from laughing uncontrollably is equal to at least three cigarettes.

# 17

# Never Give Up

ROSALIND AND PEGGY SAW SIMON AS A PERMANENT DRAIN
on Caroline's bank account, but when he became a fixture in her dark
life, Rosalind asked him to call her from time to time to let her know
how Caroline was doing. He was more than happy to make those
calls, likely viewing them as quid pro quo for the generosity extended
to him by Caroline.

The first time he called with a heads-up, Rosalind was at work on
a snowy February mid-afternoon. He urged Rosalind to go to see
Caroline, saying, "I think you should come to the apartment *right now.*"
When Rosalind pressed him for details, he responded with an awk-
ward silence. He didn't seem capable of articulation, but she took him
seriously. She was glad her husband had insisted on putting snow tires
on their car; she could drive to the apartment on McLaren without
worrying about sliding off the country roads. She had enough to deal
with her mind tripping over possible calamities.

When Rosalind knocked, no one answered. She tried the knob and
the door was unlocked. When she let herself in, she saw blood smears
on the couches, the floor, and the kitchen chairs. Rosalind's heart
squeezed. Her first thought was that her sister had been attacked, or

even murdered. Her knees wobbled, and she steadied herself against the wall. Her next thought was that she might find a dead fetus. Weeks earlier, Caroline had told her about a sexual relationship she was having with a much younger homeless man whom she had brought into the apartment. Rosalind had met the younger man once. "He smelled homeless," she said.

The bloody mess was from neither a death nor a murder. Rosalind found her sister lying in bed, awake but unable to speak. The sight of her sister's bloody thighs told her that Caroline had had a heavy period, maybe even a miscarriage. It looked as though she had spent days naked without pads or tampons. Every part of the apartment where she had chosen to sit or lie was smeared with blood. Rosalind wondered if she was depressed, psychotic, or both. If she had lost a baby, her sister would be devastated.

Rosalind's heart thudded as she lifted Caroline into a sitting position. The bed was wet with blood. She worried that some irreparable damage had occurred in her sister's brain. Not a single tear fell from the corners of her red, sleep-deprived eyes. Her unshaven legs were streaked with dried blood. The smell was awful—blood awash with bacteria, the scent of not caring anymore. Rosalind did her best to coax Caroline into the shower. When she resisted, Rosalind half carried, half pushed her sister into the bathroom, tore aside the shower curtain, found the faucet. Caroline, as always when she was in such a state, was terrified of the water touching her body; she cried out that the shampoo would penetrate her skull and eat her brain. Rosalind soaped gently, trying to be mindful of her sister's fear as she herself fought dry-mouthed panic.

After wrapping Caroline in a bathrobe, Rosalind focused on the apartment. She could find no place clean enough for Caroline to sit other than the floor, so she led her sister to a suitable spot and Caroline collapsed. Rosalind tore the sheets off the bed, fighting an urge to retch from the odour of cigarettes, decayed food, sour body, and fishy blood. She boiled water, donned gloves, and Cloroxed her way back to a mindset that didn't threaten her own sanity.

Caroline was fortunate to have sisters who were prepared to do the dirty work. It's a mistaken idea that people from families with the financial resources to find placements in homes, to line up social workers and Salus teams, do not end up on the street. The hard truth is that even the wealthiest, most educated families lose their loved ones to chronic despair and places unknown. They, too, wonder whether a child is alive—the son who played Little League baseball, who owned a chemistry set and watched SpongeBob cartoons; the daughter who wrote plays and once performed in front of a live audience. Psychosis does not discriminate. The worldwide prevalence of schizophrenia is one percent, across all nationalities, professions, income brackets. Schizophrenia is not the domain of the needy, neglected poor, the marginalized lower classes, but its sufferers can quickly descend to rungs reserved for the downgraded.

It's unclear whether Caroline had stopped taking the medications this time. She swears to her sisters that she had been compliant. Dr. Joober told me that 40 to 60 percent of patients relapse even with adequate antidepressant and antipsychotic medication. He believes that when the first recognizable episode happens, the right response can change a patient's future. Was Caroline psychotic for an entire decade before she got help? With antipsychotic treatment, behaviour improves and the patient becomes more compliant. In the short term, everybody benefits. The question is whether or not, in the long term, everybody benefits except the patient. As Rosalind cleaned, restoring order to the apartment, she wondered whether Caroline's long trajectory could have been prevented. Lessened? Softened?

"I didn't have any pads," Caroline said a few hours later, actually smiling at her sister. (That she can swing from apathy to buoyancy and back to low spirits so quickly and completely still mystifies her entire coterie of caregivers.) And then she said, with tears in her eyes, pointing to herself, "Why would I waste *anything* on something this ugly?"

Rosalind felt drained, defeated, and unbearably sad. Her arms, back, and legs were cramping with fatigue. It was all such a struggle. And to what end? How long could she endure it? As she looked at her sister, a memory surged of countless terrible phone calls from times past: *You killed my son. I hate you. I don't have sisters.* Those calls now seemed tolerable compared to what she had just witnessed. She and her sisters knew that for Caroline, the accusatory phone calls offset the ache of spending too much time alone with hateful voices. This time she hadn't used her lifeline and reached out to her sisters; she had suffered in silence. That Caroline didn't believe they cared about her hurt Rosalind more than ten thousand cuts.

Despite her fatigue, she renewed her vow to her sister. *Never give up.* She called for takeout—chicken, Chinese, pizza—anything that didn't require effort. After it arrived, she made sure Caroline ate before she let herself out of the apartment. Her tired muscles would recover, after all, whereas the painful isolation in which Caroline nursed her wounds seemed to be a life sentence.

No one knows when Caroline's disorder began, but loss was at the core: loss of the support of her mother, her marriage, her career, her figure, Oscar, the ability to care for her boys, and now maybe a baby. As the list got longer, so did the depth of her anxieties and fears, which were invitations to the voices to pummel her with criticism. Fantastic psychotic delusions—Darren and Mel Gibson, Starsky and Hutch, her dad as a garden in the afterlife—were Caroline's escape hatch, the default that allowed her to not die from unworthiness. As early as her senior year in high school, her family had interpreted Caroline's untreated social anxiety and obsessional ideation as lies, not noticing the oncoming freight train of her fractured thinking, of depression, of marginalization. The body's reaction to insults, past and present, may be the key to understanding breakdown.

Caroline wanted to belong. She craved it. Belonging is primal, the opposite of loneliness. Caroline sought and received solace from people who didn't judge her—not the usual sort of people her moneyed family were used to, though once they understood Caroline's need it became easier for them to embrace her choices. The wounded recognize each other. Caroline's self-worth was so battered she was eager to tuck as many Simons as she could under her wing. Her moral compass insisted that she live as a person of value, of generosity.

That night, Rosalind walked to her car oblivious of her surroundings but grateful for the sting of cold air on her face. In that moment, she recognized, with great sorrow, that Caroline made the same mistakes again and again because she refused to be sidelined from life.

She sat in her car for a few minutes, wrestling with whether she should bring Caroline home or go back and spend the night in the apartment. Was Caroline okay alone? She didn't think she was, but she did not have the stamina to go back inside. Before she rolled out of the parking lot, Rosalind, her voice trembling, called the Salus team. They contacted the police and asked for two officers to pick up Caroline and take her to hospital. All Rosalind could think of was how to circumvent another Halifax moment, an Evergreen moment, a Newfoundland moment, another baby. Or something as yet unseen.

———

Simon had hovered in the shadows outside the apartment, chain-smoking, the entire time that Rosalind was inside. When he saw her leave, he rushed up to Caroline's apartment to offer assistance. It came in the form of a lit match to the end of her cigarette.

The police arrived quietly, no flashing lights. While the officers were preparing their written certification with Simon, Caroline slipped out of the apartment.

She took the first bus that came to a stop nearby, not caring where it would take her. She got off somewhere in downtown Ottawa. Once on the street, she stripped down to nothing, shedding her emotional baggage for the second time. Caroline walked naked from street lamp to street lamp, the scattered light illuminating her pale limbs. The police picked her up at ten pm. Shivering and crying in a near-fatal siege of self-recrimination, she was taken to Ottawa Civic Hospital. Rosalind arrived at Emergency to find her sister immobile on a stretcher in the hallway. She held her sister's hand to check her pulse, worried that she might actually be dead. She couldn't stop thinking that the black half-moons under Caroline's eyes represented the mental fatigue they all felt.

Caroline's case was considered acute. It took three days to secure a spot, even with a cherished referral, but she was at long last granted a bed at the Royal Ottawa Hospital (ROH), the facility dedicated solely to the care of the mentally unwell, especially the treatment-resistant mentally unwell. She went by ambulance.

"We are finally in the right hospital. Surely now we will get the help we need," Rosalind hoped. In such a place, assuredly her twisted mind would be seen not as a human failing but as a treatable illness. At a minimum, the same psychiatric team would begin to follow her consistently from then on. Rosalind, Peggy, and Sharon felt palpable relief that she had landed in a safe place, that she hadn't been lost to the streets. For the family, the presence of a specialized team represented a sort of laying on of hands, so desperate were they for the right kind of help.

Rosalind's own well-being, her marriage, and her parental responsibilities had suffered. Her children were teenagers now and needed more of her. Rushing off every time her sister was in crisis, she had also stretched the tolerance of her employer. The ROH was a lifeline they all grabbed on to, especially Rosalind, who needed to take a giant step back.

Caroline was numb. Lying in her bloodied bedsheets for days on end had signalled some kind of defeat. She had nothing left with which to fight her demons. Rosalind believed that, while Caroline did not speak of suicide, the way she had given up signalled a passive type of self-murder that would merely take longer.

February 2002 was the beginning of a long stay at the ROH. This time Caroline traded civilian clothing for a blue hospital gown, and she told her sisters she didn't want anything brought to the unit. Rosalind gathered a few things from the apartment anyway, and when Caroline saw her beloved corduroy jacket, she buried her face in it and began to wear it over her gown. She spent the first few weeks curled up in a haze. "I was as lifeless as a winter tree in a colouring book," she says.

Although she was unable to attend the celebration, the fact that her son Matthew had graduated from high school gave Caroline a moment of optimism—a small flower pushing its way up through a crack in cold cement. Kyle made her a Mother's Day card, which she kept on the ledge by her bed.

During her stay at the Royal Ottawa, Caroline began a regimen of long-acting drugs administered by injection by the staff. That protocol was used for people who consistently stopped taking their medications. Caroline's family was overjoyed. There were also regular mealtimes, regular baths, scheduled appointments with specialists. But most of the time Caroline had nothing to do except smoke—and eat.

Peter Selby, chief of addictions treatment at CAMH, says that psychiatric patients die decades earlier than the rest of the population, and that tobacco accounts for the majority of those deaths: "We're helping our patients get better mentally, but they're dying right in front of our eyes." With nothing to do and a brain that is on the fritz, eating and smoking are attempts to fill the void. Mental health professionals tolerate these behaviours, even though smoking and obesity accelerate the rates of cancer, heart disease, and respiratory diseases among their patients. One-third of all cigarettes are smoked by adults with mental illness, yet they make up less than one-fifth of the population. (There has been a slow evolution in which smoking is no longer tolerated in an ever-increasing number of hospital facilities, but it is still rampant in group homes.)

The highlight of Caroline's day at the ROH was the cigarette break. That changed when, on one break, Hilary Sanderson accused her of stealing a white-ribbed sweater with a large cowl neck from her drawer. Enraged at being called a thief, Caroline pinned Hilary against the wall. She had never been known to steal; if anything, she gave things away. The skirmish was defused by Hilary's social worker, a young woman whom Caroline trusted.

So it was a surprise when the two women became friends, each of them a tangled mess of psychiatric labels—depression, schizophrenia, bipolarity, anxiety, schizoid-affective disorder. Real connection was rare on the unit, but Caroline transferred all her desires for a life mate to Hilary, who unfurled under the affection like a morning glory. As the bond lasted a week, then two, three, and eight, the staff and other patients on the floor began to view it as something special.

Caroline's natural enthusiasm—a trait that had been extinguished by drugs, by psychotic episodes, and by having nothing to look forward to—was reignited by having a friend. They had similar backgrounds and talked openly about side effects, weight gain, and all the sordid events that had landed them in the psych unit time after time. They laughed, unleashing more feelings of unmistakable happiness. That they both craved to be normal again sealed the deal. Normal people didn't live in group homes or on psychiatric wards. The two women, both in their forties, sat outside in chairs on the hospital grounds, smoking pack after pack of cigarettes, and formulated a plan to live together off the unit, pooling their disability income. It didn't take long before they became each other's North Star.

# Stefan

A Victorian row house with a wooden stoop that faces a factory is the group home to Stefan and his eleven fellow residents. If nothing to do and nowhere to go has a smell, you'll find it inside the walls and floors and bedding of this place, whose owners are overwhelmed by the task of looking after those with extreme mental illness. It takes a special kind of benevolence to run a business that houses the mentally ill, with little outside community support apart from the police officers who pull up to the front door to search for street drugs or diffuse skirmishes. The monthly income from each resident comes with a steep responsibility that either sparks despair and avoidance or confirms a Mother Teresa mission: looking after the kind of sick people no one else can or will.

In this particular home, the task of caring for a dozen needy individuals was beyond the capacity of the owners. Not only were they unable to keep the place clean, they were ill-equipped to offer the kind of emotional assistance the residents required. They should have asked for more resources. Maybe they were too proud to admit they were in over their heads. The couple next door, who had two young children, put their house up for sale and moved away after witnessing drug deals, fights, and the kinds of skirmishes that happen when people have nothing meaningful to do.

The smell in Stefan's bedroom is almost too much to take. It's urine and feces and vomit and sweat. It's cigarette butts and dollar-store popcorn. It's grease from the remains of a poutine that made him nauseated. His mattress has absorbed the stink for so long that washing the sheets doesn't help. When the owner put a thick layer of plastic sheeting over the mattress, it pooled with nighttime sweat. The smells cling to Stefan when he walks around. It makes my gag reflex kick in. He smells as if his body is rotting from the inside. In your city you might have come across his many brothers and sisters and aunts and uncles who live in stairwells on pieces of cardboard.

Stefan made a daily trek to buy cigarettes. He had exactly seven dollars in his pocket, the cost of a single pack, having panhandled for most of it at his usual intersection in Point-St.-Charles, a once hardscrabble Irish working-class borough of Montreal that became gentrified in the early 2000s. It's a community in great flux and with even greater income disparity. He has regulars who fill his cup with quarters and dimes. As well, he manages to cajole small change from his housemates in exchange for doing their bathroom duties. He has scrubbed toilets and shower stalls for as little as five cents in order to walk the long block to the *dépanneur* to buy cigarettes, since the group home dispenses a measly ten per day. But on this trip, which I took with him, the price had risen to $7.10. Stefan placed his money on the counter, a monstrous handful of change, and watched as the clerk counted it out.

"You're short," the man said.

With both hands, Stefan pushed the pile towards the man who had done the counting.

"You're short, I said. They're $7.10. Take your money and get lost. I'm not your bank manager." The clerk rang up bread and milk for the next customer in line. When he looked up to see Stefan still standing there, he hissed, "Are you deaf? Take your money."

Stefan took a long time to pocket his change, but he left the counter without a fight or a scene or even a swear word. He waited near the glass door until a small line had formed at the cash, mostly people who could not or would not make eye contact with him, and then left the store. The bell made a little jingle. Just outside, he pulled down his pants and his adult diaper and had a bowel movement on the store's small grey cement landing. Satisfied that he had expressed his contempt, his powerlessness, his poverty, his marginalization, and his loss of dignity, he left the corner store to beg for another dime.

18

# A Normal Home

HILARY HAD HER ACT TOGETHER ENOUGH TO HAVE rented a three-bedroom townhouse on McCarthy Road, in the Hunt Club area of Ottawa. It was a modest neighbourhood close to shops and restaurants, just a bus ride away from downtown and movie theatres and the Byward Market. She told Caroline she needed a roommate to help pay the rent. Caroline was overjoyed at the idea of living with someone of her own choosing in a place where her sons could stay overnight. It also seemed a lucky coincidence that their release dates were in the same month.

Caroline had been struggling with the next step beyond the ward. The plan gave both women something exciting to look forward to. All too often, the next placement causes as much anxiety as being on the psychiatric unit. Peggy reflects, "I think Caroline was drawn to the idea that living with Hilary would mean freedom, a home, friendships, space to have her meagre belongings, a place to enjoy her music and just live a more normal life. She wanted to live in an area that was not inhabited by the mentally ill or the destitute, like her apartment on McLaren Street."

Caroline and Hilary left the ward in a swirl of optimism that erased any lingering doubts the staff might have had about two women with mental health challenges making a go of domesticity. They believed the connection helped elevate both of them to a healthier emotional state. But Rosalind and Peggy were dead set against the move, unable to forget Caroline's track record. They were worried whether the two women could count on each other in a crisis, even a trifling crisis like forgetting to pay the phone bill or finding a dead mouse under the sink. But Caroline insisted.

The first week was an uneasy adjustment. The house seemed eerily quiet after months of the daily thrum of a hospital unit. Everyday household chores—paying the rent and the utilities, taking out the garbage, replacing light bulbs in overhead fixtures—were things that neither of them had dealt with in a long while. On medication, they were confounded by simple things like accessing voicemail, plunging a toilet, or replacing a washer in a leaky faucet. Within no time the situation became overwhelming for both of them.

Perhaps the biggest setback was that neither of them had the ability to navigate a disagreement. When they started to bicker, Caroline called Simon, whose boozy, easygoing demeanour was an antidote to friction. Caroline soon suggested that Simon rent the third bedroom. It would mean a sizeable decrease in expenses for the women, she argued. His welfare cheque was just enough to cover one-third of the rent, with a meagre amount left over for alcohol, cigarettes, and marijuana. Hilary agreed, a testament to Simon's charisma. For his part, he was happy to smoke marijuana with Hilary, drink beer with Caroline, and somehow try to stretch his arms wide enough to safeguard the peace between his two roommates.

But it wasn't long before Hilary began to feel like an outsider in her own home. It was two against one. Simon and Caroline were night owls, while Hilary could sleep fourteen hours at a stretch. Caroline listened to loud music, dusting off album after album to reconnect with the artists she loved. Things began to perish. The first to go was Hilary's tolerance. The second was Caroline's ability to talk openly with her friend, as she had been able to do with Hilary on the unit. She retreated into a long-honed practice of avoidance. Hilary became critical and tried to impose her will. "Everyone must be in bed by ten," she insisted, not understanding how much she was angering Caroline.

Three months into the arrangement, Caroline's voices began, despite the fact that she received injections of her antipsychotics at the hospital on a regular basis. The stress of living with Hilary had undone months of strategic talk therapy with her trusted team at the ROH. They had coached Caroline to speak up when her voices became active, an intervention tactic designed to de-escalate the experience. Except in this instance she felt that what the voices were saying was too heinous to speak about; if she confessed to the nature of the messages, it would jeopardize her independence. Soon she began to be confused about what was real and what was not.

"I began to hear a woman's voice," she remembers. "It sounded like one of my four sisters. The voice told me Hilary was snorting cocaine, and that she had used my rent money to pay for the drugs. We had a fight over that. Hilary told me I was a liar. You can't know how many times I have been accused of being a liar. I think a blood vessel burst in my brain." Simon, aware of her persistent anger, bought case after case of beer, trying to inject levity into the situation.

But Caroline could not be defused. "Another voice told me she had stolen my stereo and my two hundred albums," she says. "They said she was a coke addict and a drunk. They said to me over and over that she was a thief and a freak. Why else would someone get out of bed at midnight, open the window, and start singing to the skunks and raccoons outside? The police came and had to calm her down. She was evil."

Did Hilary do that? It's highly unlikely, Rosalind says, though neighbours who heard shouts of anger from the house had called the police numerous times. It's hard to know the truth. Hilary suffered from bipolar syndrome, though she was usually more depressed than manic. Caroline defaulted to psychosis and paranoid delusions. Their combined symptoms ignited an unmanageable crisis between them.

When Caroline first began to hear the instructions to "kill the devil," she self-medicated with beer at a local bar with Simon. He paid the tab with Caroline's debit card. They staggered home, loud and unruly, and were yelled at by Hilary, who was now resentful of Simon.

In front of her sisters, Caroline still did her best to cover up the cracks that were widening with each successive day. She insisted that all was well, a charade Rosalind wanted to believe. "Looking back," she says, "we all knew it was a house of cards. But we wrung our hands and hoped for the best."

Caroline's birthday was the highlight of the month of July. Peggy brought a chocolate cake and candles. There was a festive evening of celebration, and laughter over the fact that Caroline had difficulty blowing out all forty-four candles. Hilary gave Caroline a card with a photograph of two women sitting on a dock at sunset, unaware that her roommate was percolating a horrifying depth of hostility. Caroline's other sisters called from afar and wished her well. The voices subsided for a day or two, their instructions muted, less all-consuming.

Then Caroline called her social worker and complained that Hilary had sold her piano, which meant she had been forced to forfeit all the money she had spent on piano lessons. There was no piano and no lessons, but the social worker did not realize that and listened with empathy. After she hung up, Caroline went into her room with two ashtrays and a pack of cigarettes and reread her birthday cards. But no amount of cigarettes or alcohol or Simon's mellow influence could suppress the berating and taunting that had overtaken her mind. Once again she believed the water was tainted. Soon she had gone two weeks without washing or brushing her teeth. She left the birthday cake on the counter, even though Hilary protested that ants and maggots and cockroaches were crawling across her face at night as a result. To escape the tension, Simon regularly drank until he passed out.

If Caroline had thought she had another exit, she might have taken it. As it was, she had no alternative but to return to hospital. Wearing her pink pyjamas, she boarded the number 106 bus bound for Ottawa General Hospital on Smythe Road. *You're worth helping* was a belief that her social worker had helped instill in her—one small, pleading voice fighting against a tidal surge of ferocious negativity, a tiny defence mounted against an army of invaders.

Caroline can't remember what words she used at the check-in window of the emergency department when she asked to be admitted. She remembers the place as crowded and noisy but thinks that could have been all in her head. After the distracted nurse turned her away, instead of taking the bus back, Caroline trudged back to the townhouse on foot. On the long walk home, her social worker's encouraging words evaporated as though they had never existed. She was living with Hilary, and Hilary was evil.

The next twenty-four hours were a series of should-haves. Caroline should have called a sister, her social worker, or a member of her Salus team. Instead of Ottawa General she should have gone to the ROH, where there would have been an intervention. The nurse should have detected a woman in crisis. In the townhouse, Hilary and Simon had been nursing their own wounds, too broken to notice that Caroline had been overtaken by something dark and menacing. They weren't capable of knowing what they should have done.

On that hot August day in 2002 when Caroline poured boiling water into Hilary's ear, she had mistakenly thought the menacing voices would stop if she acted on their directions to kill the devil that lived inside her friend. When the police arrived, she was still holding the kettle, standing by herself, but not alone because of the voices. Hilary, hysterical, was rushed by ambulance to a burn unit. Caroline, deeply traumatized by her roommate's anguish, was taken in the back of a patrol car to police headquarters on Elgin Street and charged with aggravated assault using a weapon. Simon ran from the townhouse, as traumatized as he had ever been, and sat trembling on the floor of a payphone, willing himself to call Rosalind but afraid to betray his best friend.

At the time of this writing, Caroline has no memory of what happened that day. As the Greeks have written, the soul passes through the river of forgetfulness. Perhaps her survival instinct won't let her remember because the assault she committed can't be reconciled with her sense of herself as a kind, generous person. When her sisters gently press her to at least examine the repercussions, Caroline becomes angry. "Leave me alone. You don't know," she says. It's been a forbidding place for such a long time, a windowless cellar whose door cannot yet be opened.

Hilary refused all overtures from the Evans family, who wished to offer deep sympathy, an apology, and—in a perfect world—to receive forgiveness. She lost her hearing in the burned ear and needed plastic surgery to repair the scars. The incident aggravated Hilary's mental illness, too, causing a resurgence of traumatic depression and anxiety.

Peggy says, "Rosalind and I had to make arrangements with the Ottawa police to go to retrieve some of Caroline's belongings. Hilary's family would not allow us to take any of the furniture or equipment that Caroline had brought into the home. They only permitted us to collect a few pieces of clothing and toiletries, insisting that the balance of Caroline's belongings had to remain in Hilary's possession as payment for the damage Caroline had inflicted upon her. There was a Pioneer stereo, which I had given to Caroline, and lots of music, the rocking chair from the family cottage, and a number of other items. Hilary wanted nothing to do with us."

Without the liniment of forgiveness, in their minds the painful episode is still open. The memory is no longer raw, but Peggy looks back with regret. Should they have tried harder to make amends? How else could they have supported her?

Because no secure psychiatric beds were available in Ottawa, Caroline was moved from a cell at the courthouse to a correctional facility where psychiatric and medical care were minimal. She was a criminal, until further notice. Her sisters, initially helpless, drew up lists of what needed to be done, number one being to find a lawyer. Finally Michael Davies, an Ottawa defence lawyer, agreed to take the case. With the help of testimony from a forensic psychiatrist, sixteen days later Caroline was transferred to the ROH to await trial.

On the day she was moved, Caroline was still in shock, but fully aware she could face a prison sentence. She had been given sedatives and sleeping pills, but her red-rimmed eyes betrayed her feelings of shamed sorrow. The sisters did their best to reassure her when they were with her. But on their own at night, or driving back and forth to see her, they relived the eleven years—1991 to 2002—their sister had been in and out of psych wards, wondering what else they could have done. Rosalind found she had run out of tears. Why twist a dry sponge?

Most of us in the land of "normal" know the difference between good and evil, whether we choose well or not. A delusional, hallucinating person cannot make that determination. The situation with Hilary had provoked such intense fear in Caroline that she was no longer able to register the difference between right and wrong. Her only imperative was to protect herself. If Caroline had found another way to express her fear and had been helped to feel safe, perhaps a crime would have been averted. But no one had yet found a way to make her feel safe enough to cope with what would be everyday stresses for most people.

Caroline spent three months on the unit curled up in a fetal position. She had been assigned a psychiatrist, Dr. Shirley Brathwaite, who slowly helped her find the peace and quiet to work through another depression tightly wrapped in delusion. When Caroline did speak, she told story after disjointed story, broken pieces of her mangled life that she'd pasted back together in a different order. But mostly she lay in bed.

Caroline was now under the authority of the Ontario Review Board (ORB), a panel that reviews the rules and circumstances of liberty for people found not fit to stand trial. On three separate occasions in a courtroom, with input from the ORB, Caroline's lawyer, Michael Davies, told the judge that Caroline was unfit to stand trial. Each hearing took less than five minutes and Caroline was never present.

But slowly she worked her way back from intense psychosis, with the help of Dr. Brathwaite and two compassionate social workers named Joy and Linda. It took months. Long sessions with the staff helped to persuade Caroline of the permanence and severity of her mental illness, and also that acceptance of her condition was the first step to coping with a chronic condition like schizophrenia. They helped her to believe that she had a right to keep on living. Caroline said of her first experience with Joy, "I went from being a lost cause to someone with pride.

Joy told me to stay away from people who didn't believe in me. From people who didn't believe I was worthy. When my suffering was not recognized, it was emotional torture." She spoke to me about that time as a kind of permanent darkness. "I can't grow when I am so far away from the light," she says. Acceptance meant she had to tear up her bucket list of aspirations and create a new one—a realistic list. She did not speak to Gilles or the boys at any time during that forensic incarceration; her deepest fear remained being separated permanently from her sons.

On December 12, 2002, Caroline appeared in front of a judge in a provincial courtroom on Elgin Street in Ottawa. At last she had been deemed fit to stand trial by her forensic psychiatrist and the ORB. Caroline was seated next to her lawyer. Also in the room were Dr. Brathwaite, two other staff members from the ROH, the Crown attorney, Rosalind and Peggy, and everyone else whose case was being tried that day. No one from Hilary's family was present in the courtroom.

The trial was to determine whether Caroline had knowingly committed a crime or whether her delusionary beliefs had eliminated her capacity to appreciate her actions. The Crown attorney asked Caroline probing questions to determine her future. "Do you have family support?"

"Yes," she answered. "I have four supportive sisters who have been an active part of my recovery."

"Are you fully aware of what you did?"

"Yes. I understand that I have done harm to Hilary Sanderson."

"Do you have community support?"

"Yes. I am followed by Salus."

"Do you have the trust and support of a psychiatrist?"

"Yes. I will have regular appointments with a psychiatric team, and my medications will be administered by injection."

Caroline was able to answer every question without prompts or delay.

"Caroline was well enough to stand up for herself," Rosalind says. Caroline was so "buffed, washed, and combed" that Rosalind could almost inhale her clean and presentable sister. She wore a new pink blouse and her long blond hair curled down her back. Caroline was nervous but composed. Her voice was steady when she answered the questions.

The judge found Caroline not criminally responsible, declaring, "No person is criminally responsible for an act committed or an omission made while suffering from a mental disorder that renders the person incapable of appreciating the nature and quality of the act or omission or of knowing that it was wrong." The judge advised Caroline of two possible sentencing outcomes: absolute discharge or remand to a hospital for further rehabilitation, a decision the court would announce at a later date.

In the courtroom Caroline and her sisters hid their tears, as there was still much to be decided, but the flood of relief was immeasurable. On that day Caroline's sisters were also treated to a rare glimpse of something they had lost sight of: the restoration of her dignity. It was a small gift compared to the verdict, but for family members those tiny moments of recovery often make the difference between giving up and being able to carry on.

At a second hearing a month later, on January 21, 2003, the verdict was hospital detention under psychiatric supervision, the length of her stay to be decided on a month-to-month basis by the Ontario Review Board. The judge ordered her detainment to take place where she already was, at the Royal Ottawa Hospital. The court further stipulated levels of security and community access. Her restrictions, among many, required that if she was to venture beyond the unit, she had to

be accompanied by a staff member; that the local police would be noti-
fied if she was to enter the community; and that samples of her urine
would be analyzed for drugs (other than those prescribed by her
doctor) and alcohol at random intervals. Upon release from hospital
she would live in a supervised group home.

Rosalind and Peggy took copious notes in order to help their sister
adhere to all the rules, and they had to suppress nervous laughter
when they heard that one of the conditions was that Caroline would
be prohibited from owning a firearm. Her medications and long-
acting injections would continue to be administered by professionals.
The length of her stay would depend on how her psychiatrists thought
she was doing.

At least Caroline would have a chance at recovery on a psychiatric
ward rather than in prison, even if the forensic hospital unit was locked
and manned by security and visitors were carefully scrutinized and
approved. Caroline was one of the lucky ones. She had sisters advocating on her behalf. They had been able to afford a criminal lawyer. Many
others who have been driven to such criminal acts spend months,
years, and decades incarcerated for crimes rooted in suffering.

Without treatment, people often retreat so far into their illness that
recovery is no longer possible. Prisons are stuffed with such people,
and they often do not have the means to explain themselves. What is
the difference between a judged man behind bars in a penitentiary and
a judged woman like Caroline on a forensic ward? Hope.

# Thomas

Thomas has both Asperger's and Tourette's syndromes, the Tourette's becoming more pronounced when he is nervous. He has been hearing voices since grade ten. At that time, his divorced mother, Celeste, was in a long-standing relationship with Jannik, who did not understand Thomas's condition or his radioactive temperament. In Thomas's home, shouting, hitting, and physically retaliating in self-defence were routine. When he was hit, Thomas hit back. When his mother's boyfriend whipped him on the side of the face with a dishrag, Thomas kicked him. Just as often, Thomas was the one who started it.

When he was sixteen, he called 911 and told dispatch his mother and her boyfriend were abusing him. He voluntarily spent two weeks on a psychiatric ward for teenagers, sanctioned by his mother, who was worried about his mental state, especially his volatility. They both acknowledged to the hospital staff that they had no acceptable ways of communicating with each other.

Two weeks couldn't fix what was wrong in Thomas's world. He suffered from acute anxiety and paranoia, on top of his claims that he was mistreated at home. He described feeling suffocated, saying, "My aura cannot breathe when I am in the same room as my mother's boyfriend."

He told his mother that he could sense evil around Jannik. After three months at home, he went back to the hospital. His mother had woken up to find him standing by Jannik's side of the bed. When she saw the look of contempt on his face, she panicked—for good reason.

After seven months as an in-patient, Thomas found a semblance of calm. "It was a beautiful time," he told me. "I was listened to. I had feelings of love again. I was able to write." He called the manuscript he wrote during that stint "Mourner in Silence." Instead of going home after he was released, Thomas chose to move to a group home, the first in a long string of placements. Once in a while he would spend a weekend at his mother's house and their violent pattern would resurface. On one visit, he became so angry with his mother that his voices directed him to plot her murder. In the bathtub, he submerged his head to try to dull the voices, and kept it there. When the long silence in the bathroom replaced his mother's anxiety with panic, she managed to unlock the door from her side. She thought he was trying to commit suicide. Trembling with fear, she called the police. Thomas ended up back in hospital. She suspected he had schizophrenia, and she knew that her boyfriend did not want her mentally ill son even visiting. Celeste had few coping skills, was overwhelmed by her inability to defuse Thomas's belligerence, and could not afford the therapy for herself that might have helped them both.

Much as he fought with her, Thomas still felt like she'd forsaken him. He attacked a window on the locked ward, breaking it; he cracked the drywall with his fists and smashed his own radio and laptop. After another long stay, he was sent to a new group home that wasn't a good fit. Thomas instigated a serious fight with another resident, the first of his targets who was not a family member. Having no words to express himself, he used his fists. He was re-hospitalized.

After he assaulted a security guard on his long-stay ward, the hospital moved him to the forensic wing, a place of heightened scrutiny and tighter security. Thomas was lucky, though. The staff of that ward, Perry 2A at the Douglas Institute, treated him as a person, not an illness. "I loved the fact that they accepted me. I was never judged," he says. His time on the ward was a massive first step towards recovery, which for Thomas meant being able to avoid or defuse conflict without resorting to his old ways: kicking, punching, hitting, behaviours he had learned as a young boy.

There's another, huge twist to Thomas's story. When he was twenty-three, feeling empowered by years of therapy, he petitioned his psychiatrist for gender-reassignment surgery. For a long while his doctor did all he could to persuade Thomas that there were less drastic ways to deal with his sexual confusion. The psychiatrist was completely aware of the links between suppressed or repressed gender identity and mental illness: that feeling of being in the wrong body can lead to depression and self-harm. He just didn't think a surgical solution was right for Thomas. But both Thomas and his mother, who had agreed to attend meetings so she could understand the procedure and all its implications, wanted the gender reassignment to go ahead. Celeste, who felt great remorse about her son's early years, believed his aggression and psychotic behaviour had been linked to alienation over his unresolved sexual identity.

If Thomas was determined to go ahead, his therapist recommended that he at least undertake intense counselling from experts and that he live as a woman—wearing the clothes and undergarments, the makeup and other outward trappings—for at least a year before he went ahead with the surgery. Thomas didn't take the advice, because he didn't want to simply "try on" his female identity. He insisted that he wanted to change the outer manifestations of his gender identity only after he had a woman's body. He did take female hormones, though, which began the physical transformation. Within weeks he had breast buds and his hips began to fill out; his skin softened and his body hair began to disappear. He found the changes exhilarating but experienced his first niggling doubts when the number of his erections decreased. That was supposed to happen, he told himself, but it spooked him. His doctor was still trying to dissuade him, worried that Thomas's past psychosis would interfere with the long healing process required after any invasive surgery, let alone one as life-altering as gender reassignment, and the multi-faceted self-care that is required to fully heal emotionally.

Stubbornly, Thomas went ahead with the surgery, only to realize within two days that he had made a drastic mistake. "My genitals had not healed, I was covered in blood, but I knew it was wrong." He is candid now about how his illness played a role in his desire to transition. "I manipulated my doctors," he says. "I used all my energies to convince them that it was the right decision. But it wasn't, and they knew it. Still, I manipulated them. I felt the dark energy of God trying to guide me away from my decision. I thought God was completely against me, that he was malevolent. I wish I could go back to being what I was. It's a huge tragedy for me. I tried to manipulate my genitals and now I can't masturbate. I feel so sad. Twice a month I attend a transgender support group. I'm trying to self-accept my mistake, but I am living a substandard life." The drastic physical changes, complicated by his regret, sparked a deep depression and, as his psychiatrist had worried, a resurgence of the negative voices.

Thomas stopped the hormones and is now back to living as a man. He will never have children, which he says is for the best. He told me, "There are moments when I think I wouldn't want anyone to share my life." He wonders why he thought such a traumatic change would fix his life, but also why it didn't actually work. Those unresolved questions are at the heart of Thomas's ongoing search for meaning. "I had the mistaken idea that I would only be happy if I became a woman. I found all women irresistible: young, old, fat, unattractive. I loved women so much I thought my sexual experience would be greater if I was one." He now acknowledges that loving women didn't mean he should become one.

He tells me that he has come to terms with his actions. "I used to blame my mother for my unhappiness. Now I do a better job of accepting the way I look and feel, and so it's up to me to be happy." Thomas believes that his acceptance and self-advocacy are the route to recovery. He also insists, "The fight in me is gone."

In my presence he is always gentle and soft-spoken; I see no hint of the enraged young man he once was. He has reconciled with his mother and even spends long stretches living in the basement apartment of her house. Thanks to his time on the forensic ward at the Douglas Institute, Thomas has learned techniques that help him feel calm. He credits the staff for his recovery—their patience, compassion, and acceptance. He is proud of the fact that he has never used drugs or alcohol, other than the ones prescribed by his psychiatric team.

Despite the medication he takes, he is able to harness his various talents: he sings, plays the piano, and is a composer, a lyricist, and a poet. He also has a best friend, a fellow writer, who makes him laugh. They've taken the bus to various Canadian cities to go to concerts and other cultural activities, which fuel them both. Thomas has created a document he calls VOMIT, short for "Victims of Musical Insult," in which he writes derogatory rap songs about people he doesn't like, demonstrating that he is able to channel his negative thinking into music as a means of releasing the stress that still pulses through his thinking. Since one of his voices is that of God, he is now studying his faith. He is hoping that in the future God will show him how to have greater happiness, rather than playing false with his head.

When we meet, I pick him up outside the Vendôme metro station. He's always early, and waiting for me exacerbates his Tourette's. He presses his forehead, paces, and blinks until he is safely in the car. We usually go to my house because of his social anxiety, although he has taken me to his trans meetings—monthly dinners held at a drop-in centre in the gay village on St. Catherine Street. It's a ramshackle place that has a back room staffed by a nurse who can give hormone injections, which spares people from having to use a public medical centre during transition.

The first time I went to the centre with Thomas, I was struck by the sight of a hundred or so men and women in various stages of gender flux. I loved the hair, makeup, high heels, skirts, and fishnet stockings, and the various adaptations of men's clothing, but the betwixt-and-between physical stages gave me a lump in my throat—not quite a man, not quite a woman. But they were all so happy to welcome me, and they treated me with great warmth. After we left, I drove Thomas to the metro and drove myself home, wondering how such a misunderstood group of people was able to extend such generosity. I realized every person in that room just wanted to be seen as a human being, that their hearts were no different than any other human heart.

Thomas struggles constantly with his body image. He is well over six feet tall, with smooth skin, breasts, and hips, but he wears men's clothing and keeps his hair short and in a side-parted boyish style. He is sensitive to people staring at him, a heightened intuition that brings on paranoia. Ideas flood his mind about the strangers he sees on the streets and in the subway, and he claims to know from a hundred metres away whether someone is carrying a weapon. His inability to tune out the impressions he feels has made employment nearly impossible for him to sustain. As Joseph Campbell, author of *The Hero's Journey* and other seminal works on myth, writes, "The psychotic drowns in the same waters in which the mystic swims with delight."

Thomas has had a complicated life. Sexual identity issues. Paranoia. Voices. His parents' divorce. His mother's boyfriend. Uncontrollable behaviour that led to time on a forensic ward. A horrific car accident that killed his only sibling. He's finally at peace with his brother's death. "I speak to him telepathically. It was terrible that he was overtaken by drugs and alcohol. He told me he's happy now." People mistakenly assume that Thomas's psychosis is the reason for his hostility, rather than that violence was his default strategy to cope with situations beyond his control. He now understands that violence is as much of a dead end as was his surgery. Remarkable.

# 19

# The Forensic Unit

CAROLINE BEGAN HER LONG FORENSIC HOSPITALIZATION as a heavily sedated non-participant. But gradually she began to believe she was entitled to a life beyond the plain white walls of her room on the locked ward. Rosalind recalls her first visit with her sister after she was sentenced: "There were lots of pregnant pauses when we spoke, as though her attention veered off into the outskirts of her daydreams. She was listening to the voices. She didn't trust herself. I remember she was so tired. Tired of having to navigate such a difficult life."

The three sisters who lived nearest took turns visiting. "The forensic ward was in an older part of the hospital and it was pretty dreary," Peggy recalls. "You know when you can tell something has been painted many times—dents and chips and all covered in thick, oil-based gloss—so very institutional. My sister had no privileges. It was a seriously secured area and we had to pass through monitored locked doors. It was a very sad, scary place. All the patients were well medicated—zombie-like, really. When we would go to see her, the other patients paid no attention to us, so I am not sure why it felt so scary. Maybe my fear arose from the unknown as to why they were admitted. What crime had they committed?"

Peggy felt that Caroline's connection to the family, her well-being, rested on her and Rosalind's shoulders. "In almost thirty years, I do not believe my mum ever visited Caroline in hospital, nor do I recall seeing her at any of the places she lived in Ottawa," she says. "That is not a diss on my mom, just an interesting point. She really backed away from it all and let us deal with it. I often wonder about her reasons. Was it fear, guilt, disappointment, denial, disgust, exhaustion, shame? A little bit of everything, I imagine. She could not bring herself to go and see her but she tried her best to listen. She did speak to Caroline on the phone." There are a hundred justifiable reasons to explain why Isabel withdrew, but to Caroline it simply felt like a long, drawn-out loss of her mother's love. A heavy and unrelenting burden. Sharon also offered support, but admits that she too backed off, suffering from burnout and the need to look after her own three children. In addition, she couldn't forget Caroline's terrible verbal assaults when she was in the tight grip of delusion.

When two of Caroline's brothers who lived out west came to town for a visit, Peggy insisted they visit her on the locked unit. She wanted them to *know* and *feel* and *see* the situation. It didn't surprise her when the brothers broke down and sobbed in the car on the way home. But they did not step up.

Caroline was regularly assessed during her long incarceration to determine when she could leave the hospital. Rosalind attended all of the Ontario Review Board hearings, Peggy only a few. At one particular hearing, Caroline brought a pair of her underpants with her and waved them in the air as evidence that she had been raped in her room. Her history of unproven allegations played against her, though; Rosalind sat silently in her seat, unable to vouch for her sister's credibility. The allegations were not investigated.

Sherry, another bright young social worker assigned to Caroline on the forensic unit, helped enormously. Her tactic was to listen and to "believe" everything Caroline said—the rapes, the sexual torture, her adoption, that her sister had started the Salvation Army, that eating Play-Doh causes birth defects, that her mother was a pelican. Sherry accepted every fabrication that had tinkered with Caroline's rational mind. For Caroline, being heard without judgment was infinitely more important than separating fact from fiction.

Dr. Nicola Wright, a clinical psychologist in the ROH's schizophrenia programme, also helped shape Caroline's recovery. Rosalind says that the arrival of Dr. Wright was transformative. Wright also recognized that Caroline's incredible tales were true—in the sense that she was explaining her suffering through fairy tales. Caroline says, "After you have been abused and you are exposed as a liar, you suffocate. You want to die. When the doctor believed me, I saw the sun sparkle on the water. Brightness returned to my life. I can breathe when I am heard."

Caroline was given a conditional discharge and released thirteen months after the boiling-water incident. To live outside the hospital, she was required by law to follow a specific treatment plan, called a community treatment order (CTO), issued by the Ontario Review Board, or be subject to re-hospitalization or jail. The order meant that the police were allowed to pick up Caroline and take her back to the hospital, regardless of consent, if she had any kind of relapse deemed dangerous to anyone or if she was non-compliant with her treatment regimen.

In the past, Caroline had refused her medications because of adverse side effects, including extreme lethargy and brain fog; she'd also gone off them because "normal" people weren't on drugs. Consenting to constant medication felt like a life sentence, but now she embraced all aspects of her CTO. She was terrified of a prison sentence and also wanted to appease her family, who were in favour of treatment. She wanted the love and continued support of her sisters and her sons; she would have signed anything to be redeemed in their eyes. It meant lifelong surveillance and lifelong medication, which opened the door to more illnesses, including diabetes, heart disease, and joint degradation, but Caroline was fully on board.

As they readied for her release, Caroline's sisters were worried that the stigma of her crime would be permanently etched across her forehead, and that those closest to her would be looking over their shoulders forever. There is much truth to those worries, even now. It would be a lie to say the Evans family are not afraid of Caroline. They have seen with their own eyes that when Caroline is not compliant, she becomes psychotic. And they now knew she was capable of violence. Such fear of a loved one breeds guilt and remorse, along with resentment, and it also meant that Caroline would forever be at arm's length from the people she needed most. Such a mutual conflict was the very worst type of Catch-22.

The greatest predictor of future violence is the person's past history of violence. Caroline's sisters have spent a lot of time trying to understand why their sister's voices pushed her to violence. They assumed it was the progression of the illness—that in her psychotic state, Caroline was no longer able to defuse her discontent and escalating terror in a rational way. Did she even realize she was committing an act of violence? Caroline's one violent act is still always present for Caroline's sisters, which means that, though they love her, they keep her at a distance for fear of what she'll do to them or their children.

Caroline's voices were insulting, crass and demeaning, and relentless, and still can be. However, very few who live with such voices become violent, no matter the public misperception that people who are suffering psychotic breaks are prone to violence. It goes without saying that Caroline was not adept at coping with the voices, but no one knows why she was one of the few who snapped. It's likely that her fear of Hilary was so all-consuming there was no room for any form of good judgment. For most of her adult life, Caroline had been seeking help. Over the phone with her sisters, in bars with older men, on benches in shopping malls, she was on a mission to be seen and affirmed. Harming Hilary may have been a desperate form of communication, saying, *I'm not okay, and the voices in my head are so horrible I can't tell anyone.* She was sickened by her frightening thoughts. It seems as though in Caroline's case, all roads lead back to trauma. She was bullied by her brother, grew up in a household of addiction, was almost unbearably sensitive. She had nine siblings vying for her mother's love. Trauma is not inherently linked to violent acts, but violence was Caroline's response to the spiralling tension with Hilary and the desperate strain of trying to regain a normal life. It was that desperation that caused her to crack.

Three key professionals from the Royal Ottawa Hospital were enlisted to help Caroline after her release into the community: a psychiatrist, Dr. Chantal Whelan, and social workers Sherry and Nicola.

Dr. Whelan counselled Caroline and her family that Caroline's delusional thinking would likely persist despite the medications: she might always be prey to psychotic episodes. The doctor was able to help them all understand that Caroline had a lower breaking point than other people, and that genetics and her environment had had a hand in her psychosis. Along with unusual ideas and voices—hallmarks of the disease—she was also experiencing a slow mental degradation with each successive psychotic breakdown. Dr. Whelan warned that anti-psychotic drugs do not help cognition and that the reverse might be true, that the brain is adversely affected by long-term drug use. She told Rosalind and Peggy that the lowest possible dosages of drugs and Caroline's acceptance of the disease were the best path forward. She encouraged Caroline herself to accept her symptoms.

On the advice of a psychiatric team at the ROH, an Assertive Community Treatment (ACT) team was assembled to monitor Caroline's drug compliance. ACT teams take mental health services to the client's home, community, or hospital; they are an intervention reserved for people like Caroline who have been hospitalized numerous times for complex, long-term, and serious psychiatric illness. A primary goal of Caroline's ACT team would be to keep her out of hospital by preventing further breakdowns.

Sherry, who had connected so well with Caroline on the forensics unit, had been tending to the chronically and severely mentally ill for more than fifteen years as a passionate advocate. She now openly discussed her personal experience with burnout with Peggy and Rosalind: "Being a caretaker of someone else's mind is a daunting responsibility. So much is invisible. It's an intuitive, compassionate profession." She told them to allow their feelings of grief and pain and sadness over Caroline's suffering to flood through them. "Embrace the feelings. You need to know that feelings aren't fatal. I know you feel guilty," she said. "Deal with the guilt, because at times detachment is the only channel."

Sherry worked with the people who were, as Rosalind put it, "a blink away from disappearing, or worse, already gone." Her role was to help Caroline make peace with a dark life that seemed beyond her control, to help her convert her angst to quiet acceptance by letting go of the things she could not change and owning the symptoms. She knew that patients who go off their meds when they get out of the hospital do so because they do not think they are sick, or because the side effects are too distressing. Or, as Caroline said, "My life is such a mess. What is the point?" Then they flare up and land back on the ward.

Lack of insight was Sherry's most heartfelt concern with people like Caroline, and their families. The Evans family does have insight. They've listened to a hundred impossible, crazy delusions, which is like trying to hold water in your fingers. The pain is bigger for family members who experience each turn of the downward spiral with a sense of futility. Rosalind remembers listening intently the day Sherry seemed to be giving her an out. "When families walk away, I get it," Sherry said. "I never judge a family for doing that. Your lives have become too difficult. You become sick as well—a different kind of sickness, of course. It's heartbreaking because many people simply don't get better in the ways that parents hope for. Parents need to look after themselves. They put their lives on hold. They are stuck. It's a family illness. We need to do a better job of listening to the needs of the family."

Sherry's words helped absolve some of Rosalind's most conflicted feelings about her mother's decision to walk away from Caroline. As for herself, getting a "pass" from a social worker stiffened Rosalind's resolve. To the best of her abilities, she vowed, she would never, ever walk away.

"Recovery," Sherry says, "is a sliding scale. Think of all the times when Caroline wasn't bathing, deeply afraid of the shower. So when she did shower, that was a form of her recovery." The illness is invisible except for the physical decay, which is often assumed by outsiders to be moral decay. Caroline had to go deep to understand why hot water was a source of terrible psychic pain. Peggy was the one who remembered the time when Ian locked Caroline in the bathroom with him and pulled her into the shower. To Ian, it was a game of cat and mouse. It just so happened that he was always the cat.

Recovery is a shifting process in which the smallest of positive changes should be regarded as a success. Sherry told Caroline and her sisters, "You must celebrate what seems like the most mundane victory."

It's a bitter pill to swallow, especially for those who had lofty dreams: the pre-med students and engineers, the writers and musicians and athletes who left adolescence with aspirations intact. But despite her downward trajectory, Sherry said, "Caroline needs a purpose. That is my wish for every single patient."

# Norman

When Norman's parents divorced, his mother left Denver, Colorado, where the family lived, and returned to her hometown of Montreal. In the summer of that same year, Norman, age sixteen, was sent to work at a cattle ranch in Granby, Colorado. His father, who had custody, wanted him out of the city, in a place that was only eighty-five miles from their family home but planets away from distractions like girls in white miniskirts and kegs of Budweiser. After his parents broke up, Norman had been suspended from school for uncapping the apple juice bottles in the lunchroom, dumping the juice, and replacing it with beer he had stolen from his father's fridge.

Norman's jobs on the ranch were to repair the many fences that circled the property and to bale hay when the harvest came. Some weeks into his stay, Norman witnessed calves being separated from their mothers shortly after birth. The heifers were slotted for future milk production but the bull calves were destined to become veal; they were tethered with chains inside individual crates where they couldn't move around freely—veal fetches a better price when it's milk-fed and tender. Norman says, "The wretchedness of the sound of mother cows crying for their babies made me crazy. I was able to hear them voice their distress. They were talking to me and asking for my help."

The more calves Norman saw in captivity, the more his grief for them grew, along with a smothering outrage for the mothers, which were confined in barbwire enclosures that prevented them from running towards their babies. His anxiety and paranoia grew, too, and soon he couldn't sleep at night, obsessively worrying about the harm being done to innocent creatures and the grief felt by their mothers. At first he was able to shake off such thoughts in the morning, but as the days became weeks, he began to obsess about ways to "make it right." He plotted ways to unchain the babies. He plotted ways to free the mothers.

Norman told me his story on the front porch of his group home in LaSalle. I hadn't been assigned to work with him, but over the years I came to know him all the same. The residents rarely leave the house, and over time you become friends with everybody in a group home. Eventually he had to do something, he said, and he stormed the cattle barn, arms flailing as he yelled at the mother cows to escape, causing them to stampede. The angry rancher called Norman's father, who came and got him. The following day Norman was sent to live with his mother in Montreal.

But even reunited with his mother, he couldn't cope. It didn't help that she was in a new relationship with another man. Norman eventually found he couldn't do homework in the school library for fear of being persecuted by his classmates, and when his grades slipped, he dropped out. On June 24 the next year, Saint-Jean-Baptiste Day, he thought the sound of celebratory firecrackers was gunshots and hid in the bathroom of a restaurant near the Old Port in Montreal. Newspaper headlines induced panic attacks. He felt that radio broadcasts were being directed at him. He decided that his mother, whom he loved, was in league with his enemies. Hallucinations, pursuing footsteps, and monsters invaded his daytime life as well as his dreams, and eventually he was hospitalized and diagnosed with schizophrenia.

He thought obsessively about ending his life. He told me, "The psychic pain was so intense that I thought a better life must exist beyond the present one. *I'm going. Don't stop me.* Those of us who were raised as Christians dwell on the idea of Paradise and Heaven; others are afraid of damnation. They are the ones who would never kill themselves willingly. They don't have faith about which door will open. On some days I felt I had no choice. On other days, it was enough to know that if things got bad enough, I had that option."

With oral medication, which included lithium and clozapine, Norman went from fog to clarity, from constant panic to calm. He still isn't able to work or date; he has no children, no outside support. "Everybody gave up on me," he told me. "And I don't blame them. I said terrible things to them. I physically hurt my mother. I wanted to die. I drove away everyone I was close to. I am responsible for that. My wish to be alone came true. I have no family—nobody."

He was truly grateful to be free from the panic attacks that had threatened his very being before he began to take medication. I found him to be chatty, helpful, and magnanimous. He also had insight— acceptance of his condition—and bore no malice towards anyone or anything. Not his family who had walked away, the medical system, or his group home with its meagre resources. He was content, a much sought-after mindset that many a family would buy if it were for sale.

"Have you reached out to your family now that you are well?" I asked near the end of our conversation on the porch.

His smile faded and he shook his head. I knew that parts of Norman's life were under lock and key. I wondered if his mother knew where he lived, or if she was even alive to see how well her son was managing.

Norman looked different from many others who are mentally unwell. He was still slim, was neat and tidy in appearance, and showed no obvious manifestations of illness. He faced little stigma in the local grocery store and considered himself lucky to have a roof over his head, three meals a day, and enough money for cigarettes. Norman's greatest recent accomplishment had been overcoming his agoraphobia, a dread so intense that he found it all but impossible to venture beyond the group home except to buy cigarettes. He still dreamed of the day back in Colorado when he was nearly trampled.

"This is a painful process that many of us who suffer from psychosis must deal with," he observed. "The real pain we suffer is from the years upon years when we were held prisoner by the several delusional ideas overtaking our lives—the madness. We lived our lives through the guidance of these delusions, and the psychosis that accompanied them. When I bit my mother, my life changed." He scanned my face after that admission, looking for the disgust and shame he himself felt. "Such a terrible waste. Sometimes we did this to the point of acting out the delusion, unable to hold on to reality. I tasted her blood." He anxiously looked at me again. "Instead, we released that delusional energy. We hurt not only ourselves but also the ones we love. I was a scary person."

Norman had thought he would grow up to become a chemistry teacher. He could converse for hours on subjects that were dear to him, like photosynthesis and bee pollination. He told me that hydrogen is the most important element in the periodic table. Recently I asked him if he would like to go the library with me to borrow science books. I told him that if it was crowded, we could leave immediately. He nodded tentatively, remembering all the times he'd been too afraid to go anywhere. Now he's the proud owner of a library card, for which he had to produce proof of residency in the neighbourhood. Now he never wants to move away from his group home whose address gives him the right to borrow books.

A critical aspect of schizophrenia is the lack of purpose felt by people who suffer with it. An unfortunate aspect of some group homes is that nobody is counting on the residents to be productive. For too many, there is nothing to do except smoke. Their mental illness becomes a life sentence of boredom, their days a constant, tedious, dull ache.

I thought Norman, who had successfully reached a place of real stability, could be a mentor to others. Peer-to-peer support has the potential to be one of the most effective ways to reduce stigma. Those who have lived homeless or experienced the fear of delusions are less likely to shame or humiliate another person in the same boat. At first he was frightened by the notion, worried that it might upset his equilibrium, but in 2017 he began work as a peer support volunteer through an outreach organization. He now takes the bus on his own. His first "case" was a second-year McGill University student whose parents lived in Hong Kong. The parents did not know that their son, fuelled by mania and feelings of grandeur and laced with shame that they might find out, had temporarily quit classes. That was something he was able to tell Norman about.

Norman doesn't get paid for his work, but he has never felt richer.

## 20

# Stable for Now

ROSALIND AND PEGGY WERE SKITTISH ABOUT THE NEXT step for Caroline. Where would she thrive? Sherry was frank with them about how hard it is to find the right group home. She told me, "We are failing our clients when we put them in houses where we know they won't do well. It kills me to send them somewhere that's inadequate. I try my best. They are ready to start over, but sometimes I don't find the best fit. The owners get paid. There is nothing for the residents to do. They hang around and smoke. It's a dirty business, and it's impossible not to feel overwhelmed by the responsibility of having half a dozen medicated people under your care. If it's a situation where there are no chores in the house, the cooking is done for you, the laundry is done for you, then it's a setup for failure. Everyone needs to have obligations. Living in a group home frees up a hospital bed, but the terrible irony is that the goal that matters most is often pushed further away—the chance to live a purpose-driven life."

About a month before Caroline was to be released, her oldest brother died. Rosalind and Peggy feared Stuart's death would set her off again. She was indeed bereft to hear the news, but she was emotionally strong after months of counselling and only regretted that, because she was not yet free, she was unable to attend his funeral. She felt a kinship with Stuart, forged by the weight of shared suffering. He was the family's first-born, and when they were children, he had carried more responsibility than he could handle. Especially at the summer cottage, he was often left in charge of his nine younger siblings. In 1968, when he was eighteen, he suffered a serious concussion in a family car accident. After the head injury, substance abuse issues with alcohol and drugs overturned his life, representing a terrible family sorrow that was especially felt by Arthur.

Reflecting on Stuart's death, Caroline told me, "Growing up in my family was a wild experience. My dad was an air force pilot as well as a doctor. That shaped him. He saw things. He grew up lonely. Drinking was normalized, and there were bound to be a few problems. Alcohol makes it easier to get through a Saturday night, but you still have to figure out the rest of your life. It was a special kind of comfort to know that some of my other brothers and sisters had hard times. I wouldn't trade away a single one of them, especially my oldest brother. I'll always have a soft spot for Stuart."

Sherry was the one who found Caroline her new home: Wymering Manor, a group home for thirty women who had severe and persistent mental illness. It was a low-key private residential facility with a pink-flowered sofa in the living room and light blue bistro chairs in the dining room that were invitations to mingle. The staff worked hard to make each bedroom inviting and comfortable. After more than a year on a forensic ward, Caroline had a true sense of having landed in a welcome sanctuary. She told me, "It's hard to love someone out of the loony bin, out of mental illness. It is possible to love them into recovery."

At Wymering Caroline could breathe again, even if the sedative aspects of her medication dampened her down. She was under constant monitoring by social worker and psychiatric team, and of course she needed to observe the constraints of the Ontario Review Board for up to five years. But she was stable and free from frightening psychosis.

She could also catch up with her sons Matthew, now twenty, and Kyle, seventeen, who had spent most of their lives with Gilles and his extended family. "Can you imagine if I had been a single mother?" Caroline says. "When I look back to see some of the other alternatives, I shiver. For what he did for my boys, Gilles will always be a hero." Matthew had his own small business in sound recording, and Kyle, despite his cognitive deficits and extreme obesity from Prader–Willi syndrome, was in a programme at Concordia University for young people with disabilities. She rarely saw them but spoke to them often.

Both boys responded to her with affection and understanding, although Matthew felt deep resentment about his mother's diminished circumstances. Kyle, who has a network of friends and is never ashamed of his 380-pound body, knowing that his obesity is caused by his condition, constantly worried about how the knowledge of his shortened lifespan affected his mother. When I asked him how that knowledge influenced his own life, he said, "It's hardest for my mum, and second hardest for Matthew. It's always harder for those who will be left behind." He takes after his mother where warmth and generosity are concerned.

Caroline still struggles with her failure as a mother. "Our mother instinct keeps us strong," she told me. "In my case I wasn't able to keep that advantage. It's why I have had such a hard time letting go of the past. And when I look at the past and all I see are horrible things, I am in danger of making the worst decisions. It's a broken puzzle, and all the thousand pieces are around me, on top of me, and under me. When there are so many pieces in the wrong place, I start to panic. When I let go of the past and allow myself to feel good inside, the panic goes away."

At Wymering Manor Caroline had five years of stability interrupted by the odd eccentric moment. The home was near the Westgate Shopping Centre. Inside the mall she found a comfortable bench where an older man also lingered most of the day. Caroline held his trembling hand so his coffee wouldn't spill on the one suit and tie he always wore. He spoke only Italian, but Caroline claims she was gifted with understanding when they were together. He was probably as lonely as she was. Peggy said, "Caroline does not judge others and would like to see more compassion in the world. She does not gossip, is generous to a flaw, and has more love to give than most people."

She had regular visits from her three nearest sisters, loving phone calls from Lorraine, still living out west, and friendships with the women in her building. She remained stable but she struggled, especially when she compared her life to those of her sisters, who seemed to have successfully navigated the road that tripped her up time and again. And wrapping her head around the idea of permanent disability was a gigantic challenge. It's one thing to have a bad back, but the idea of a broken mind was a concept that she, like so many others in her situation, was not quite willing to accept. She craved to break free from the blunted feeling caused by the medications, but everyone around her insisted that her quality of life would hold only if she was compliant.

Her recovery was incremental: coffee with her friend at the mall, a shower undertaken of her own volition, riding the bus alone, smoking fifty cigarettes in a dopamine rush. Heating her own frozen dinner in the microwave. Buying presents for Matthew and Kyle at Goodwill.

She worried for them. How likely were they to develop a mental ill-ness? Matthew has had struggles with anxiety, she confided to me. "How could he not?"

Her sisters knew that Matthew took a benzodiazepine medication to control his feelings of panic, but they did not share that fact with Caroline, knowing it would spark her guilt. When she couldn't reach him or he didn't return her calls, she had to fight to breathe; otherwise so much guilt bubbled up, she felt she would drown in the sensation. Now she says, "I wasn't able to be living with my two boys, but having them in my mind has kept me alive. I take every opportunity to tell them how much I love them. It's the only gift I've got. I try and convince myself it's enough."

# Jackson

I met the Martineau family in 2002. Sabine Martineau was eight years old, a perennially happy girl with a gap-toothed smile and a coppery braid so long she could tuck it into the waistband of her shorts. She told my husband, Hal, that she could eat more ice cream than he could. "I'll bet you fifty dollars," Sabine proposed.

"Fifty dollars! I don't have that kind of money," my husband said.

"Well, do you have ten?" Sabine asked.

"Yes."

"Okay. How's tonight after supper?"

Sabine and Hal were neck and neck after visiting five Toronto ice cream shops within a two-kilometre radius. They had a single scoop cone each time. At the sixth stop my husband said, "I'm having a banana split with four scoops of black cherry, two bananas, chocolate sauce, and extra whipped cream. Are you good with that?"

Sabine took a moment to think, then said, "Mr. Hannaford, you can't afford two banana splits. Let's call it a tie and we'll split the ten dollars." She put her hand out for the money and Hal gave Sabine a five-dollar bill.

The next day Sabine's brother Jackson, egged on by his younger sister, said, "Mr. Hannaford, I bet I can beat you in tennis." That tennis match was the last happy encounter we had with Jackson, and it has become an indelible memory for both our family and his. Of course, Jackson won.

At five Jackson was a star athlete, a coordinated kid who could run faster, jump higher, and kick a ball better than any of his classmates. Jackson had trouble reading, though, and by grade three he needed extra help for everything in the classroom—but never outside on the field. In junior high school there was an inverse correlation between his grades and his athletic prowess. His self-esteem began to waver, his academic struggles undermining his confidence as a rising football player.

At around the same time that Jackson was in junior high school, Purdue Pharma introduced the opioid oxycodone, whose trade name was OxyContin. It was aggressively marketed and promoted. The company hosted conferences for thousands of physicians, nurses, and pharmacists—all-expenses-paid symposiums at luxury resorts— to promote the product. Patient starter coupons for a free seven- to thirty-day supply were handed out as an incentive for doctors to prescribe the drug. An explosion of addiction followed—along with astronomical sales. Jackson's father, a Toronto real estate developer, was one of those unsuspecting patients. He followed his doctor's advice for pain relief after back surgery, filling his prescriptions for OxyContin.

Jackson's older brother, Delaney, became aware of the drug and began to experiment. Soon he was hooked, and eventually he became a heroin addict. Jackson's parents grappled with conflicting advice on how to help their addicted son. There is never a one-size-fits-all solution. Certainly Delaney drew upon an unhealthy proportion of the family's emotional resources during this long-term crisis. While Jackson excelled at rugby, skiing, and football yet struggled with math tests and writing assignments, his brother was in rehab, a costly intervention that Jackson's mother felt blessed to have been able to afford. Looking back, she says, "Without a doubt, the impact of Delaney's addiction was an under-recognized stress for Jackson, a quiet, sensitive non-talker." And for his little sister too.

In grade nine Jackson began to smoke marijuana on weekends and at parties, always with friends. The weed alleviated his shyness and gave him a feeling of relaxation, a pleasant euphoria. By grade ten he was smoking alone, every day before school, already feeling the pressure of SAT exam preparation. The scouts from Ivy League schools were looking for superstars like Jackson to flesh out their teams, but not if he couldn't get in. Jackson's father was in talks with coaches as far away as California, four thousand kilometres from home. Jackson had a close relationship with his father, based on shared interests and a genuine love of each other's company. He was not psychologically ready to be cut off from his number-one fan, but given his talent, a college career as an athlete seemed a certainty.

During a tense four-year period, Jackson's brother wrestled with addiction, multiple treatment programmes, and relapses before landing in a group home for structured sober living in Pennsylvania. It was an exhausting ordeal of sleepless nights for his family, haunted by the stone-cold fear that relapse was imminent—or worse, death by overdose. Jackson found great solace in marijuana for its ability to calm his acute stress and allow him some distance from his brother's ordeal. But cannabis can also induce anxiety, fear, panic, and distrust. Jackson had his first psychotic thought at eighteen, when he believed that a newspaper headline was a personal attack.

When Jackson appeared one morning with ligature marks on his neck, which he'd unsuccessfully tried to hide with a turtleneck, his panicked parents encouraged him to seek immediate counselling and organized a team of professionals. It was a terrible reckoning to learn that while their emotional energy was directed towards supporting Delaney, their younger son had attempted to end his life. Jackson willingly entered a private psychiatric hospital, where, untethered from his athletics, he sank into depression. The experience of being hospitalized when all his friends were leaving for university was further deflating. When he was able to go home again, he isolated himself in his third-floor bedroom and was soon back to smoking marijuana in an effort to counter his anxiety. His mother recalls the daily worry of not being able to reach inside her son's heart to reassure him that all would be well. She was desperate to make him understand that he was loved unconditionally, and that his brother Delaney's journey would not tear the family apart, but neither she nor anyone else in the family could reach him.

Jackson's parents were alarmed to learn that studies have linked marijuana use to an increased risk of psychiatric disorders, especially if a great quantity of the drug is consumed at a young age, when the brain is still developing. Jackson's mother strongly objects to the legalization of marijuana. She scoffs at the argument that most people who smoke it do not become psychotic. "The psychotic vulnerability to marijuana is only determined after it's too late. And how many fourteen-year-olds have the confidence to say no when their peers are smoking dope?"

Her concerns are valid. How do we know who is vulnerable to brain toxicity? Is psychosis a result of marijuana use or are some people using it to offset anxiety and psychosis? Is it in the same category as alcohol: toxic and addictive for some but not others? In both cases—marijuana use and alcohol use—a genetic predisposition to illness and addiction may be the underlying cause.

In that first hospitalization, Jackson was not diagnosed with a mental illness, although his therapist discussed bipolarity and schizo-affective disorder. But when he took five hundred dollars out of his bank account to buy a rusted second-hand car, then drove it into an oncoming truck on the wrong side of the highway, Jackson's psychiatrist pieced together, from his knowledge of Jackson and the suicide note he left, the relationship between marijuana, psychosis, and his act of self-destruction. Suicide is relief from an inescapable powerlessness, a sense of emptiness. Jackson could not see a way out of his suffering.

For Jackson's family, the aftermath of his suicide has been multifold: the loss of a cherished family member; the guilt; the endless, looping grief that comes in and out as if through clouds; and the intractable reality that nothing can bring back their beloved son. It continues to be a deep heartache for all of them, in particular Jackson's father, who lost not only a son but also a best friend.

The Martineaus are thankful that their older son has been in recovery for several years, a salve for some of their wounds. He works for a mobile gaming company, has a girlfriend and an apartment. Jackson's mother said, "Delaney has found his way—an unimaginable gift, given how far he had walked off his path." As for Jackson, four years after his death she says, "I have finally been able to let go, and now hope shines as my beacon. It's the fire inside of me. I remain hopeful that we can break the silence, by communicating, connecting, and not allowing survivors to feel alone with this disease. Slowly I am taking hold of all that I know in order to help others who are ready to listen. The pain never goes away, and the nights are still the hardest, but hope has made it possible to move on."

Jackson's family holds an annual event to honour their son's memory, an initiative that raises awareness about suicide, mental illness, and the idea that while marijuana is safe for the majority of users, those with a sensitivity to the drug may be vulnerable to suicidal thoughts. Remarkably, the family has not unravelled. This is a family that did not give up, even while enduring the gut-wrenching regret that all parents endure: that they were unable to reach their son. Their love and commitment to their son's memory, and to one another, along with a willingness to keep moving forward, have allowed each family member to focus on building a legacy for Jackson as a positive bulwark against his loss.

# 21

# Cut Flowers and
# Knitting Needles

FOUR YEARS AFTER THE VERDICT OF "NOT CRIMINALLY
responsible" (NCR), the Ontario Review Board declared that Caroline
no longer needed to be under its watchful eye. She had fulfilled the
mandate of the disposition, had been compliant for all that time, and
had experienced no episodes of any nature that were of concern to the
public, her ACT team, or her family.

And so nobody in the family can quite piece together what happened eighteen months later, in June 2008. Her sisters have contrast-
ing versions of the story, but the outcome for everybody was the same.
Peggy claims that after the ORB was no longer monitoring Caroline's
every move, someone outside the group home began selling her marijuana, and she soon became a daily consumer. Caroline had befriended
a person who lived next door to Wymering Manor, an older man suffering from advanced cancer, who smoked marijuana to combat nausea
and pain. Rosalind says the instigating factor was that her sister had
a flareup of sciatica, suffering numbness in both feet and searing pain
down the side of one leg. As a result, she was prescribed painkillers,

perhaps opioid-based, and those new drugs set off the chain of events.

Both sisters spoke of Caroline's increasing memory and cognitive deficits; at the time they were worried that she was becoming incapable of following her drug regimen. Rosalind recalls watching the movie *Sea Biscuit* with Caroline, which she thought her sister would enjoy. Sea Biscuit was an undersized thoroughbred racehorse that had stolen the hearts of a nation during the Great Depression. But Caroline could not follow the plot. Once again, something had changed in her brain.

Her regular phone calls to them became full of allegations of rape and assault, and both sisters assumed Caroline had stopped her antipsychotic medication. Rosalind called the ACT team. Either marijuana in high doses or opioid painkillers, they were told, could have a toxic affect in combination with her antipsychotics and the benzodiazepine she was taking for anxiety. Regardless of the cause, they knew the signs. Caroline went back to the ROH in an ambulance.

When Peggy arrived at the hospital, Caroline was crying about Kyle, and Peggy briefly thought that Kyle had died. She remembers actually shuddering with relief when Caroline told her that Kyle had stolen his father's chequebook and made several large withdrawals to cover a one thousand dollar cellphone bill and other things. To her sisters this was bad, but not so bad; kids make mistakes, even twenty-two-year-olds. But for Caroline the news had triggered her feelings of responsibility, or lack thereof, inciting stress and tipping her into paranoia. Caroline speaks of that moment: "I had the crazy idea that Kyle was going to die, and the money was for his last hurrah."

This time Caroline was on a less restrictive floor. She could leave on a day pass if she felt well enough. She had a full physical and a dental checkup in which the dentist found seventeen cavities, likely caused by not brushing her teeth for months on end. Her family wondered how none of her caregivers had noticed as she sank once again into apathy about everything to do with her body. It took several weeks to get Caroline back on track. Sharon made sure the family reinstated the old safeguards, including power of attorney and the order that allowed the police to take her to hospital in a crisis. For that she bore the brunt of Caroline's fury. Sharon brought cut flowers from her garden to help make amends. Rosalind brought needles and wool, thinking Caroline could pass the time knitting. She laughed all the way home when the nurses kept the needles at their station; what had she been thinking?

Caroline's fiftieth was coming up in mid-July. Peggy planned a party in her backyard to mitigate Caroline's dismay at reaching a milestone birthday while back on the psych ward. It hit all the sisters hard, too, that at age fifty, and after so many interventions, she was once again unstable. On the day of the party, Peggy sent her husband and sons to the hospital to pick up Caroline. In the parking lot of the hospital she hallucinated snakes and spiders on the ground, even though she was fully medicated. The men went home without the birthday girl. Peggy and her family, along with Sharon and Rosalind, headed to the hospital unit with a cake covered in fifty pink and blue candles.

Caroline was especially cruel to Sharon that day, telling her, "I hate you more than anyone on this earth." Sharon admits that her feelings have still not fully healed from that particular verbal assault. "It's simply impossible to walk away from searing accusations and chalk them up to the symptoms of mental illness." Family members who grapple with such abuse need constant reinforcement of the reality that the sickness is speaking, not their loved one.

The family's emotional equilibrium was rattled further when, on July 30, 2008, a week after the cancelled party, a delusional man named Vincent Li stabbed, beheaded, and cannibalized a fellow passenger,

Tim McLean, on a Greyhound bus in Manitoba. The horrifying attack sparked outrage, especially when anyone tried to point out that the perpetrator had been in the grip of a delusion. Rosalind and her sisters were distressed and frightened, immediately reminded of their sister's assault on Hilary. "The idea that Caroline could have killed Hilary while psychotic is such a horrible thought," Rosalind says. "We need to get help for these people. The system is broken."

When these rare acts of violence occur, all those with schizophrenia are coloured with the same brush, their portraits painted with fear and ignorance. And they and their families deeply feel the persecution of aroused suspicion.

# Josh

When Vincent Li got on that Greyhound bus in Edmonton, headed for Winnipeg (a twenty-one-hour trip), he walked to the rear and sat beside Tim McLean, a young man who was already asleep against the window. Li heard persistent voices telling him to kill McLean. Overcome by the experience, he obeyed their orders. The screams of the other passengers pierced the night air but could not pierce the delusion that had engulfed Vincent's brain. Passengers who had exited the bus vomited by the side of the road, overcome by what they had seen. The sustained media frenzy that erupted was understandable.

That same year, Eric and Amy Stein's twenty-four-year-old son, Josh, began to exhibit symptoms of schizophrenia, triggered by rejections from every law school in the country. "At the time it was inconceivable to me that there was any connection whatsoever between our son and the man who headlined every newspaper," Eric says. "There were early signs that we simply refused to acknowledge. One night, long before the diagnosis, Josh came home bloodied and with a broken finger. Another time he had a cracked tooth. We were terribly upset to know that our son, who wished to study law, was not able to resolve his issues other than with his fists. I am ashamed to say that when he insisted he had been beaten up, we didn't believe him. He was the high scorer on the soccer team in high school. Popular. He was the editor of the school paper." But in high school Josh had also begun to tell lies, insisting to his friends that his father was a billionaire. When he refused to recant, two classmates tried to thump the lie out of him.

Josh's father is a quiet academic. His wife is also soft-spoken, a reader, writer, and advocate for the protection of Manitoba's environment, but now a champion of a different kind of plight. I met them both at a psychiatric conference. "Josh made some exalted statements that were scary and intimidating," Eric told me. "The week he was graduating from high school, he believed he was a judge. We accused him of taking LSD. How else could such a smart boy be spewing such nonsense?"

Since they didn't know anything about delusions or hearing voices, they believed their son's irrational statements had to be fuelled by substance abuse. There were three terrible years of family fighting, but it was only after the law school rejections that their son broke down. His parents woke up to what was really happening when he spent twenty-four hours barricaded inside the garage next to one of their cars, then checked himself into Emergency, refusing to speak to them.

They learned everything they could about psychotic mental illness and delusions of grandeur, and with each new piece of information, his mother became ever more deeply engulfed by depression over her son's plight. Amy ended up at the same hospital where Josh was in care. Her husband took a leave of absence from his work and began to call anybody who would listen, to ask for help for his wife and son.

"By 2016 I thought I had endured the hardest ten years of my life," Eric says. But it got worse. "The hardest part for me was when our son stopped believing he had any kind of illness. He was jailed for attacking a police officer. We had come so far, and it seemed a crash landing.

Everything we had done to that point became meaningless. If a person does not see themselves as sick, then why would they look for ways to get well? It seems impossible to move forward. *Don't bother. Give up.* Through the Manitoba Schizophrenia Society we found a peer support group run by a therapist. She saved us all. She told us that living with a child with schizophrenia who isn't capable of accepting treatment is like eating a hippopotamus. The solution lies in the number of people at the table willing to take one bite at a time. From then on, we were never alone. It helped my wife believe that she could get through this, too. Though to be honest, you're never through it. The key is to stop thinking like it's a life sentence. It just is."

The Steins, like the rest of the country, closely followed Li's court case. When the accused stood up in court to enter his plea of not criminally responsible, he spoke three other words: "Please kill me." After the court accepted his plea but not his death wish, he was sent to the Selkirk Mental Health Centre, and for nine years he underwent intense rehabilitation. When the Manitoba Criminal Code Review Board granted him a full discharge in February 2017, it made one of the most important decisions in the province's health-care history when it comes to people with schizophrenia.

No one can bring back the young man Li killed, but his treatment and discharge show that recovery is possible. It was an enormous breakthrough for the mentally psychotic, for it gives hope to the perpetrator, and to suffering family members, that redemption is possible.

Eric says, "It was a court decision that angered many people. Yes, it wasn't fair that the young man was killed, but mental illness isn't fair either, and Vincent Li didn't choose schizophrenia. It chose him. Li's attack was rare. It was highly publicized; it sold thousands of papers for the shock value. But everyone"—even the most notorious, he argues—"has the God-given right to rehabilitation."

The Steins are supporters of the decision. "The McLean family lost a son. It was tragic. For a long time we thought we had lost our son, too. The decision infused us with the idea that we can still move forward. You can't possibly understand what that means unless you've been down this road, seen your son behind bars. You come to a standstill."

Vincent Li is followed by an impressive team of specialists who are fervent in their desire to prove that the decision was the right one. Manitoba, against most odds, has shown the world not only that rehabilitation is possible but that schizophrenia is treatable. As Gandhi put it, "The fragrance always remains on the hand that gives the rose." May there be many more such hands.

# 22

# The Lawsuit

CAROLINE STAYED ON THE PSYCHIATRIC UNIT FOR MORE than a year after she turned fifty, largely estranged from her family, even her sons. Kyle's transgression with his father's chequebook had plunged her into depression, which meant she was both psychotic and depressed. For that combination, she needed to take even more medications. Soon her blood sugar levels became uncontrollable—she had hyperglycemia, a rapid increase in blood glucose—and her weight, which at her best was about 135 pounds, bounced between 260 and 300. Her prescribed antipsychotic, Zyprexa, had sparked a secondary and life-threatening condition: diabetes.

Around this time, in 2009, a Toronto law firm, Stevensons LLP, launched a limited class-action lawsuit on behalf of eleven people in Quebec, Ontario, and British Columbia who had become diabetic after using Zyprexa. The firm estimated there could be another 1,400 Canadian claims in addition to the 18,000 US claims. The suit alleged that pharmaceutical giant Eli Lilly had hidden a dangerous side effect of their drug: the development of diabetes, which could lead to permanent damage of the endocrine system, severe weight gain, blindness, limb amputation, hyperglycemia, pancreatitis, and heart disease, which

50 percent of diabetics suffer. Dr. Wright, Caroline's psychologist, encouraged her to apply for compensation. Caroline now needed a daily dose of insulin, Humalog, to combat her diabetes—a drug also marketed and sold by Eli Lilly (in 2013 those two drugs earned the company $3.8 billion).

On June 30, 2010, while admitting no liability, Eli Lilly settled the lawsuit for $17.6 million in Canada and $1.4 billion in the United States. Caroline was awarded six thousand dollars as her share of the payout. She gave every dollar to her sons. After all, what is the price tag for contracting a debilitating secondary illness? Many Canadians who qualified for a payment had not joined the class action. Where were they, and how come they did not step forward? Some were on the streets, some had died, and some had simply disappeared from the mental health care system, too sick or unaware to know that compensation was available.

Given that Caroline's diabetes is chronic and full-blown, the payment was nowhere near a real level of compensation. By the time she was diagnosed, she had already lost more than half of her insulin-producing cells. Still, if Caroline shed 150 pounds, she would have a fighting chance to slow the progressive disease. But that is a nearly impossible task for a person on antipsychotic medication who experiences the side effect of extreme weight gain. Eli Lilly's two drugs go hand in hand, and their profits more than compensate for the payout.

Upon her next release from the hospital, in 2010, Caroline did not go back to Wymering Manor. Instead she was accepted into the Fisher Salus group home, a large three-storey house with fifteen bedrooms. Under the auspices of the Salus organization, it offered a one-year programme focused on teaching life skills to people recovering from mental illness. Each resident was expected to participate in their own care, although in Caroline's case her sisters were the ones who made sure she had clothes, winter boots, bus tickets, and grooming products. They also brought in cleaning supplies and scrubbed out the mini fridge in her room, mopped the bathroom floor, washed windows streaked black from cigarette smoke—domestic dirt that seemed invisible to their sister.

By the end of her year in the programme, Caroline was once again angling to live independently. Everyone took a deep breath and prayed that this time she could cope.

# Sydney

Recovery is the elusive goal of everyone with severe mental illness, whether they are able to articulate it or not. I've known members of Sydney Weston's family since 1973 and have watched at a distance as he inched his way towards equilibrium. "There were no miracles or shortcuts," his older sister, Patricia, says with great pride. "Sydney has learned to cope with his own illness." Patricia is the one who told me the details of Sydney's journey that I share here; at his sister's request, I did not talk to Sydney himself, because she was worried that in his earnest attempts to speak frankly about his troubles, he would become anxious and fall ill.

Sydney and Patricia's parents are divorced. Their father lives in Canada and their mother in Kent, an hour southeast of London, England. "Sydney became a marijuana smoker at sixteen," Patricia said. "At nineteen he went to university, but he was not ready to be away from home and suffered from pressure and enormous stress." He was in a new city, attending a new academic institution, with new professors, teachers, and friends, and facing the higher academic expectations of university. He was also heartbroken when his girlfriend of two years ended their relationship. He smoked marijuana and drank all too frequently.

Patricia says, "At home during the university holidays, none of us picked up on his drug habits, because we weren't looking out for it. Nothing was wrong, and then it suddenly was. Sydney's descent was rapid, and for a family who had had no experience with something like this, we were completely caught out and left reeling. There was certainly no support here for family members."

Sydney also started to show signs of being distracted and careless, most notably when he sped down a hill and slammed his vehicle into a parked car at the bottom of the road. Was it premeditated? Careless? Reckless? At that point Sydney's mother arranged an appointment with a psychiatrist, who told her, "Lay off. The problem is with you." So she did.

Sydney's first psychotic episode followed soon after. He ran amok in a crowded shopping area, uttering nonsensical phrases, until the police arrived. The officers took him to a locked psychiatric ward in the country that, according to his sister, was Dickensian, dilapidated, and filthy. From there he was transferred to St. Thomas', a respected teaching hospital in London.

"Despite the newer, modern facility, simply being on the premises to visit my brother was a frightening experience," Patricia remembers. Sydney was put in the same room as a drug offender who was also psychotic. When illicit drugs showed up in Sydney's urine analysis, the two were separated. By then he was distraught, bewildered, and deeper in a spiral towards a total loss of contact with reality.

After several weeks of antipsychotics, Sydney stabilized and was sent back home to Kent to live with his mother. He recuperated there, incident-free, and began to teach sports in a local primary school. Then his well-meaning father persuaded Sydney to come to Canada, where he could study sports management at Carleton University. In Ottawa, everything felt foreign to him except the language, and he folded completely. Drinking heavily, he fell into a second and far worse psychotic state. Raving and delusional when he was admitted, he spent three months at the Brockville Mental Health Centre.

Sydney was fortunate to be followed by an ACT team that included Dr. Freeland of the Royal Ottawa Hospital. Their doctor–patient relationship lasted fifteen consecutive years, and that continuity allowed Sydney to develop a trusting relationship with his doctor despite being symptomatic. Dr. Freeland orchestrated Sydney's move into the community: to a group home in Ottawa run by a man named Stan (he wishes to keep his family name private)—"one of the truest saintly citizens," says Sydney's sister. Stan is one of a handful of group-home operators who have made it their mission in life to help the suffering see that recovery is possible.

Stan was no pushover. He was fair, but he enforced his rules and expectations with little room for deviance. "If you drink or take drugs, you're out," he said, and meant it. His mantra was "Trust comes from mutual respect." He really did care for those who boarded in the home he was running. He also cared expertly for family members, explaining to them an illness that was new, devastating, and shameful in the eyes of most of them.

A reckoning occurred when Sydney did not stick to the rules and was kicked out. He soon reverted to his old addictions, using street drugs and drinking alcohol daily. Patricia says, "If my mother and I had been living closer, one of us would have stepped up and been the safety cushion, an enabler of sorts. I would have shielded him from the harsh reality of the group-home rules. My father had remarried, had a new young family, now lived in Toronto. He wasn't available either."

Rescuing Sydney would have been the wrong tactic. In a twist of good luck (or fate or insight or fear of the locked ward), suffering psychotic flashbacks, Sydney reconciled with Stan, who allowed him back into the group home providing that he adhered to the rules. And he laid down the law to the family, too. "When Stan forbade us from sending money, as Sydney was using it to buy drugs and alcohol, we stopped," Patricia says. "We knew Sydney's future depended on Stan."

They inched forward. For several years, whenever Patricia arrived from England to visit, she found her brother scattered, non-communicative, unfocused. He'd disappear during visits, even though he faithfully took his medication. "What was really hard," Patricia explains, "was that at the height of Sydney's illness he used to ask me again and again if I was really his sister. Sometimes I would come from England and spend an entire day in Ottawa to see him for five minutes. 'I have to be going now,' he'd say, and vanish back into a world I was not a part of.

"The turning point came out of the blue on one visit, when he suddenly said, 'I would like to stay to have dinner with you this evening.' My heart almost stopped. I cancelled, with fifteen minutes' notice, my plans to see friends of my parents, and we found somewhere quiet for dinner. For the first time in a decade Sydney sat with my husband and me, ate with us, almost enjoyed himself! On another, later visit, he said, 'I think I would like to come to England to see the family.' It was such a big moment that we were all at the airport waiting for the flight two hours before the plane landed. Now that he was well enough to travel, he was no longer in exile."

He was also able to find and keep a girlfriend; the two of them share a passion for wildlife and the natural world. Patricia says, "When Sydney feels wobbly, he talks about it and goes to his doctors, who find the time to see him and listen to him. His family and friends always stick to their word and promises, which has allowed him to feel loved and to love us back. He speaks daily to me, to our mother, and to our father."

In 2015 Sydney began to volunteer weekly with disabled adults, helping them swim. One of them is blind, so Sydney guides him in the pool.

He thinks about the swimmers' disabilities and needs, noticing what they find difficult—a relief from his relentless internal focus. His sister says, "It's incredibly moving to see someone who has had hardship offering solace to others with such genuine love and tenderness."

He doesn't drink or smoke cigarettes, avoids caffeine, and exercises daily. As a result he is no longer obese—a side effect of his medications that had been distressing. He cooks, shops, and uses public transit. He's reading again, books his mother saved for him during the twenty years when he was unable to focus. Patricia says, "I have stopped thinking that something is going to go wrong."

Have there been losses? I asked.

Of course, she says: a career, a marriage, children. One residual problem Sydney faces is chronic anxiety. He worries over and over about the same things. He is susceptible to stress. Yet, with age, he's grown to recognize and accept his limitations. He is fortunate to have had a positive, helpful group-home experience. His family continued to love and support him throughout the worst of times; surprisingly, the geographical distance between them proved to be an asset. Patricia, for instance, did not experience the burnout that might have occurred had she seen her brother awash in addiction, breaking the rules and jeopardizing his living situation.

Twenty years ago, Patricia gave Sydney a watch. To her joy, he managed to keep it and wear it through all the difficult years. It's a symbol of his connection to his sister, a sign that recovery is possible.

## 23

# Hallucinating a Better World

IN 2010 CAROLINE'S HOUSING WISH CAME TRUE. SHE managed to convince the Fisher Salus team, as well as her ACT monitors, that she could manage independently. Rosalind thought her sister would falter without the camaraderie of a group home, even if the men and women around her in the house weren't close friends. But she kept her doubts to herself and fell into step with the plan, in order to keep Caroline happy.

Caroline moved into an apartment on Lepage Street run by Ottawa Community Housing, an organization that provides low-rent homes for people with special needs. Dr. Chantal Whelan administered long-acting injections of antipsychotics at the ACT team office, each one inducing several days of lethargy: a physical and emotional slump in which she slurred words and craved hibernation. She was also taking clozapine and sleeping pills. Clozapine is prescribed for severe schizophrenia only when other drugs are seen not to work. The drug has the usual list of problematic side effects and also includes suppression of the immune system, resulting in a lowered white blood cell count. Caroline had regular blood tests to check her count. Clozapine also lowers a person's seizure threshold and causes drowsiness, dizziness, and, in Caroline's case, excessive salivation. The drug also increases the risk for pneumonia, a problem for a heavy smoker such as Caroline. But despite the long list of hazards she faced, she lived in the apartment, incident-free, for an entire year.

Even on all the medications, she still experienced stressful days when she heard voices that harped on everything that was wrong and negative about her life. She was powerless over her thoughts when stressed, no matter how high the drug dosage. She became worried when Isabel fell and afterwards could move only with the help of a walker. When she learned that Gilles was moving Kyle out of his house and into a group home, her anxiety spiked. But Gilles felt he had no choice—Kyle had gone physically downhill to such an extent that he wasn't comfortable leaving him to navigate the stairs on his own. Gilles couldn't stay at home with him, because he needed to keep working.

Caroline told Rosalind she was angry about her lack of influence and ability to care for her son. Group homes had been hit-or-miss for her, and the thought of her son being consigned to the same situation caused her to feel guilty that both his parents had abandoned Kyle to the care of strangers. Her voices kicked in and she made several frenzied calls to Rosalind and Peggy. That stressful week was one of a handful of times when she told Peggy she wanted to take her own life. The ACT team mobilized and Caroline went back to the ROH. "I never really believed my sister would do it," Peggy said, "but she had those thoughts. That's a dark place."

On the ward, Caroline struck a nurse—the first time she had been violent towards another person since she'd hurt Hilary. The nurse had been trying to give her extra medication, as the doctors had ordered. For Caroline a heftier dose meant even more loss of control, more defeat, more uselessness. Afterwards, trying in her own way to come to grips with an act she wished she could take back, she rambled about her psychotic aunt: "Auntie Marilyn was stationed in the war. Her own grandfather tortured her and put hatpins under her fingernails. I grew up in Poland. It's the epicentre of the world, the birthplace of the man's scrotum and the woman's umbilicus."

The only reason her sisters could come up with was that Caroline had nowhere to vent her frustration and anger with Gilles. When Rosalind asked her what had happened, Caroline screamed at her. Perhaps, under the same circumstances, we would all want to lash out as some kind of release for being incapable of helping our children. The sisters sent the nursing staff flowers. It was all they could think to do.

Caroline was also panicked about Isabel's health. On the ward, where her mother had never come to visit, Caroline suffered feelings of unbearable shame that she was cut off from Isabel while her mother's health was failing—that she was unable to do what Rosalind was doing for the woman she had loved best in the world.


In the fall of 2011, Caroline returned to her Lepage apartment, more obese than ever, diabetic, a chronic smoker, with knees that throbbed whenever she moved, and exhibiting flat affect, one of the negative symptoms of schizophrenia. She was home for only two weeks before she returned to the ward. She was jittery and brain-zapped by a bombardment of negative voices. No one had told her about the situation in detail, but she now realized that her eighty-eight-year-old mother was gravely ill.

Isabel died a month later, in December 2011, with Peggy and Donald at her side. "I was with my mother when she drew her last breath," Peggy says. "I was with her as she shed her last tear, and I gently wiped it from her cheek. I told her not to be afraid. I told her how beautiful she looked and how Dad was going to be so happy to see her. I do believe her transition was peaceful."

In a moment of clarity after she was told her mother was gone, Caroline said, "My mother and father came back from the war, got married, and there was no time to process the terror. All those deaths. We were taught to move forward with a smile on our faces. It all goes underground. When terrible things happen, we had been taught to shut up and keep walking. If you walk fast enough, you think you are far away from ideas that attack you. My mother could do that. She was a workhorse—no time to think. I could not."

In psychotic moments her internal script turned dark: "I was abused. I was severely abused as a child by both parents. It takes three seconds to violate a child. I was made to sit in abrasive cleansers and had the handle of a plunger rammed up my ass. I was forced to eat aluminum foil. After that, you hallucinate to a better world. My parents were the perpetrators, but I forgive them. They abused all of us, from Stuart right down to Pegs." Perhaps those grim fairy tales of abuse were simply a metaphor for her isolation in the family, in her marriage, in life.

Lorraine had flown in from out west, and she was the one who took care of Caroline in the days that led up to Isabel's funeral. She went to the hospital with a clean outfit, styled her sister's hair, and managed to get Caroline to and through the wake.

At the funeral, the clan assembled one last time to honour their matriarch. Peggy remembers that an unspoken but overriding need to connect as a family softened any grievances among the siblings on the day. The recessional piece was a recording of "The Prayer" sung by Andrea Bocelli and Céline Dion. Its lyrics went, in part, *Watch us where we go . . . In times when we don't know . . . when we lose our way. Guide us with your grace / to a place where we'll be safe . . . We ask that life be kind.*

It was as though the Evans children were asking Isabel, now under God's wing, to help tie them all back together after time and geography and circumstances had flung them apart.

Right after her mother's service, Caroline went back to the ROH for yet another six-month stint.

Dr. Whelan visited Caroline in the hospital and recertified her for another Community Treatment Order that allowed forcible police action if the family decided she needed further hospitalization. This time, the order dictated that if the police did bring her in, she would be required to spend a minimum of twenty-one days under observation. The rationale was that Caroline was now classified as at risk for what was termed "chronic relapse." It was not a question of *if* she would relapse, but *when*. So far, no housing situation had been sufficient to maintain stability. And no treatments, either.

Rosalind and Peggy reacted with sadness, regret, responsibility, fear, anger, shame, and grief, all wrapped in bitterness at the futility of their efforts to help their sister. Maybe it was Caroline's quirky humour or her grand insights or her bald-faced love for them that kept the sisters believing for so long that she would find a soft landing. Now they felt an exhaustion that required space and distance. From then on, the sisters took turns being the front runner, passing the baton when pointlessness threatened to overwhelm them.

Caroline lived in the apartment on Lepage for a few more months before another incident invoked panic. For her, psychosis was now a default mechanism provoked by life events big or small. Relapse. Get up. Relapse. Get up again. She and her family felt a tedious resignation, a desensitization. The sisters had been living and reliving Caroline's breakdowns for as long as she had, and they felt like they had PTSD.

Rosalind says, "Without Peggy, I would have grown too weary. In some moments I think of the people who have to do this alone. I think it's why so many severely mentally ill people are abandoned by their families. You have to remind yourself all the time that the rough stuff is not the person, it's the illness. But that too is a daily struggle, because you can't help but feel it *is* the person."

Peggy reiterates that point. "After all these years," she says, "I still wrestle with feeling as though my sister is manipulating me and using her illness to shirk responsibility. I've been so angry with her, so frustrated. When is a lie just a lie and not a delusion?"

Caroline's lies are an attempt to reconcile distressing events and to diminish her culpability. When caught in a lie, Caroline will fabricate another, even during times when she is not psychotic. It's this aspect that has been Peggy's hardest burden. A lie contains the intent to deceive. When Caroline tells a lie, she is deceiving first herself and then her sisters. By telling them that Mel Gibson was Kyle's father she was attempting to remind herself, as much as her sisters, that she was once a highly desirable woman, worthy of being cherished by someone like Gibson.

Chronic pathological lying has been referred to by health professionals as the "wish psychosis." Several times Caroline has told me, "Hilary poured boiling water over my body." It is her greatest wish that she had not harmed her friend. If a lie has been told over and over, eventually it becomes the truth. Repetition has that kind of power.

• ● •

# Gary

When my friend Theresa and I had lunch in Toronto in 2010, she shared the story of her brother and his decades-long struggle with mental illness. She and I had met at a party in 1985 when we both wore the same dress. We'd been friends ever since, but this was the first time she'd spoken at length about her brother.

She and Gary and their other sibling, Danielle, grew up in São Paulo, Brazil. In 1968 the family moved to the American Midwest, where their father, a PhD, had accepted a teaching position in the department of theology at a university. At the time, Gary was about to begin his freshman year of high school. He was an ardent student, but he often did his homework until four in the morning—his body clock didn't seem set to the standard time zone. Even in elementary school, Gary had thrown himself into his studies.

According to Danielle, her academically gifted brother "never fit in with the farmers" in the rural town where they lived, so vastly different from the dynamic urban centre of São Paulo. Danielle said she didn't either, and as an adult she has suffered with depression. Gary had his first psychotic episode at the beginning of his second year at Emory University in Georgia, which was his father's alma mater. His father took him back to the Midwest for an in-patient stay at the Menninger Clinic, a private facility in Kansas. (A highway sign just outside city limits used to proclaim "Welcome to Topeka, Kansas, the psychiatric capital of the world.") At the clinic, he was diagnosed with schizophrenia, a label he was reluctant to accept. After stabilizing on a cocktail of antipsychotics, he went back to his parents' home, where he slept on the floor of their bedroom, the only place he felt safe. Initially his parents kept his sisters in the dark about his troubles—hard to do when their son was sleeping in their room. But when he missed the entire semester of school, it was impossible to hide.

Gary eventually returned to Emory and was able to finish his undergraduate degree, thanks to regular psychiatric appointments that helped him cope with stress. But when it looked as if Gabriella, the international student he'd been dating, had to return home after fourth year because her student visa had expired, Gary became psychotic, engulfed in delusional thinking about mind control and the CIA. He proposed marriage. Gary's doctor spoke privately to Gabriella and urged her not to do it, but she refused to listen. She believed he'd broken down only because the thought of being without her was unbearable to him. They walked down the aisle in 1982.

After they were married, Gary earned two more master's degrees, one at Columbia University in New York City and an MBA from Georgia State. Already fluent in Portuguese and English, he acquired two more languages (French and Spanish), had two children with Gabriella, and worked steadily until he was forty-six years old. On paper, Gary was an educated married man with a life that was unfolding as it should. Gabriella gave him unilateral support, even when his illness made him verbally and physically abusive. His parents, who had settled in a small town near Atlanta, where he and Gabriella and the children lived, also backed him unconditionally. It was unthinkable for any of them to imagine that a multilingual scholar like Gary could falter in any permanent fashion, even though they knew that during those twenty-two-odd years he had had a number of emotional breakdowns related to schizophrenia, all attached to significant events in his life.

Then a merger occurred at the bank where he worked, and Gary's job was threatened. He boarded a train to Washington, believing that he was being tracked by spy agencies and that his father was complicit in the surveillance. Even when he went back to hospital, Gary remained intent on understanding how his brain was converting sensory information; he didn't see himself as a sick person, but rather as a man with cognitive differences. He questioned the benefit of drugs but was largely compliant with his regimen, thanks to the influence of his psychiatrist, whom he trusted and had come to depend on. In essence, the relationship with his doctor was his best medication.

In 2002 Gary's doctor retired. Days later, Gary booked a flight for Seattle, desperate for the comfort of his sister Danielle, who lived out west. When the flight was cancelled, he switched destinations, heading for Toronto, where Theresa lived. When he arrived, sweating and distressed, he asked for political asylum. He was taken to an immigration holding cage and airport security called his sister. Theresa and her husband sped to the airport, not knowing what to expect. She called her father, who arrived on the first available flight. He was instrumental in his capacity to convince Gary to retract his asylum request and fly home to Atlanta. The loss of the relationship with his psychiatrist had been enough to trigger psychosis, despite the fact that Gary had not stopped taking his medications. Downplaying his alarming request, he returned to work.

Also in 2002, two other relevant events happened in quick succession not long after the fateful trip to Toronto: Gary attended his high school reunion in Iowa and then took a second trip to South America on business. His sisters and his wife were worried that the reunion would evoke bad memories and trigger psychotic thinking. He made it through the Iowa trip, but in South America he had what Theresa describes as a seminal breakdown. "He had a full-blown manic attack in front of colleagues and clients," she says. "He felt on top of the world and didn't want the euphoria and wild productivity to end. He had fantastic but impossible ideas that he hoped to implement at the bank, all so implausible and disruptive they sent him home. His superiors gave him time off to recover, but he never worked again."

He went back to the hospital and was given a new diagnosis of schizoaffective disorder, to account for the erratic mood swings in combination with his schizophrenic symptoms. More medication. Gary was forced to stop working in finance. Instead he taught English as a second language, gave art history tours at the local museum, and took painting lessons. His father was a major influence, promoting those shifts of focus to help Gary harness his great intellect. As a result, his advanced degrees now gather dust but he functions in the world, aided by his own acceptance of his differences and unwavering support from his wife. His sister Danielle has had severe bouts of depression since high school. Of Gary she says, "When I was in the depths of an episode, I couldn't imagine it was possible to feel any worse. And then I would wonder what terrible pain my brother suffered, given that his mind had folded and taken him to another place."

Gary is a rare example of what researchers at Johns Hopkins University refer to as a person with "high cognitive protection." Their study suggests that people as intellectually gifted as Gary who present with schizophrenia experience impressive cognitive benefits over the span of a lifetime, compared to people with lower intellect. It has been proposed that high-intellect adults have a greater volume of grey matter.

So, as the disease advances, the progressive loss in the frontal cortex is less pronounced. Another theory to help explain schizophrenia is that intelligent people with "hyper brains" are more sensitive and reactive to environmental stimuli. This heightened sympathy might predispose an individual to mood disorders caused by elevated sensory experiences, confirming the stereotype of the "tormented genius." That phrase truly describes Gary as far as his two sisters are concerned.

In 2014 Theresa went to Atlanta for a visit and invited Gary and Gabriella to join her family for dinner at a restaurant. While they were eating, a tree fell on Gary's house; it split the roof and crushed the room where Gary and Gabriella would have been watching TV had they not been out to dinner. The incident provoked another psychotic episode, but once again Gary was able to work his way through it.

On the phone from Montreal, I asked Gary if he felt awed about that moment when the tree fell. He told me with a laugh, "It was the hand of God that we weren't home. You know, I come and go. I have good times and bad. That was one of the bad times. My sisters helped me through that one."

"And Gabriella? Has she saved your life?" I asked.

He took a long moment to respond. "I guess she has," he said at last. "She has rules that I don't always agree with. She manages my illness for me." He is happy to be on his medications, he says, because they help him think more clearly. But he suffers from tardive dyskinesia, the tremors that result from decades of antipsychotic drugs. He sleeps a lot and struggles with his weight. He and Gabriella have normalized an abnormal situation to the best of their abilities, but they worry about the emotional toll his illness has taken on the children, especially their son, who worries about falling ill. Gabriella told me, "My son suffers from depression based on the fear that he will become his father. I told my children to abstain from drugs and alcohol. I said, 'You risk opening windows in your brain with substance abuse. I don't want you to get sick like your father. Do what you can to protect yourself.'"

Gary is sustained by his family and by music and painting. His abstract artwork, with its splashes of bold colour, hangs on numerous walls of his parents' home, a testament to their willingness to accommodate the differences in Gary's brain. They celebrate each of Gary's attempts to find meaning and purpose. Apart from stabilizing stints in the hospital, he has always lived with his family, which has had impressive benefits. In many group homes, lack of stimulation leaches the creativity and curiosity from the residents. The Henderson family has made room for every deviant behaviour—at times an inconceivable burden.

Gary's two children have been given the gift of seeing first-hand what it takes to permit their father to live an atypical life: unconditional love. They have also seen that, in their family, nobody gets left behind, regardless of how far that person exceeds the standard deviation. They have lived the very idea that charity begins at home. Gabriella never abandoned her husband, even when she had to take out a restraining order against him when he was seriously ill and she became the target of his paranoia. She says, "In Venezuela, we were taught that when you marry, you marry for life." Danielle said that without Gabriella, Gary would be homeless. She was determined to hold the family together, raising her children with the oft-repeated phrase "The sickness is talking, not Daddy." Gabriella took on Gary's trauma so the entire family could survive. She carried the heaviest burden because she had the love and the strength and the will to do it.

Gabriella actually smiles when she remembers that she was told not to marry Gary. They recently celebrated thirty-seven years together.

## 24

# How Do You Keep
# Loving a Crazy Person?

LEADING UP TO CANADIAN THANKSGIVING, CAROLINE
began calling her brother Donald. He was the sole sibling still in
Montreal, the only who lived close to her sons. She left messages for
him, hoping to be invited for dinner, which would mean staying overnight. But he didn't call her back. The rejection prompted a crisis and
a brief readmission to the hospital the day after Thanksgiving. Every
small disappointment now sparked a resurgence of harsh voices, paranoia, and delusion.

Donald had been there for Caroline in the early days of her difficul-
ties, but he never achieved a comfort level about his sister's behaviour.
He and his wife couldn't shake off their frightening feelings. I asked
Caroline about the cost to her of being excluded from her family's life.
Even though it caused her such distress, she knew why it happened.
"My family didn't trust me. I could see it on their faces," she said. "If
you don't have their trust, you have nothing."

The siblings who had the least contact feared her the most.
Rosalind has said that everyone in her family is either part of the

problem or part of the solution. The siblings who are less invested have little tolerance for Caroline's looping cycle of crazy symptoms. The sisters, especially those closest in age, were more emotionally attached to Caroline from childhood on, and better able to keep the bond alive. Rosalind and Peggy bore the brunt, then Sharon, but even the eldest, Lorraine, who lived out west, lent a helping hand. The brothers went missing. Rosalind tries not to judge them for keeping their distance, but she can't walk away from the idea that many hands make light work—or would at the very least have made the work of supporting Caroline lighter.

When Caroline reflects on how she has managed, she says, "Antipsychotic medication is twelve thousand per cent better than the meds I took in the 1980s, when I first got sick. There are many days when I feel quite normal. When I let myself obsess about all the things that went wrong in my life, the voices told me I was horrible, ugly, fat, worthless, and unlovable. All the things I tried so hard to hide were out in the open, leaking out of my ears. And as I felt myself lose control, I stopped taking my medication. I know that I can't do that anymore. I'm hurting myself when I get sick, but I'm also hurting Rosalind and Peggy. It's been so hard to say, 'This is my life.' It makes me cry. My knees hurt when I walk, but my heart hurts all the time."

Caroline eventually realized that when she went off the drugs, she descended into a world that was both frightening and intolerable. Fear keeps her compliant. "My life becomes one big illusion if I go off the meds," she told me. "I'm taking so many different drugs, and the cost must be in the thousands and thousands. What a waste. But it's too scary what happens to me when I stop taking them. I stop sleeping, and after a few days of no sleep my mind goes over to the dark side. I have to think about my sons."

Her sisters valiantly kept trying to find some pleasures in life they could share with Caroline. During the summer of 2012, Rosalind bought three tickets—for her, Peggy, and Caroline—to hear Barbra Streisand perform in Ottawa. For months in advance, Caroline spoke about Streisand's music, about what the sensation of listening to her live was going to be like. Not since Elton John had performed at the Montreal Forum in the 1970s had she been as excited to hear a performer. She didn't say it out loud, but she was also thrilled to have been included. She was managing to stay functional for longer and longer periods of time. Her sisters began to have the tiniest hopes and expectations of her regaining some independence and worried less about the next big misstep.

But Caroline did not go to the Barbra Streisand concert. Perhaps she was frightened of the crowded venue and the noise. Perhaps it was her bad knees that deterred her, given the prospect of a steep climb to the second balcony, or not being able to smoke for two hours. Whatever the reason, she bailed on the actual event. The truth was that she needed the *idea* of attending a concert with her two sisters more than she actually wanted to go. It made her feel normal, and that was enough.

But Peggy blew up. "I was so mad. After the lengths we went to in order to make it all happen, there was no consideration for us," she says. "In the early years I was ready to do or say anything to get Caroline back to normal, a place where we weren't sick with worry all the time. *What will happen next, and to whom?* I don't have that willingness anymore. I'm tired. Her fabrications mean she doesn't have a teaspoon of credibility. You should have heard her reasons; they felt cruel and unfair and intentional."

Rosalind takes a different view. "How is any human being ready and able to accept themselves when the brain literally breaks down?

Caroline's threshold for suffering is lower than mine. I ache for her. It's her brain and she doesn't have any control. How terrible is that?"

Despite her occasional fiery outbursts about Caroline, Peggy is her financial guardian. She says, "When I'm feeling less charitable towards my sister, it's still nice to know I'm doing something concrete for her well-being." And she also claims to be the sibling who has the least difficulty with stigma. She never apologizes for her sister and she has an inspiring capacity for honesty. Peggy is the one sibling who wants to examine every hour of their upbringing with a flashlight, including the darker sides, like their father's alcoholism and the stress on their parents of raising so many kids. "I believe most people need to get over themselves and just imagine wearing the shoes of an afflicted loved one for a week or two," she says. "I know there are many in my own family who are embarrassed or ashamed to be seen with Caroline or to acknowledge they have a 'crazy' sibling. I get so angry with her sometimes, but I also know with every cell in my body that if I were the one with schizophrenia, Caroline would never turn her back on me. She did nothing to cause her illness—nothing."

Shame and stigma. The fear of being exposed as unworthy.

After the aborted concert adventure, Caroline stopped going out of her apartment. It was too much effort. She lived on cereal and socialized with the men on welfare who lived across the hall or on the streets. Caroline's calls to her sisters to explain why she wasn't going out alternated between the practical, the straightforward, and the illogical. "My knees hurt. I can't go grocery shopping anymore because I was sexually abused in a store when I was three," she told them. "A man stuck his fingernails up my vagina and ripped me to shreds. My friend Ken will bring me some pasta."

303

Ken was a man she had "found" in a shopping mall coffee shop. After they became friends, he spent long days smoking cigarettes in Caroline's apartment, coming and going on public transport. Rosalind said he would leave Caroline's place after supper and stay up all night at a lonely table in a twenty-four-hour fast-food venue, eyeballing the people walking past the windows. He made Rosalind uneasy, as she didn't know anything about his past or the details of his long hospitalizations or why he didn't sleep, but he was kind to Caroline. They were fellow travellers marooned on the same barren island. As with Simon, Caroline didn't need to know what Ken had done to invite such a solitary existence. *Today* was important—right now, this minute.

The ACT team stepped up its monitoring, checking in on Caroline three times a week. Those visits from trained professionals made all the difference, and soon Caroline was coping much better. So much better that, in 2013, Lorraine invited her to Vancouver for Thanksgiving.

Lorraine spent much time on the phone with Caroline, assuring her that she could handle the five-hour cross-country flight. Caroline was scarred by those previous flights mired in delusion, police officers, and medication. Flashbacks to Halifax and Newfoundland added to her stress. Lorraine persevered; she was calm and loving and insistent that Caroline could manage. A few days before her departure, Caroline went to Emergency with chest pains and was sent home with anti-anxiety medication. Fully supported by her three Ottawa sisters, she managed to fly to Vancouver unassisted. She had a joyous week-long reunion with Lorraine.

After the trip, Rosalind noticed that Caroline's sense of humour had returned—her laugh, even rendered rattly by her smoker's lungs, is contagious—and how much she loved telling her sons about her trip. Caroline still kept a room in her apartment with two twin beds for the boys, although Rosalind cannot recall a single instance when they stayed the night. Kyle now weighed so much it was difficult for him to walk, let alone come to Ottawa by bus. At the time, Matthew was living in Asia, where he was working in the recording industry and had a girlfriend. Caroline was so proud of him.

Her sisters noticed that she was also taking more interest in magazines and TV series. She loved to watch reruns of *Anne of Avonlea*, *Anne of Green Gables*, and *Little House on the Prairie*, all shows with positive messages that reinforced her desire for internal harmony. But as Rosalind had learned to her sorrow, Caroline's periods of peace were never a sign that her internal war had been won.

In April 2014, Patty and Rosalind headed over to the Lepage apartment for a long-overdue visit. Peggy says, "When we arrived at her apartment, she had a small piece of wood holding the door ajar. Apparently she was not concerned about the tenant base in the building—or she was asphyxiating in the smoke from her cigarettes. I had to fight that instant when my brain tells my body not to breathe because something nasty lurks there." Caroline's response was that she was about to do a thorough cleaning that day.

Rosalind said, "The filth of the place was overwhelming. There were dust bunnies the size of a cat. All corners of the ceiling were draped in cobwebs. There were literally fifty-plus bags of plastic bags. I couldn't let myself look inside the bags. The box of Mum's treasured items that she'd received after her death was on the living room floor, one and a half years later, not opened. The stench from the fridge was scary—leftovers not covered, left to decay and harden into an unrecognizable mix. Her beautiful presents from Christmas were still in their gift bags. There were dozens of empty cigarette packages stacked haphazardly on the bookshelf. An oversize coffee tin full of old butts and ashes sat reeking on the table. The ashtrays were so coated with grime that cleaning them seemed impossible, but in the end we tried with SOS pads and lots of elbow grease. The windows ran yellow with nicotine as I washed them." To dampen Rosalind's wrath, Caroline wandered about aimlessly putting things in drawers but incapable of any meaningful assistance. When she got home, Rosalind stripped down and jumped in the shower, scrubbing off her sister's despair.

After that, the two sisters decided that they would not visit her apartment but instead arrange lunch dates at nearby restaurants, picking up Caroline at the front door. It was too demoralizing to feverishly clean the apartment and return a few weeks later to the same filth.

Still, they'd experienced roughly two years of relative calm. So, when Caroline called Rosalind on the evening of December 20, 2014, her voice shrill and distressed, shivers of surprise and shock went through Rosalind's body.

Caroline was in a panic about black bugs. Rosalind's first thought was that her sister had gone off her medication. Still, they had to check it out. She called Peggy and the two of them drove to Lepage Street the next day. When Caroline answered the door, her sisters could tell she hadn't showered or combed her hair or changed her clothes in a long time. Rosalind couldn't prevent herself from blurting out, "Ugh. Caroline, you stink."

Caroline silently led them to her bedroom. From the doorway, she pointed to an infestation of bedbugs so extreme that swathes of the black insects covered every seam and crease of her white cotton mattress. They could see all the life stages, including moulted skins, larvae, and mature bugs the size of lentils. At first Rosalind and Peggy recoiled, and then they leapt into action, hauling the mattress and bed frame out of the apartment. Peggy's skin still crawls at the memory. "When I set the wood frame down in the hallway for a moment before taking it down the back stairs, numerous bugs darted out. I realized I was infecting the entire building. When we got the mattress and frame outside and dumped it into the snow, you should have seen them trying to flee. Black bugs on white snow."

Next out were the infected bedding, the pillows, and a sweatshirt sitting on the bed that was covered with bugs. When she set them down outside, Rosalind could see thousands of the bugs in several swarms on the frozen grey pavement, scrambling in all directions.

The epicentre of the infestation was the upper right corner of Caroline's mattress. A wet patch from her excessive salivation, a side effect of her drugs, had become a moist haven for breeding. When the sisters investigated further, the clothing cupboard was infested. The dresser drawers. The sofa. Magazines.

It was a heart-rending moment. Clearly Caroline had been living with the infestation for weeks and had not raised the alarm, either, because of her sisters' boycott of her apartment or blindness to the crisis, which seemed impossible. While they were cleaning up, Rosalind and Peggy couldn't help but shift in their clothes and surreptitiously examine each other in case a small critter or two had crawled up a leg. "It was the worst case of the willies I have ever had," Peggy says. "But you can't run away. You can't run away from your sister."

"I wanted to get in my car and drive for a thousand miles," Rosalind says. "And even that wouldn't have been far enough."

Caroline's sisters did what they could. Then Rosalind called an Ottawa housing inspector to discuss what to do, and found out that the earliest appointment they could get with an exterminator was Boxing Day.

Peggy and Rosalind looked at each other and then at Caroline. "I'm so sorry," Rosalind said. "I think you'll have to stay in the apartment until after the fumigation." Rosalind didn't want to touch her sister—they'd found bugs even in her hair—and so couldn't offer any kind of physical comfort, even though Caroline was devastated at the idea of being alone for Christmas in an apartment crawling with insects. Peggy turned away so Caroline wouldn't see her break down. She went into the bathroom, closed the door, and cried into folded arms.

The other option? Return to the hospital. Her sisters made it clear that she couldn't come home with them: neither of them could stomach the possibility that Caroline would suffer a psychotic breakdown in their house at Christmas or bring bugs into their homes. The inspector had told them that bedbugs are not dangerous or toxic unless a person is allergic to them, which Caroline clearly was not. He also told them that group homes suffered regular outbreaks of bedbugs but the residents were never relocated, because the bugs were not considered a serious threat. In the end, Caroline chose to stay in her apartment. At least the teeming mattress was gone.

Rosalind wondered how the infestation had become so bad without the knowledge of Caroline's ACT representative. But Caroline had the right to refuse to let caregivers into her space, and her caregivers tried to respect that right. Rosalind and Peggy had stopped coming over after they'd cleaned Caroline's apartment, and it is likely that no one else had been inside her door since. Except for Ken. Nothing in the way of dirt, cobwebs, mould, bugs, bad smells, or overflowing ashtrays was distracting enough to keep him away.

The apartment was cordoned off with yellow tape, with Caroline inside. Rosalind and Peggy thought they were hardened to Caroline's circumstances, but as the tape went up, they were overcome with emotion over their sister's oblivion to the squalor, the devastation of her life, the weight of their responsibility for her. In tears even now when she thinks about that incident, Peggy says, "I struggle daily with guilt that it chose her and not me. It is vile and has robbed her of almost everything in her life: her family, her marriage, her capacity to live with her kids, her physical beauty, her financial independence." The sisters were also crying for themselves. At no time during their decades of caring for their sister had anybody grasped them by the hands and asked, "How are you?" They suffered alone.

When the fumigator arrived on December 26, Caroline did not let him in. When Rosalind phoned to see if the place had been sprayed, Caroline told her it had. Rosalind passed on the news to ACT, and two members of the team went over to see Caroline and assess her state of mind. She let them in, and as soon as they sat on Caroline's couch, they knew the place had not been fumigated. The ACT team left immediately. A second fumigation date was set and once again she sent the two technicians away, saying, "The nest is gone. It's all taken care of. Happy New Year! Thank you for coming!" They did not know that the first team had been turned away and took her word for it.

When Rosalind phoned the exterminator to check up, she found out what had happened and arranged for a third visit. This time she and Peggy met the fumigators at Caroline's door, wearing clothing they would later throw away. Rosalind's heart thumped in her chest with a combination of anger and desperation, and she prayed that she could be merciful with Caroline. What they saw when Caroline opened the door made them cringe. She had not been able to prepare the apartment in any way for fumigation, so the team sprayed their solution over everything, in and out of sight—drawers of clothing, books, magazines, furniture, music, lamps, ornaments—everything. By the time they were done, the entire apartment and all of its contents were coated in chemicals.

Right then Rosalind decided that Caroline would walk away from everything in the place, as if there had been a catastrophic fire. She would take only photographs, some china, her animal figurines, and the envelopes that contained the blond hair clippings from her boys. Rosalind and her husband would store her things in two Tupperware containers in their garage through the winter, in the hope that minus-thirty-degree days and no access to human skin or blood would kill any unhatched eggs. Peggy said, "We took the stuff we could easily move, being two petite ladies, to the garbage bins out back and left the big furniture in the apartment, like the couches and tables. I try to forget the details of those happenings. I can't remember what Caroline was doing or thinking, except that we left her in the apartment. We were in preservation mode. It's just too awful and painful to hold on to those memories."

When Rosalind suggested that Caroline walk away from everything, Caroline accepted it as inevitable. She had long since detached her worth from mere possessions. Rosalind carried Caroline's two Tupperware containers out to the car, thinking, *She can no longer take care of herself. I can't keep doing this. Living independently is no longer an option.*

When Rosalind arrived home, she took off her boots and old clothes in the cold garage and ran naked past her startled dogs into the house, straight into a hot shower. Peggy did the same.

Caroline spent the next six months more or less isolated in her apartment, waiting for a suitable housing option to be sorted out. She kept the windows open twenty-four hours a day to release the chemical smell. Rosalind and Peggy bought her new clothes, new linens, and minimal kitchen essentials. She slept in the twin bed that hadn't been discarded. Her friend Ken was the only person to visit. He came at least four days a week to smoke with her over meals of macaroni and cheese or boxes of Hungry Man dinner he'd bought at a discount grocer. He didn't care if he inadvertently took bugs home to his own apartment. His life had left him with permanent scars, and being in Caroline's company was far preferable to eating alone, living alone, being alone. Rosalind would sometimes dash in of an evening and hand off a roast chicken or groceries. When she got home, she'd bag her clothes and leave them in the garage.

On the final day Caroline was in that apartment, Rosalind and Peggy both went in. "We bought her more new clothes," Rosalind says. "We were so afraid to bring bugs to her new place. We got her to shower, put on the new clothes, and then we took her directly to the hairdresser and had her hair washed again and cut. We left everything behind, even the new stuff we'd bought since the fumigation."

For good reason, too. "There were still a few bugs in the apartment," Peggy remembers. "The three of us got in the car and we couldn't get away fast enough. It felt like a getaway from a bank robbery. At the hair place I kept thinking I'd see bugs crawl off Caroline's head. After that, we drove her to her new placement. It was my son's graduation and Rosalind and I went back to my house to celebrate. Rosalind had worn a beloved summer shift she wanted to wear for the occasion. Because we had seen so many bugs at the old apartment, Rosalind took off her dress and I washed it several times in scalding water. Even so, she wore something of mine instead.

"A day or so later, Matthew came to my office and picked up the keys for the apartment," Peggy says with a wistful expression. "He went in alone, looking for anything to take, sentimental or otherwise. I can't help but wonder what he must have thought."

## 25

# New Hope

DR. CHANTAL WHELAN WAS THE ONE WHO FOUND
Caroline a shared bedroom with an organization that houses compromised elderly individuals and the chronically mentally ill, in a
complex integrated into a suburban neighbourhood. Caroline's roommate is eighty-nine years old, a gentle, accepting woman who does not
know anything about Caroline's past. She is maternal—an unexpected
blessing. She leaves the room only for meals, makes no demands, and
sleeps day and night with the television on. Her presence makes
Caroline feel less alone.

The living room on the main floor has an upright piano. On its
top sit plastic tulips and three framed slogans: *Live. Love. Laugh.*
There is a pop machine that also dispenses candy bars. A sign taped to
it says: "Do not rock, kick, shake or tilt the machine." The red-brick
fireplace has two giant four-foot teddy bears propped in the grate to
discourage fires and any other wayward ideas. Nearby are canisters of
oxygen for the heavy smokers. The floors are smooth tile to allow the
easy movement of wheelchairs and walkers. Two lively budgies, powder
blue and banana yellow, swing and sing inside a white cage festooned
with mirrors and bells.

It feels like these people, with their mental, physical, and emotional challenges, have gathered together at the last bus stop. There is no pretension or artifice. Everyone is an equal. Caroline's room is neat, organized, and cheerful, and she keeps a wooden angel beside her bed, a gift from a friend.

Twice a week, volunteers set up a clothing "shop" and offer free clothes to the residents. "I'm their best customer," says Caroline. "One week my weight is up, the next I'm down. I'm always losing four pounds. I've said that so many times even I laugh." She's over three hundred pounds at the moment, wheezes at the slightest exertion, and takes the stairs, she says, only "if there's a gun to my head." In the lobby a weigh scale sits outside the little office where the residents' money is doled out to them. Having the scale in such a public place seems curious, but privacy is far down the list of pressing concerns for the home's residents.

Caroline does not carry ill will in her heart. She knows that people can be repelled by her weight, her fearsome smoker's cough, her inactivity, her eccentric behaviour. The look of contempt on the faces of strangers hurts less now, where it used to skewer her to the heart. "I have days when I'm strangely alive," she says, "and others where I'm riding a train and it's nothing but a blur of grey trees. I think that as long as I am able to laugh, I'm okay. It's a benchmark of sorts. It's why depression is so hard for me. I pray every day that my grandchildren have a better life than I did." (Matthew's girlfriend has recently become pregnant and Caroline is thrilled. Kyle, too, is in a relationship but will not have children. He doesn't dare bring another baby with birth defects into the world.)

Being innately good-natured has helped her. It has kept people around her, like Ken and Simon and Dinah, whom she met at the ROH, friends who don't have the expectations of her that her sisters do. Caroline holds on to her dignity by being charitable. Giving things away has always been more satisfying for her than owning things, though she says, "I wish I had more to give to my sons."

It's a miracle that, despite all that has been scraped away from Caroline, the loss has not left her hardened. She verges on the saintly in her wisdom and acceptance of the faults of those in her inner circle. If her sisters are impatient, she argues, it's because she created a vortex of unrealistic need. She does not get unconditional love, but she gives it. She regards whatever good things come her way as a grace note in her life. She believes in God and an afterlife and "a chance to start over." The few times when she got to the point of considering suicide, thoughts of Matthew and Kyle reminded her that she needed to carry on living.

As she has grown older, her psychotic symptoms have waned somewhat, which happens with some people with schizophrenia. Perhaps it's because their possibilities for success in life have also waned. The stricken need to fight has loosened. The devastation of a first and second breakdown may be so great because so much potential is at stake. After decades of psychotic symptoms, Caroline has been able to replace the obsessive *I am worthless* with *I love my sisters* and *I love my sons*. For a long time, she tells me, berating herself with horrid accusations gave her a sense of control. "If I am in the process of self-blame, I am actually doing something. I'm not standing by in a passive state. The voices would command me to go off my medications because nobody would care."

At last she's at a point where the voices mostly know when to stop.


One April morning last year, Matthew, Kyle, and I drove to Caroline's new place for a visit. She hadn't seen them since before Christmas and had a dozen gifts saved in her closet. In the car, Matthew talked non-stop while Kyle mostly listened, interjecting now and then to correct his brother ("No, that was in 1998, not 1997"). Matthew has a short fuse about his mother's situation, and his anger often ripples to the surface. "Medication is not for the person," he railed. "It's for all the people around the person." After that a few minutes passed while we all looked out the car windows.

"When we were younger," Matthew eventually continued, "I used to drive to Ottawa with Kyle, and I would cry all the way home for having seen my mum in a pseudo-vegetative state. She lives in the past because she has nothing in the present worth sharing. How many times has she told me that Mel Gibson was my father?" We drove another twenty or thirty kilometres in silent commiseration before he spoke again. "My mother had voluntary shock therapy. How was she allowed to make that decision for herself? I would tell Kyle that we were never going back. It's too hard. She's not my mother; the woman who raised me is my real mother."

That woman was Gilles's aunt. She and Caroline's sons were close, a relationship Caroline was grateful for; she has no jealousy or resentment. In 2018 that beloved aunt passed away. Matthew flew in from a freelance job in Mexico to attend the service. He and Kyle stood next to each other, as physically opposite as the Hollywood duo of Arnold Schwarzenegger and Danny DeVito in *Twins*. Despite their differences, there is a little boy inside each of those grown men who craves a part of their history that will always be out of reach.

At times Matthew has also said that he would have cut off his mother ten years ago, if not for his brother. Kyle doesn't go to bed at night until he has spoken to Caroline. He is all acceptance, a sponge for her endearments. Having to cope with his illness has turned him into a fatalist. For Kyle that fatalism isn't about powerlessness or hopelessness, but about acceptance that some things won't change.

For most of the drive, as usual, Kyle was Matthew's verbal punching bag. He's often a target for the outrage Matthew feels about having a mother who struggled so greatly. Kyle has learned to be a tolerant receptacle, a rubber-coated target for his brother's rage. "My brother has been hurt by all that has happened," Kyle told me when Matthew was out of earshot. At one point during the drive, Matthew turned to me in the back seat and said, "Do you know the question I hate most? 'What happened to your mother?'" He hit the steering wheel with both hands. "Because I can't answer that question."

But when Matthew reminisced about his grandfather Arthur, he softened and the sense of injustice melted away. "My grandfather took us fishing every summer before he died. He loved to hunt—deer and ducks. He kept his guns in a locked cupboard and he was the only person who knew where the key was hidden. He was a bit of a freak about safety. We loved it when we were with my mum's family. Her friends, too. Her best friends were Ken and Simon. Simon was not your ordinary friend—he was gutsy." Matthew's laugh at the thought of Simon was as delightful as his mother's. "Once he drove my mum to Montreal to see us. Twice he had to put oil in the car so the engine wouldn't seize. Years later, I learned that Simon didn't have a car or even a driver's licence, but he knew how badly my mum wanted to see us. He knew an old man who had gone to the hospital for kidney dialysis. He 'borrowed' the car. He had those kind of guts."

Maybe part of Matthew's attitude to his brother is fear that Kyle will not live long. The average age of mortality for people with Prader–Willi syndrome is thirty, a number Kyle has surpassed. Kyle walks with a cane, made unsteady by the extreme weight his knees and hips must bear. That day, after we arrived at the residence and parked the car, Kyle needed extra time to get to the door.

The brothers are polar opposites in body and temperament: Matthew full of anger and Kyle calmly accepting. Yet love for their mother fuses them together. Each time they visit Caroline, they let her put her arms around them. They crave so much more than what they have been given.

Caroline loves hugging her sons. She is grateful for the tiniest of kindnesses. The fight has gone out of her; she has come to accept her smaller life. "Medication undermines the human dimension. It has taken me a long time not to be upset with that fact. Fear keeps me going for the injection. I've fallen down so many times. I've seen on the faces of my family how much it hurts them." Those words are the essence of Caroline's generosity. "I don't hear the voices as often anymore, and when I do, they whisper. I have my mind, but my body is shot. I never did seem to be able to have both at the same time." When the mind breaks down, it manages to steal the physical. "The two need to hold hands, don't you think?"

She says her purpose in life now is to be "the gatekeeper of the souls of my brothers and sisters," especially her sisters. When I asked her what that means, she says life is about acceptance and love, and she wants to reconnect her siblings without judgment. "It's been a few years since my mum died. I hear her voice. It's her, all right. She says, 'Caroline, don't look back. Look forward.'"

Recently Caroline celebrated her sixtieth birthday, a milestone she reached despite her many medical conditions. Her life is mashed-potato bland. There are few field trips or vacations, no visits to a museum or art gallery, no concerts or plays. But compared to acute paranoia or living on the street, three meals a day and a warm bed are not a wasteland but an oasis. Caroline is grateful: "When you are well enough to remember some of the horrors from the past, a calm, quiet life can be enough."

Rosalind, Peggy, and Sharon check on her regularly, by phone and in person. Lorraine calls. In her way, Caroline is functioning well, a testament to her sisters' tireless devotion. That's what it takes. Recovery insists on the family being present and involved—when it's possible.

Sadness still hugs Caroline's shoulders like a winter cape. She is haunted by one question: *What has my life done to my sons?* It's why she watches comedy shows—a way to ignore the debris of loss scattered at her feet. She's prone to being reclusive. She cancels plans. She drives Peggy crazy with her overspending, usually on purchases that are given away, like tobacco. She has more insight now than when she was bouncing from stabilized to psychotic, but that insight also fuels her sorrow. Travelling anywhere alone beyond the neighbourhood is out of the question. "Everything is a reminder of my mistakes," she says. "Buses. Airports. People holding hands. Mothers pushing strollers."

Matthew sometimes manages rueful circumspection about his mother's decades of dysfunction. "For most of my life, my mum felt like a stranger. Nobody told us what happened." Gilles kept them in the dark on purpose, attempting to protect them, but he inadvertently created a vacuum in which their mother's mental illness was talked about only when she was in crisis, rendering her black-and-white "crazy" for her sons. For a long time Matthew's sympathy lay with his father. In his twenties he did extensive reading about her condition and grew to understand it. He also never forgets that during his earliest life she was the epitome of a loving mother, and that at no time did Caroline ever stop caring about him and his brother.


Caroline doesn't have a cellphone. Though she has access to a landline, her calls to family are few these days. "I'm done with calling people.

I know that when I do, I'm only in their hair. I spent decades of my life waiting for people to phone me." She makes an exception for her sons. Kyle still doesn't go to sleep unless he has heard from her.

Schizophrenia, untreated, has the power to unravel a person's mind, but it should not be allowed to destroy the heart. No illness should be able to erase the human being. Although Caroline's life can be read as a calamitous smash-up, it reveals the essence of what really matters: connection. The link between Caroline and her siblings may have thinned to a spider's thread, but it never broke.

When Caroline is well, she is wise, calm, and patient. She bears not a trace of a grudge for those who did not walk beside her, including her brothers. She has nothing but admiration for her mother. "My mother was one woman looking after the eleven. She didn't have enough hours in the day to advocate for each one of us. We had to figure it out for ourselves. It took me the longest." She adores her Tuesdays with Ken and her Thursdays with Dinah, weekly visits that give great comfort and shape to her life.

Her dear friend Simon has died. Smoking weakened his lungs, but it was a "family matter," Caroline claims, that caused him to give up on life. She had encouraged him to reconcile with his three children, and a kind social worker helped him track them down. Simon had long admired Caroline for her devotion to Matthew and Kyle, and he was overwhelmed when his children welcomed him back into their lives. To Simon's eternal wonderment, his youngest son, Rodger, wanted him back—the one he had hurt the most, the son who, too many times before he walked out on his family, had seen him so drunk he was crumpled on the floor. When Simon's children welcomed their father like the prodigal son, erasing an upbringing rife with alcoholism, debt, and abandonment, he cried the healing tears of release. Then Rodger was diagnosed with lung cancer and died within three months. The light went out for Simon. He caught a cold, which soon turned into pneumonia. As Caroline says, "He went to be with Rodger. Their reconciliation after decades of distance was a powerful drawing card for Simon to follow Rodger into the afterlife."

To an outsider, Caroline's mind can seem irrevocably broken. She often speaks of her visits with people who are not alive; clearly, her experiences are sometimes from another realm. But who are we to dispute the other dimensions a person such as Caroline may be privy to enter. At least these days, her interior garden has become a place of comfort where she feels accepted, where her voices affirm rather than demean her existence.

The mentally "well" have coping strategies. Protection comes in the form of loving relationships, safety and self-esteem, communication with others, feeling validated, feeling heard. It comes from making mistakes and learning from them instead of being defeated by them. In grade eleven Caroline started to wither. She grasped for the unattainable: Darren Fulton, then Starsky and Hutch, then Andy, then Gilles, then Mel Gibson. And then it was sex with homeless men and old men in bars that satisfied her craving to love and be loved.

For decades Caroline's losses rumbled through her like a freight train. That grief was a physical sensation. The pace of Caroline's life in the seniors' residence is snail-crawl slow. She's let go of needing and the desire to be needed, which are altogether different from the satisfactory feelings of love. "I am loved by Ken and Dinah and my sisters and brothers." She stops speaking for a moment before adding, "And my sons."

There are those who need compassion and there are those who deserve compassion. The burgeoning number of people seeking treatment for mental disorders has skyrocketed. Anxiety leads the parade. There are many reasons for the increase in the ranks of those who need help. People do not suffer in silence as they once did, when stress and depression and psychosis were considered failures to be suffered in secret.

It's hard to know what would have been the best route for Caroline. There is no guidebook to follow, because every family is unique, just as the faces of schizophrenia and the pathways to breakdown are too numerous to be catalogued. New research from peer support groups and patient advocacy movements is what is driving mental-health care forward. But the question for everybody is the same. What kind of environment is best during and after a crisis? CAMH in Toronto has successfully created housing options that are integrated into the streetscape of the city but still attached to a medical facility, given that the centuries-old model of sticking people in an intimidating building hidden deep in a treed park only reinforces stigma. Deinstitutionalizing them wasn't the answer either, when it meant drugging patients into submission and providing no helpful therapeutic care. Grassroots organizations such as Nazareth House and Chez Doris have sprung up, too, advocating care-centred approaches of self-acceptance, activity, integration, and love. The idea is that poverty, social isolation, a poor diet, and street drugs allow the illness to flourish, whereas social reintegration is the only hope for the severe cases.

It all sounds so simple. In reality it's a nightmare. Even in a good group home, the accumulation of loss means some doors are permanently closed. How do you reverse diabetes while taking heavy doses of medication? How do you apply for a job when your reference letter is from thirty years ago? How do you pay the bus fare for your son or daughter's visit when the welfare cheque covers the basics and little else? How do you lie in bed at night and keep the ruminations from sending you to the drawer where you hid the screwdriver? You reach for something to swallow and hope that someone, anyone, will recognize the signs of despair, and that a miracle will happen.

In 2018 Rosalind and I looked inside Caroline's two Tupperware containers, which had been tucked into a corner of the garage for years. Inside we found hundreds and hundreds of photos, a robin's-egg-blue mixing bowl for making birthday cakes, a white china angel holding a gold harp, a signed sculpture of a black-capped chickadee on a snowy branch, and a figurine of two wolf puppies. Caroline loved animals for their unconditional love of her. When she couldn't care for a live animal, she bought figurines.

There was a photo of Caroline with six-year-old Matthew at his First Communion in 1990. He wore a red and black vest and grey flannels, a black bowtie, and a white shirt. Caroline was dressed in a tight-fitting white pantsuit, white heels, and a glittery cardigan. Her hair was shiny and her eyes sparkled. There was not a single photograph among them that had been taken after 1990, which is when Caroline had her first psychotic breakdown.

"I never let anyone take a picture of me," Caroline tells me, "because the image in my mind is vivid and suffused in a golden light. I am on a swing attached to a tree. I see shredded rope and an obscured view of the sky through leaves. The scene is fully realized in my memory, but sweeter, darker, kinder, happier than right now. All I have to do is close my eyes and I'm there. And then I add my boys to that daydream so they can see me as I once was."

Caroline's story does not end with redemption. Whose does? But the lessons of her life are many. Caroline's inexhaustible quest to find love and meaningful relationships is a key to understanding her yo-yo life, stringing up then down into paranoia and psychosis. She never stopped wanting to connect to others, which is a testament to her happy early childhood and to parents who were in love their entire married lives.

Eventually she reached a kind of equilibrium where she can carry her disappointments and sadness. But first she had to forgive herself for not reaching the heights she'd once imagined. Next, she needed to forgive herself for hurting Hilary and her family, and for the way her circumstances have affected her sons. It's no wonder addiction swallows so many of the mentally ill. To be numbed by alcohol and drugs can be preferable to the hard work of self-examination, dredging painful memories from a hole in the psyche the size of the Grand Canyon.

It has been three years since a psychotic episode interfered with Caroline's day-to-day life. She still has delusions, but since her sisters stopped pointing out her flawed ideas, Caroline is happier. Mel Gibson is still Matthew and Kyle's father.

Once she stopped comparing her life to those around her, stopped ruminating that she was "less than," the healing began. Caroline marvels, "One of my happiest days was when Ian called me, forty years after the fact, and apologized for the way he treated me. 'Will you forgive me?' he asked. Of course I will. Who would not want that kind of release?"

Peggy also helped Caroline let go of her anger at Ian. She told her, "If you could see Ian now, he is not that same person. I don't know which of his four wives brought it out of him, but he is a meek little church guy now. He turned to religion. The majority of his time is spent praying, reading, staying healthy, and helping those in need. People who have more people who despise them than love them? Well, then God is the only way to survive. It's working wonders for him. He's a changed man."

Another miracle.

# Sixty Thoughts

CAROLINE'S STORY IS ONE OF SHAME, PHYSICAL DISCOMFORT, and loss, but running through her narrative is the understanding that it is still possible to feel whole. The final step for her was to find a way to silence the negative voices that relentlessly told her she was unworthy. When Caroline let her mistakes echo through her life, she undermined her sense of self and self-worth. But all mistakes are lessons, which is easy to say but hard to practise.

When I thanked her for her willingness to share her life in these pages, Caroline said, "I felt all alone for such a long time. My hope is that others don't have to suffer like I did." She also confessed how scared she was, scared to be judged all over again. I told her that by telling her story she was being a pioneer for all mothers with mental illness. "You're still you. You're still a loving mother and person despite all you've suffered," I said. A winner's tale is usually an easier sell, especially to oneself. Caroline's victory is to have reached the point of being "enough."

In July 2018, Caroline turned sixty. She invited me to her family birthday party, which was at Peggy's house. I couldn't attend but sent her a few gifts and sixty dollars in her card. When I next went to visit her, she said, "I haven't spent the sixty dollars yet." I told her there was one dollar for each of the thoughts she had shared with me. She said, "Well, in that case, I'll never spend the money, because when I open my sock drawer, I'll know there was a time when I had sixty thoughts." She laughed the way she usually does, and then coughed so hard I thought she might bring up her ankles. Then she asked, "Is the book finished?"

Yes, I told her. She was very quiet, the smile gone. It came over me that finishing the book represented another ending and, in a way, another loss. I could tell by the dropping of her chin that she was thinking our daily phone calls would end, calls precious to both of us, even if many had been painful trips into a past she'd tried hard to bury. No, Caroline, I told her after a long silence. It's not finished.

"Thank you, my friend," she said.

Of course it wasn't about the book, just as Georgie's missing leather jacket wasn't about the jacket. It's never about something concrete that can be held or read or worn. It's about the unquantifiable essence of knowing you matter, that you have lasting value. There is no final chapter. How can there be, when so much is still to be done? Not just for Caroline, but for Camilla and Stefan and Aleks, and everyone who feels like a stranger where they are, feared and forgotten but for the gardens where they wander.

Caroline was changed by the symptoms of schizophrenia. She needed to accept that she was changed but not accept being erased by the symptoms. Her heart beats within her chest with the desire to love, as do yours and mine. In the exploration of her life she's undertaken for this book, Caroline has done much emotional healing. We both always thought this work would be a vehicle to help others, but the person it may have helped the most is Caroline. Her life matters, and she is finally able to agree that it does.

Four weeks before Caroline's birthday, Peggy returned the dress she had washed during the bedbug crisis to Rosalind, who was so touched she cried. The memories were sordid but the clean dress somehow meant the sun always rises and fills the day with light. The dress is a symbol of all that Caroline's sisters did in the name of empathy, in the name of sisterhood. In the name of schizophrenia.

Imagine lying in the grass and staring at the night sky, with every star in the inky universe visible. Now think of the tangle of millions and billions of blinking neurons in a person's brain. The task of isolating a misfire is nearly impossible. These neurons seem to play a pivotal role in the pathogenesis of schizophrenia, and research continues every day in an attempt to find the root cause of an illness in which the mind separates perception from reality. Perhaps hundreds of genes are at play. The solution to the mystery of extreme mental illness continues to elude us.

As I wrote this book, I flipflopped between embracing the necessity of antipsychotic medication and vilifying the culture that has made sedation a major aspect of treatment. There is still no evidence that medication corrects a biological abnormality. The notion that biochemical imbalance in the brain is the root cause of mental illness is still speculative. Extreme mental illness is, however, a debilitating series of experiences that cannot be wished away. Schizophrenia is not speculative, nor is depression.

Clearly there are times when the drugs are beneficial. Caroline poured boiling water in Hilary's ear, an act of violence that would have been prevented if she had been admitted to hospital when she reached out for help. There is no argument that antipsychotic medications reduce the manifestations of psychiatric distress, and a recalibration of Caroline's medications would have prevented that one act of terrible violence. But at issue are the long-term negative effects that limit a person from living a purpose-driven life. The idea of people being permanently limited fuels my doubt about the current treatment scenario. The drugs are touted as having positive clinical properties, yet schizophrenia is an illness in which the vast majority of medicated people do not return to normal. Should *normal* be redefined? A paradigm shift would be to view psychosis as part of the human experience, and to view recovery as something that is in reach within ourselves, with outside support.

Many pharmaceutical companies that produce the drugs prescribed for people suffering from mental illness have been mired in lawsuits, price-gouging scandals, and clinical bias. For example, the selection of patients is known to be a powerful predictor of the results of clinical trials. Recruitment and retainment are not well monitored. In other words, not all patients are included in the final results. It's hard to know what is best for the patient. It's also problematic that so many patient advocacy groups are funded by Big Pharma, but then, who else has so much vested interest? Who better to tout the medications than an advocacy group, who then become paid functionaries. Is it even lawful when an advocacy group accepts money from an industry, then pushes that industry's products? Under the glare of watchdog organizations, some impartial advocacy groups no longer accept industry funding.

How do we reduce a dependence on drugs when the drug companies want their patients to be customers for life? I worry that the medication model is so all-pervasive that few young psychiatric residents will ever have the courage to stand up in front of their peers and disagree with a protocol that is so entrenched, so widespread, so profitable. Why and when did psychological healing become so closely associated with profit margins?

Back in the 1950s, when chlorpromazine was given to the thousands of patients warehoused in asylums cloaked by their treed parks, that first antipsychotic drug was seen as a miracle. Chlorpromazine reduced the screaming in the asylums, and the world gave a collective sigh of relief. It turned out to be a raincoat over a river. Those untold thousands were sedated and then released into the community to become the jobless, the homeless, the addicted, wandering our cities, thickly painted in the dark colours of stigma and shame. Today that same desperation for relief has fuelled an industry where the patients are as complicit as the doctors. People are willing to swallow anything if there is a sliver of hope that medication will dissolve their utter distress. The pressure on doctors to provide treatment to patients who are in extreme psychic pain is immeasurable.

And some people do better on medication. The sense of relief after being on an out-of-control roller-coaster ride with no seatbelt can feel like salvation. Standing on solid pavement again can seem miraculous and lifesaving. But being drug-free is an option. We need more services for people who make that choice.

The dilemma of overmedication continues to haunt me and runs through many of the lives I've recounted in this book. Is there another route out of the abyss? Can psychic pain be undone by medication? Before we find solutions, we first need to identify the entry points that set a person on the path towards psychotic breakdown, depression, bipolarity, suicidal thinking, or feeling so distraught that the mind severs from rational thought. It's impossible to predict who will fall to the ground and who won't, because the pathways to mental breakdown are so multifactorial. It's not enough to say that mental illness is genetic. Identical twin studies indicate that if one twin has schizophrenia, the likelihood of the other also being symptomatic is 50 percent or less, which means that nurture plays an equal role. The most compelling argument for the implication of genes is the remarkable consistency of onset: in late adolescence to early adulthood, a critical period of brain development.

So what are the seeds that lead to the first episode of breakdown? The earliest warning signs, the "prodromes" of schizophrenia, are ambiguous: social withdrawal, lack of motivation, disinterest in pursuits that once brought joy, lack of personal hygiene, inappropriate comments or behaviours, fatigue, lying, manipulation, alcohol and drug abuse. But this list could also describe the behaviours of a great many high school and college students who go on to achieve significant personal and professional success. However, when those issues ramp up into a higher gear, when symptoms such as hearing voices, hallucinations, delusions, apathy, and disorganized speech and thoughts join in, they characterize psychosis, which in turn can be labelled schizophrenia. Medication subdues these frightening symptoms, but drugs do nothing for social withdrawal, lowered motivation, and isolation. Have we medicalized the human emotions of grief, loneliness, and disappointment?

Before we tackle that question, should we consider: is schizophrenia preventable? Once it rears its terrifying head, can it be cured or merely controlled? Its incidence is worldwide and spans every socioeconomic group. People with schizophrenia are less likely to marry and they also have fewer children, yet its prevalence in the general population persists. Why has it not been weeded out? As the stories in The Ghost Garden show, the common denominator for every single symptomatic person is that they are suffering. Suffering is universal, a natural and essential aspect of the human experience. Without suffering there is no benchmark for joy. But for certain vulnerable people, their suffering can trigger a dire mental breakdown.

Trauma and suffering go hand in hand with anxiety, which, according to the numbers of people on anti-anxiety medication, is at an all-time high in the Western world. Too often, doctors prescribe to treat the symptoms but not the underlying quandaries that make us anxious: poverty, obesity, joblessness, ageing parents, immigration, gender dysphoria, divorce, substance abuse, the death of a loved one, moving, chronic pain, shiftwork, dangerous work, finding a purpose in life—the list is as long as a cross-country highway. Stress and unhappiness are not illnesses, despite the pharmaceutical companies' desire to medicalize certain anxiety-inducing events, from death to divorce. The DSM-5, the manual that classifies mental illness, now lists 375 diagnosable conditions. In it, several once normal human experiences are now classified as pathologies. Bedwetting becomes "enuresis." Shyness becomes "social anxiety disorder." Caffeine withdrawal becomes "caffeine use disorder." "Disruptive mood dysregulation disorder" is the new diagnosis for children aged six to eighteen who have angry outbursts. Each of these diagnoses can be treated with drugs.

When I think about my friends and about Caroline, I keep coming back to the idea of trauma being an individual setpoint that seems to vary wildly from person to person. Every time you remove a block from a Jenga structure, it becomes more vulnerable to total collapse. A traumatized person, a schizophrenic person, is like that game of blocks—vulnerable to massive damage from a single incident, or from a pileup of many. A traumatized mind means that simply existing can become hardship, because the person feels a constant fear of attack or a constant sense of loss. Every threatening stimulus has the potential to take that person to the ground. Delusions and psychosis are the manifestations of insult, but they are also a protective shell against ruinous breakdown.

Stress does two things to the brain: it depletes the neurotransmitters, serotonin, and norepinephrine, and it increases the release of cortisol. That chemical upheaval can cause changes ranging from mild depression to full-blown psychosis. A drenching with cortisol has been shown to damage cells in the hippocampus, a small organ located within the brain's medial temporal lobe that is an important part of the limbic system, the region that regulates emotions. Pain and suffering lead to stressful thoughts. It seems impossible to deconstruct an illness whose symptoms are linked to the nuances of human emotion. Until we solve the biological/pathological puzzle of negative thinking, the drugs we take and the electroshock therapy we undergo are a matter of guesswork. Sometimes they work, other times they don't. And sometimes we simply *will* them to work. That's called the placebo effect.

In 2019, scientists believe that schizophrenia is, among many things, a monster combination of genetic vulnerability, an ineffective response to stress, neuro-inflammation, and a hostile environment. Stress is a powerful predictor of both physical and mental illness. When a person senses danger, be it real or imagined, the body responds.

Sigmund Freud's lifelong quest was to understand why the mind fragments. Why do delusions seem so real? His intervention was talk therapy, which led to modern-day psychoanalysis, designed to release emotional experiences that no longer serve the person in a healthy way. Handholding, conversation, reassurance, chocolate ice cream, laughter, home movies, episodes of *Seinfeld*—anything at all that can be construed as a tool to keep a terrified person from snuffing out the candle, figuratively or literally, in thought or in deed, is a treatment. And maybe small amounts of intermittent medication will allow a suffering person to come down off the cliff edge and become able to receive the humanitarian gifts that ensure a person will feel worthy enough to carry on.

Caroline exhausted her siblings and her mother to the point where they wavered in their ability to offer her comfort. The love model is harder to execute when a person tosses used tampons on the floor, closes their eyes to body odour and maggots, or vilifies a sister in public. To a long-suffering family, hope for a better day seems a fantastic notion. That's why volunteers can do so much: non-psychiatric "talking teams" provide shoulders to help carry the weight of people in deep pain.

Imagine if we all viewed a bout of depression or psychosis the same way we view the common cold. A cold needs to run its course: the pounding headache, raw sore throat, racking cough, sleepless nights, nose and chest congestion all build, then pass. Pharmacies brim with cold and cough remedies, but many people know that the human immune system destroys the cold virus in time, irrespective of drugstore remedies. In a future world, maybe we could attempt the same self-care for mental disorders. If a person could own their symptoms and be allowed to look them in the eye while surrounded by supportive people, instead of wrestling them to the ground in shameful silence or masking them with drugs, they could be less hospital-prone. Less lonely. Less scared.

I really do wish the drug model was a cure-all for everyone. I wish that if my friends adhered to their medication, they, and everyone like them, could walk away from depression and suicide and schizophrenia. But at this point, they can't. Until new research on the causality and treatment of these disorders arrives, what's left? Hope.

Hope is a life-sustaining force predicated on the human desire to have a future. Spirituality, a belief in something bigger than us, is a coping mechanism that is insufficiently recognized by the psychiatric community. Faith, for some, offers strength. If they believe tomorrow might be better, they can bear a hardship today. If faith, hope, and spirituality—along with the sense that someone like Caroline is not just her symptoms but a whole person—were allowed to come together with orthodox medicine, a less debilitating path forward might arise.

The idea that schizophrenia is a single condition, reached by a single route, has been discredited. The pathways that lead to psychosis are as varied as there are people on the planet; the trigger may be trauma, a virus, marijuana, in utero complications, gut bacteria. Or perhaps hypoxia, bacterial infection, folic acid or vitamin D deficiency, or altered environmental factors during fetal development. No matter where the psychosis originated, be it emotionally, biologically, or epigenetically triggered, the psychotic experience ends at the same destination: the suffering person is at a monstrous distance from other human beings. In other words, life causes breakdown. For many people, childhood gives them resilience and coping strategies abundant enough to handle a stressor that might topple another. We still don't fully understand why some people are susceptible to the unhinging of self-esteem that leaves a person alone, afraid, paranoid, and schizophrenic.

It seems from my experience over these past dozen years that restoring human connection is the best pathway to healing the broken social threads. That connection needs to be re-established by whatever means possible, be it medication, ECT, CBT, or simple care and compassion. Treatment is best when it is uniquely tailored. Some people improve with shock therapy, while others in the grip of disorganized thinking can be restored with antipsychotic medications. But for those people who cannot adhere to their antipsychotic medication, perhaps the source of their psychosis is resistant to such drugs, and we do them harm by insisting that the only treatment option is to stay on their meds.

Psychiatrists, in my experience, are heroic truth seekers who are attempting to navigate the pockmarked terrain of mental illness. What is the best way to treat a person who has become unhinged and flown off into an unknowable world? To try to quantify schizophrenia is like catching the wind. We will never be able to stuff our shapeless humanity into a tidy box neatly tied with bow. There is no one-size-fits-all with mental illness, just as there is no one-size-fits-all human being. But schizophrenia can be softened by introducing more drugless pathways to wellness—art, acts of service, music, meditation, journal writing, dancing, exercise, nature walking, better sleep, friendship, yoga, meditation, singing, pottery making, going to church, bird-watching—the list goes on. The best predictor of good adherence to any discipline is when a person's life has improved, regardless of the treatment or behaviour modification.

Dr. Michael Meaney, an epigenetics researcher at the Douglas Institute, studies the relationships between stress, gene expression, and maternal care, and he has developed an attachment theory by using rat pups as his test subjects. Baby rats, he says, are coated in a saline solution that the mother rat finds irresistible. As a result, she licks her babies from tip to tail. Well-licked rats have lower stress, fewer diseases, and better survival rates than rats whose mother gives them insufficient licks. Substitute any beast with a beating heart into this model. Nature and nurture are closely linked. Dr. Meaney states that what we inherit from our genes is shaped and altered by what we experience. What is truly groundbreaking is the idea that our genetically mandated patterns can be reversed by nurture.

An example of epigenetic effect is that of a pregnant woman who smokes cigarettes throughout her pregnancy. Her behaviour affects three generations—herself, her baby, and the reproductive cells of that baby. When those cells become her granddaughter who suffers from asthma, do we attribute the child's weak lungs to genetics? The asthma genes are expressed in the third generation because of an environmental event: a grandmother who smoked while pregnant. Caroline and her Aunt Marilyn shared many of their symptoms of breakdown, suggesting a genetic connection. What has come to the forefront is that a large number of genes may contribute to susceptibility, but none so far can claim full responsibility for the pathology of schizophrenia.

As I try to shape these final thoughts from all I've witnessed with Caroline and the others, I realize that what I most want to underline is the idea that even a person with a devastating condition like schizophrenia needs to live with purpose. I am in awe of the exceptional people I have met in my volunteer work: writers and artists and scientists whose lives have been distorted by mental illness. No one is fully intact, but the survivors are the ones who have embraced the idea that beautiful Barbie and handsome Ken are more real after their heads have been shaved by a defiant five-year-old. Perfection means accepting a world with imperfections.

And yet I stumble when I think about Aleks, perhaps the loneliest person I know. In the past year he rebelled against his doctor, his medications, and his group home, because he felt as if he had been consigned to life in a coffin—claustrophobic. The ensuing breakdown resulted in his being treated with more antipsychotics, which led to more numbing of his emotions, more slurring of his speech, and more isolation. His new group home is too far away for me to visit. He has hardly anyone to tell him that he's still okay, that he is enough. He is a man who has been failed by all of us: by me, by the medical system, by the housing system, by his mother, and especially by himself. There are countless men and women like him living among us. His experience is a painful reminder of what happens when a person becomes disconnected from other humans but still yearns for love. I wonder how many times he has contemplated ending his life. "Why am I here?" he asked me last week on the phone. It's a question I've heard before.

His suffering demands that at least one person reach out to help him, reinforcing their own purpose, whereby the chain of service begins. If that chain is thick and unbroken, then suffering has less of a chance to breach it. This book, at its heart, is a plea for more non-medical interventions in the lives of the severely mentally ill. I can testify that the joys of helping others in need are limitless. There is simply no substitute for human connection.

There is no medication anywhere that can replace the two plastic wedding rings that tumbled from the vending machine into Maureen and Jean-Pierre's hands.

# Acknowledgements

My gratitude begins with the people I have called the Evans family for the purposes of this book, who braved all to tell the unflinching truth about the emotional cyclone we call madness. Rosalind and Peggy gave me unlimited access to family secrets, as well as to their precious time and to their reflections on living with Caroline to ensure the truth was laid bare. Caroline bravely dug out suppressed memories in the hopes that her mistakes would be life lessons for others. This book is my gift to them.

To all the people who also shared their stories with me, I express my awe. Once my intentions were out there, the stories flowed toward me as if drawn to a magnet. From a brother. A friend. A son. A sister. A mother. The afflicted themselves. I could hardly carry the weight of what came my way. I prayed every single day to get the meaning right. My only regret is that so much is yet to be written, and to be said.

My own heavy lifting began in 2009 at the Douglas Institute, a psychiatric hospital in the midst of positive change. My heartfelt thanks to psychiatrists Dr. David Bloom and Dr. Pierre Etienne for their tireless and swift responses to my questions. Thanks also to geneticist Dr. Ridha Joober, to Terry Williams (who only gives me the toughest cases to work on), to Fr. John Matheson, Karine Ravenelle and the volunteer department, and to Sonia Nicholls, who, among other things, changes the sheets on the psychotic disorders ward—a dirty, thankless job. The first time we met she showed me the bible she keeps on the lowest rung of her laundry cart. I can't help but believe that her bible kept all of us safe during some of the toughest times on the unit.

Thank you to Stanford University and Johns Hopkins University for their online courses in psychiatry, genetics and psychology, which gave me the confidence to pursue this project. In particular, I thank Robert Sapolsky.

I owe additional debts to Jasmin Nuhanovic and the IT department at Selwyn House for saving me from lost documents and other technical disasters.

I am grateful to my daughter, Dr. Alisse Hannaford, her husband, Dr. Christopher Cosgriff, my son, Reid Hannaford, and dear friends Monika Quinn, Betsy Coughlan, Tom Adams, Elise Moser, and Val Marier for being my earliest readers and unflagging supporters. And to Campbell Hendery for reminding me over and over again that the world needs this book right now. I underwent a stem cell transplant while I was working on this book, and Campbell's sense of humour was both life-affirming and uplifting. Thank you to William Ashby-Hall for donating his stem cells. Without a bone-marrow transplant, I would not be alive to further my own purpose-driven life. Special thanks to Katharine Cunningham, a woman who bravely struggles against stigma and psychiatric labeling—may you further the enlightenment with your own writing. David Doherty, thank you for always being my Saturday morning friend. And to Breda O'Dwyer, Melissa Boyd, and Lucy McInnes for helping me embrace a spiritual awakening.

I owe a debt to Ann-Marie MacDonald that will be difficult to repay, but I will spend the rest of my writing life trying to do for someone else what she has done for me. Thank you from a place so deep in my heart its permanence is guaranteed.

To Anne Collins, my incomparable editor and publisher at Random House Canada. I want to thank her for believing that this was a story worth telling, for turning a huge block of ice into a sculpture, for knowing how to extract meaning from some of my most shapeless ideas. In her deft hands this book will travel to where it needs to go. For that, a thank you could never be enough. Anne sometimes wears a long black coat covered in dragonflies, which says it all. Transformation. She has managed to transform the lives of readers and writers worldwide, and I bask in that inclusion.

I am thankful and grateful for my incredibly supportive family, especially Donna, Ross, and Keena in Montreal, and my children. But I reserve my final reverence for Hal Hannaford. I'll never forget the cinnamon lattes.

# Index

SUSAN DOHERTY is a Montreal writer whose award-winning debut novel, *A Secret Music*, was published in 2015. She worked on staff for *Maclean's*, and freelanced for *The International Herald Tribune*, *La Tribune de Genève*, and *The Independent* in London, and for eighteen years ran her own advertising production company. She has served on the boards of the Royal Conservatory of Music, the Quebec Writers' Federation, and Nazareth House, a home for those afflicted by addiction and homelessness. Since 2009, she has volunteered at the Douglas Institute, a psychiatric hospital, working with people living with severe mental illness. Doherty is married to the educator Hal Hannaford, and has two children.